About the author

Martin Booth was born in 1944 and educated in Hong Kong. He is the author of seven novels, including the highly acclaimed *Hiroshima Joe* and *A Very Private Gentleman,* and is the biographer of Jim Corbett, the tiger conservationist. He has also written for the cinema and television, his work as a wildlife documentary writer receiving a number of international awards.

MARTIN BOOTH

The Dragon
and the Pearl

A HONG KONG NOTEBOOK

SIMON & SCHUSTER

LONDON·SYDNEY·NEW YORK·TOKYO·SINGAPORE·TORONTO

First published in Great Britain by
Simon & Schuster Ltd in 1994
A Paramount Communications Company

Copyright © Martin Booth, 1994

The right of Martin Booth to be identified as author of this
work has been asserted in accordance with sections 77 and 78
of the Copyright, Designs and Patents Act 1988.

Simon & Schuster Ltd
West Garden Place
Kendal Street
London W2 2AQ

Simon & Schuster of Australia Pty Ltd
Sydney

A CIP catalogue record for this book is
available from the British Library
ISBN 0-671-71206-3

Typeset in Sabon 11/13.5 by
Hewer Text Composition Services, Edinburgh
Printed and bound in Great Britain by
Butler & Tanner Ltd, Frome and London

for Jane and Peter

Contents

Acknowledgements

This book could not have been written without the considerable generosity, assistance and encouragement of the following: Tony and Ulli Frazer, with Terry and May Boyce, for the very frequent loan, often at exceptionally short notice, of their spare rooms, en suite bathrooms and maids; Stephen Wong of the Hong Kong Tourist Association for his provision on innumerable occasions of *pak pais*, cars, drivers and interpreters, not to mention exquisitely fine meals; Kent Hayden Sadler and Tim Harrison of the HKTA office in London; John Dunn and the Royal Hong Kong Police; Mr Chan Chun-yan, the senior superintendent of HM Prison Stanley and his staff; the staff of the Hong Kong Government Information Service; William M.C. Liu and the staff of the Hong Kong Government Public Records Office; Betty Ng; May Boyce for helping me translate place names; Mr & Mrs Joseph Chan for their memories and friendship over three decades; Anders Nelsson for his recollections of our childhoods and teenage years together; Dr D. Gibson for memories of Wanchai; British Airways for a 'jump' seat into Kai Tak; Christopher Hilton for his local knowledge; and last, but certainly not least, Jane and Peter Binstead for thirty-five years of amity, their never-failing invitation to the racecourses of Happy Valley or Shatin and for the not inconsiderable debt they owe me for monies lost thereat.

Martin Booth
Discovery Bay, Lantau Island, Hong Kong
March 1993

Foreword

There is an apocryphal story about Hong Kong which goes like this: An eleven-year-old English boy comes out from suburban London to spend his holidays with his uncle, an expatriate businessman. For six weeks, he lives the life of Riley – he takes water-skiing lessons, visits the Ocean Park seaquarium, buys a radio-controlled racing car and a new wristwatch which measures his pulse, temperature and walking speed, eats shark's fin soup, rides the Peak Tram, takes a sampan round Aberdeen harbour and cricks his neck staring at towering skyscrapers. Finally, it is time to go home. At the airport, his uncle asks him, 'Well, what do you think of Hong Kong, my boy?' His nephew considers for a minute then replies, 'I like it, uncle. And it'll be wonderful when they finish it.'

At any one time, 15 per cent of the buildings of Hong Kong are being either demolished or rebuilt, renovated or restructured, this in addition to new edifices. There is not a quarter of a square urban kilometre which does not contain a construction site, a land reclamation project, a hill levelling, a new fly-over (or –under) scheme, a hole in the ground filled with thumping pile-drivers or a skeletal edifice up to sixty storeys high covered with bamboo scaffolding, decorated throughout the night by the futuristic flash of welding torches and showers of sparks.

A skyscraper, it is said, recoups its cost within five years, so the mode is to pull them down and put them up again. One building I knew as a child – the Four-seas Hotel at 77 Waterloo

xi

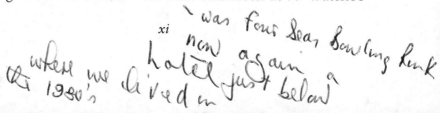

Road in Kowloon – has been since 1960 (when it was demolished) an apartment block, another much bigger condominium block and a luxury hotel. The full circle has turned in thirty years.

With such progress inexorably churning, it is a wonder Hong Kong is recognisable from one decade to the next and, certainly, much has altered. Central District (originally called Queen's Town then the city of Victoria), neighbouring Wanchai, Western District and Causeway Bay are indubitably among the most architecturally thrilling environments in the world containing the unique and innovative headquarters of the Hongkong Bank Group, the spectacular Bank of China Tower, the Lippo Centre with 'flying floors' like the bridge wings of ships and Central Plaza, Wanchai, the tallest building in the world outside the USA.

On every visit, new buildings appear cutting the skyline, a new quadrant of sky where once there was a hill or a new spit of land jutting into the sea which was once the hill or the sea bed of the Pearl River estuary. With Hong Kong's mountainous terrain, building land is at such a premium it has long since had to be created so that, today, 23 per cent of all urban buildings are constructed on land reclaimed from the sea: the present reclamation rate is a staggering seventy million cubic metres per annum and this is set to more than double in the near future. New roads are constructed which are quickly lined with apartment buildings, factories or freight terminals – if not buildings then facilities. The Mass Transit Railway, or the *MTR*, which was opened in 1979, has nearly doubled its original network and runs through a second tunnel under the harbour. To 1993, it has carried more than 5,175,000,000 passengers. Two vehicular tunnels pass under the harbour, linking Hong Kong island to Kowloon and over half a dozen other tunnels cut through mountains carrying road or rail traffic whilst the shore of Hong Kong island at North Point is walled by a motorway on stilts erected over the sea.

Fishing villages I knew as a child living in Hong Kong in the fifties are now satellite towns of 100,000 people or more, beaches where I swam are extinct, bays on which I boated are residential or industrial zones and at least one hill, in Ho Man Tin, where I used to scrabble about in the gravelly soil for snakes' skeletons, has totally vanished. What became of the small Muhammedan burial ground there is anybody's guess: I cannot even find where it was.

Yet, despite these dramatic transformations, there is much which remains untouched not only by progress but even by the present century. The secret, of course, lies in knowing where to look. It is not just bricks and mortar, roads and stretches of coastline that have, at least until now, survived. So, too, have people and their traditions which, protected by Hong Kong's governmental if not geographical insularity, have been uninterrupted by mainland Chinese dogmas or doctrines, the eddies of political whims which have altered the face of China and are only now being gradually eroded by the new liberalism.

'You must feel quite a stranger here now' is a line I often have put to me over lunch or at a cocktail party in Hong Kong, but it could not be farther from the truth. For the little shop in Soares Avenue in Kowloon from which I purchased firecrackers and cherry bombs in 1952 is still in business and the old man in Prince Edward Road from whom I used to buy naughty magazines when I was seventeen still runs a stall of smutty picture books in the very same staircase. The waterfall before which I had my photo taken with my grandmother along Harlech Road on the Peak in 1954 remains running with water and hung with mosses. The differences are that traffic now roars past the little store, the old pornography vendor is deafened every few minutes by low-flying Boeings and the waterfall has a new iron railing around it.

After a break from 1967 to 1983, I have been returning to Hong Kong at least once annually. It is my home, albeit no longer my residence. I have watched as the changes have unfolded but, at the same time, I have observed beneath them the past tenaciously surviving or metamorphosing to cope with the hectic present.

Touching Down in Old Cathay

Over the headset I hear the dispassionate, disembodied voice of the Kai Tak air traffic controller: if ever there is a ghost in the machine, it is an ATC official, incorporeal but utterly essential to the well-being of 400 passengers and crew, not to mention a multi-million dollar aircraft.

'Speedbird Three-one, cleared to descend to 4,000 feet, heading 1–5–7.'

He speaks with the distinctive accent of a Hong Kong Chinese, quite unlike the stilted tones of the Guangzhou controller less than a hundred miles away and utterly different from the unintelligible mumble of the Kunming area radio operator whose instructions came over the airwaves an hour ago as, 'Arh, spea bud feewung yoo dee-seng do fee zewo fowsung fit mungtung pesunk buwin.' Or an approximation thereof. Although they did not admit ignorance, I was doubtful if the flight crew fully understood the command.

The first officer acknowledges the instructions and reaches for a small knob on his control panel, no larger than the volume button on a hi-fi. The numbers on the lilac computer monitors alter: the Boeing 747-400 changes course as the altimeter begins to count down.

'We're going in on Runway 1-3,' the captain informs me, glancing over his shoulder to where I am buckled into the non-existent engineer's seat: the latest 747s have only two flight crew. 'And we're approaching from the west over Kowloon. It's hands-on here. No ILS – instrument landing system, just

IGS. Instrument guidance. We get to play real pilots in Hong Kong.'

It is a sunny morning and, peering out of the side window behind the first officer, I can see through broken cloud the harbour nearly 10,000 feet below, cargo ships in lines like toys, the summit of the Peak wraithed in mist and the end of the Kowloon peninsula jutting flatly into the sea, the surface of which is herring-boned by waves. The skyscrapers of Central and Wanchai are little more than miniature building blocks with the morning sun striking deep shadows off them.

'We fly south-east towards the Lema Islands,' the captain says, 'turn right towards Macau with an eye on the Cheung Chau beacon then swing round to come in along the north shore of Lantau. In over Tsing Yi . . .' He stops. 'But I guess you know the route as well as we do. After all, this is more or less home to you.'

He smiles and turns his attention to the computer screens, talking in pilotspeak to his companion. I make no response: there is a lump in my throat as there always is when I sense the engine whine change pitch or watch the wing flaps edge out a few more degrees. And he is quite right: the flight path from the west is as familiar to me as a village street is to the man delivering the mail.

The Kai Tak controller gives a new heading, asking the captain to drop his speed a little: there is a slower aircraft in the flight path ahead of us and we must maintain a safe distance. It is 10.30 and the morning aviation rush hour has begun, aircraft arriving in Hong Kong airspace at a rate of one every five or six minutes. Some – the early flights from Taipei, Manila or Tokyo – will have to hold to make way for long-haul carriers should there be an emergency: Speedbird Three-one, the non-stop over-night British Airways flight from London, will not have to stack. We have been in the air for over twelve and a half hours and fuel, though not short, is precious.

The Boeing reaches 4,000 feet, levels off and alters its course with a tight turn. Below appear small, uninhabited islands, waves breaking over rocky shores and a high-speed boat of some sort which has cut a white line through a sea the colour of *café au lait*. By this, I know we are over the Pearl River estuary. Early European traders named it the Tiger's Mouth, learning to dread its fickle currents and shifting sand bars and it was into these waters the world's first aircraft hijack ended in tragedy when the *Miss Macau*, a Catalina flying boat, plunged into the sea killing all on board but for one of the hijackers: his gang leader panicked and shot the pilot dead. Only a part of the wreckage was ever recovered and it is said, with good reason – for the aircraft was known to carry bullion as well as wealthy passengers – there lies at least 200 kilos of gold sunk in the silt.

At this moment, I am sure the captain of Speedbird Three-one would hardly notice a hijack attempt. He is otherwise preoccupied with landing at one of the most spectacular but potentially dangerous airports in the world. Glancing at the Hong Kong Terrain Routes map in my lap, the ominous instructions printed in bold stand out: *Aircraft should adhere closely to approach lighting system as numerous unlighted obstructions exist on approaches.* For *unlighted obstructions* read *mountains*.

I ignore the summits of Lantau Island moving by on the right and watch these two men. They seem to communicate telepathically, each aware of what the other is doing and synchronising their every action. A warning horn sounds briefly to signify the landing gear is down. The first officer speaks into his microphone warning the cabin crew to be seated for landing. Ahead I can see Tsing Yi island with its oil depots and the five grey chimneys of the power station. Beyond these, the hills and peninsula of Kowloon are vague in hazy sunlight. Another warning horn alarms as the captain switches off the auto-pilot and assumes control himself. The suspense on the flight deck is almost tangible.

Stonecutters Island, now joined to the mainland by a vast land-reclamation scheme, slips out of sight beneath us. The Boeing is at 1,000 feet and, across the tenement rooftops of Sham Shui Po, there is a line of sequentially flashing strobe lights, the approach track directing us forward into the haze. We are less than thirty seconds from touchdown but the runway is not in sight before us. It is well off to one side: I can see it about a mile away through the side window behind the nape of the first officer's neck. Directly in front of the aircraft is what must be one of the most welcome and daunting sights any pilot can wish for – the chequer-board. This is an orange and white pattern of squares painted on the side of a low hill which has been shaved for the purpose. It tells the approaching pilot exactly where he is and acts as a vast sign board: it might be replaced by the words *Hong Kong – Turn Sharp Right Now.*

At a certain moment, the aircraft dips its right wing. Four hundred feet below are the streets of Kowloon Tong, then the blocks of apartments melding into the tenements of Kowloon City, Prince Edward Road and Argyle Street jammed with mid-morning traffic. Pedestrians and shop advertisement hoardings are easily visible. The flight computer begins to count down the altitude in a mechanical, robotic voice like that of an arcade computer game. The aircraft quickly levels and the runway is ahead, the first 300 metres black with skidmarks.

Until 1958, the runways were virtually tucked against the mountain, where the modern apron and terminal buildings are: to overshoot was to hit the steep lower slopes of Fei Ngo Shan. With the advent of jets, the two runways were broken up and in their place was constructed the single Runway 1-3 which juts for over three kilometres into Kowloon Bay, a huge earth pier. It has not done away with aviation accidents – several aircraft have overshot or dived sideways into the sea – but the level of fatalities is now very low indeed. We touch down.

The captain politely announces to the first officer he is applying reverse thrust and the whole flight deck vibrates as the 747 sucks itself down from 180 to 20 miles an hour. As the aircraft turns left onto the taxiway, a distinct smell suddenly permeates the cockpit. It is not strong but it is pungent.

'It's not me, it's not you,' the captain remarks to his fellow officer, the tension of landing suddenly lifted, 'so it must be Hong Kong.'

We laugh quietly. Despite the hermetically sealed atmosphere of the fuselage, the stink has already spread into the atmospheric control system. No sophisticated computer controlling of oxygen and pressurisation can keep it out.

Along the right side of the aircraft, now trundling slowly towards the apron, is a wide channel of water across which stand factories, tower blocks of low-cost housing and warehouses with mountain slopes behind them, some of which have been cut into vast quarries. An elevated motorway wends through the buildings, vehicles moving in a steady and constant stream. They too might be under some form of traffic control for none seem to be overtaking. The sea water in the channel is as black as sump oil. Since the runway was built, the tides have been unable to sluice this area out so the pollution – chemical and otherwise – has simply built up. Technically, it is a part of Kowloon Bay but the locals refer to it as the Kai Tak nullah, a word derived from the Hindi *nala*, meaning a brook or rivulet. In Hong Kong it means an open sewer.

'It's a toss up,' the first officer says, 'as to whether you drown or are poisoned to death when you miss the runway here.' He flicks a switch. 'Cabin doors to manual. Now,' he consults a chart of the airport which looks much like one of the maps customers receive in supermarkets to guide them to the shelving sections, 'how do we get to our stand through this little lot?'

Ahead on the apron are stationary rows of jets, the green and white bodies of Cathay Pacific aircraft predominating: CX, as the locals call it from its flight coding letters, is the Hong Kong national airline, noted for its punctuality, cramped economy seats, the intractability of its ground staff and the alleged amoral accessibility of its exceptionally pretty stewardesses. Next to the Cathay Boeings and Tristars are aircraft from JAL, Singapore Airlines, Philippine Airlines, Thai Air, United and North West: most are long-haul 747s or new Airbus aircraft but amongst them are two DC8s and an exceedingly old Trident in the livery of a Communist Chinese regional airline. In all there are more than two dozen aircraft parked before the terminal.

As Speedbird Three-one halts at the edge of the apron to give way to a Delta Airlines departing flight I recall, almost as a reflex, the old airport I knew in childhood. Choi Hung Road, the main route east from Kowloon, bisected the runway; cars halted by traffic lights as DC3s, Constellations or Argonauts lumbered out of the skies whilst in Kowloon Bay, where the modern runway protrudes, seaplanes used to arrive. I watched them from the roof of the Watson's soda water factory in Mok Cheong Street where friends of my mother rented a flat. They glided gracefully in through Lei Yue Mun like vast seabirds, settling slowly to the water which suddenly erupted around them. Hardly any sound came from them: they might have been one of the ghost spirits that haunt the Chinese everyday world.

As the Boeing pulls into its stand against the terminal, I remind myself that the land upon which we are resting was reclaimed from the sea by Allied prisoners-of-war working as slave labour under the Japanese. Every morning, they were given fish gruel and rice then marched from Sham Shui Po prison camp to the airport where they broke rocks, dug the sandy soil and exchanged illicit messages with Chinese partisans amongst the enforced labour coolie teams.

'How long since you were last here?' the captain enquires as we unbuckle our harnesses.

'Eight months.'

'Well,' quips the first officer, 'I hope you can find your way about. A lot changes here in a fortnight.'

I thank them for inviting me on the flight deck, collect my cabin baggage and head for the arrivals hall. Long queues stand at the immigration desks which are possibly the only inefficient activity in Hong Kong: it takes twenty minutes to get my passport stamped. My suitcase taken off the carousel, I head through customs. There are just two officers on duty, chatting together. Hong Kong being an entrepôt port, they have no interest in my case unless I am carrying guns or dope: guns come into Hong Kong by sea and land from China and heroin usually departs rather than arrives.

The taxi rank is busy but there is no discernible queue: Hong Kong has more taxis per capita than any city in the world. The driver lifts my case into the boot of his Nissan Cedric (where else can a taxi be called a Cedric?) and I get in.

'What hotel you go?' he asks.

'*M'heui jau dim.* No go hotel,' I tell him, slipping easily into the semi-pidgin of taxi drivers, my accent like his: this, too, is a reflex. 'Star Ferry. Go Argyle Street, Waterloo Road, Nathan Road.'

This is the long way round but I prefer it. The route goes along streets I played in as a child. The driver starts his engine: we drive 300 yards and get stuck in a traffic jam at a roadworks. A Boeing 737 roars overhead, not 200 feet above us and, in a little garden to the right by the start of a flyover is a large square rock surrounded by low trees. The Sung Wong Toi monument was originally a smooth round boulder covered in inscriptions and lodged on a hillock 400 yards away: it was dislodged when prisoners-of-war levelled the hillock as infill for the airport extension. The Japanese blew it up to shift it, and only the central third survives with three characters on it which translate as *The Terrace of the Sun King*. A Yüan dynasty monument, it commemorates the temporary residence of the last of the Sung emperors, a little boy and his brother with their diminished court and ragtag army who came to Hong Kong to flee the Mongol hordes.

In another city, such an important memorial would have a somewhat more auspicious setting but it is appropriate here that it should be on a virtual roundabout fifty metres from the airport perimeter fence and only a few hundred from touchdown. This is the nearest convenient spot to the original site and thereby the rules of *fung shui* are obeyed, the balances of nature retained. What is more, it symbolises Hong Kong: behind the ultra-modern, seldom more than a few steps away, can be found an attitude and way of life essentially unchanged for a thousand years.

From Crisp Croissant
to Clucking Chicken

Arguably the best croissants in the world are served at the Coffee Shop of the Mandarin Hotel in Central: this is hardly surprising as, year after year, the Mandarin is voted one of the top five hotels in the world by those people who ballot such awards. It is a discreet eating place with smooth carpets, immaculately laid tables, a muted décor and impeccably efficient, polite staff. Two croissants, all the coffee one can swallow (milk or cream), a range of honeys, jams and marmalades and a free copy of the morning paper (to read, not to take) costs HK$90 (£8.50) in an ambience of not-too-restrained luxury.

Yet the wonder of the Mandarin lies not just in its sumptuous pandering to patrons but also in the fact it stands just 1.7 kilometres from Spring Garden Lane and this brief journey between two points passes through all that symbolises Hong Kong, a microcosm of the city and its people.

The peregrination begins at the rear entrance to the hotel, by the Coffee Shop. Even here, there is a hint of things to come: just along the pavement, day in and day out, squats a shoe-shine man. He has been on this pitch for decades, certainly since I was a schoolboy, for I had my shoes polished and buffed by him when I was sixteen, on the way to my first day as a sixth former. The Mandarin stands on the western side of Statue Square and close to the Star Ferry. Originally, Statue Square took its name from an effigy of Queen Victoria which stood under an ornate dome vaguely reminiscent of the Albert Memorial in London, but smaller and less imposing. It was set up in 1886 but knocked down by the Japanese in 1942, discovered in a scrapyard in Japan in 1945 and returned to Hong Kong: it now stands without its cupola in Victoria Park, Causeway Bay. The statue that remains in the square, somewhat fittingly when one considers Hong Kong's scale of priorities, is that of Sir Henry Jackson, a one-time manager of the Hongkong and Shanghai Bank, the headquarters of which he faces. Money has always held precedence over monarchy.

Statue Square is a pedestrian precinct with trees and fountains which plash in modernistic concrete tiles. It is never without loiterers, old men reading the paper or office workers taking a break, but it comes into its own on Sundays for this is when the square and the surrounding streets, overhead pedestrian walkways and pavements become thronged with the colourful, noisy massed ranks of Hong Kong's Filipina maids.

Where once household servants consisted of Chinese amahs or cookboys in black and white uniforms, today's domestic servants are diminutive Filipinas escaping the crushing poverty, rocky economy and corrupt society of the Philippines. Hong Kong has a Filipina maid population exceeding 40,000. Many of them are highly qualified – those employed by friends of mine include a junior school teacher, a midwife and a PhD in psychology – but, unable to find work at home, they leave behind husbands and children to move to Hong Kong whence they remit a percentage of their earnings back to their families. It is accepted that many a village in Mindanao or Luzon entirely survives on expatriate incomes and they fear the consequences of the Chinese takeover in 1997.

To confront this congregation on its day off is to be simultaneously filled with sympathy for their plight and deafened. Tens of thousands of Filipinas swapping news from home, selling each other towels and sheets, joking and laughing, recounting stories and singing is astounding. They nearly all of them communicate in Tagalog, the main language of the Philippines which, heard *en masse*, is rather like the noise which explodes upon one on the opening of the doors of a battery-hen farm shed.

Many of the neighbourhood skyscraper landlords employ guards, rope off their entrances or plazas and lock their doors to keep the hordes at bay but, although these defences cause occasional friction, they seem not to deter these tiny women from the general joy of their day off, walking arm-in-arm or sitting by the fountains eating Filipina or Chinese junk food and wearing gaudy Sunday dresses or blouses such as they would wear back home to go to church – many are devout Roman Catholics. The skyscraper landlords, it must be said, also have a call on sympathy: the litter these troves leave behind is staggering in its range and volume.

East of the square is a low, particularly imposing building which looks as if it might have been put up as a film set for an historical drama. Surrounded by skyscrapers of steel, concrete and glass, it is constructed of granite, three storeys high with a central dome reminiscent of a Georgian gazebo or a bleak papal sepulchre. Bordered by grey pillars and deep arcades or verandas in keeping with colonial architectural style – the deeper the shade, the cooler the building – and begrimed by traffic, it was started in 1900 but took twelve years to build because it was decided halfway through to have the main entrance face Statue Square and not what was then a cricket ground on the opposite side of the building.

Originally, this was the Supreme Court and remained so until 1985 when it underwent a metamorphosis and became the Legislative Council building, the nearest Hong Kong has to a parliament. Hong Kong having never been a politically-motivated society, it was not deemed important to have an imposing assembly-house until after the British government had decided to give the colony away. By then, of course, the debates would have little import: and, this aside, many of the council members are not elected but merely appointed at gubernatorial whim. It is, therefore, as anachronistic as the building in which is sits, an oddment from the past out of keeping with its entire surroundings and of little use save in aesthetic or politically cosmetic terms.

South of the square, across the tram-lines of Des Voeux Road Central, is the headquarters building of the HongkongBank, which all Europeans know simply as the Bank and which all Chinese call

Wayfoong meaning *Abundance of Remittances*. The name comes from the characters *hui* and *feng* which were originally drawn in 1881 by Tseng Kuo-fan, a famous calligrapher who was Viceroy of Nanking and later Chinese ambassador in London and Paris.

There have been a number of bank headquarters on the site which was originally known as Marine Lot 104 for it was on the waterfront quay or *praya*. Part of Wardley House, rented from Sassoon & Co. in 1864, was the first office but, by 1882, the Bank owned the whole property yet discovered it was fast becoming too small for their expanding business. By 1886, a new headquarters was built with a substantial domed banking hall supported by Corinthian pillars made of polished red Aberdeen granite. This building in due time also became insufficient so it was pulled down and, in 1935, a new headquarters was erected that not only used the old Wardley House site but half of that of the City Hall next door. The modernistic block which rose from the site was the tallest building in the world between San Francisco and Cairo and looked very much like the present-day Senate House of the University of London. Constructed by Wimpey, it was made of cream granite and adorned with two-metre-high stone carved figureheads of mandarins and lions. The banking hall was barrel-vaulted, supported by pillars of black Ashburton marble, the ceiling inset with the largest mosaic in the world (of Venetian glass tesseræ) depicting commerce and industry between East and West and Occidental and Oriental transport through the ages.

Another fifty years passed and this building was deemed inadequate so it was duly destroyed, the present structure designed by Norman Foster and built by Wimpey (again). It is rumoured Foster, on hearing his design tender had been awarded the contract, asked, 'What is the budget?' to which Michael Sandburg, the Bank chairman at the time, allegedly replied, 'Never mind that. Just build it.'

The result is one of the most spectacular buildings on earth, a structure of steel, aluminium and glass constructed on the principle of a series of suspension bridges placed one of top of the other. It is full of superlatives and world records – the only building of its kind over thirty storeys high; the longest free-standing escalators; the biggest circular vault door; the first internal, computer controlled sunscoop (which directs sun into the twelve-storey high atrium); the most complex building ever erected – and reputedly the most expensive at the time. Clad in grey satinised aluminium panels with acres of glass windows, it defies description. No visitor to Hong Kong avoids walking under the atrium and rubber-necking upwards through the curved glass soffit to the sunscoop high above.

To enter the plaza under the soffit, one crosses the road avoiding the trams and passes the two bronze lions sitting at either side of the Bank entry. They are named Stephen and Stitt (Stephen is the snarling one) after two Chief Managers in the twenties and they have sat outside the Bank since 1935. Stitt in particular shows some bad shrapnel damage from the war and both lions – along with Queen Victoria – were shipped to Japan but rescued in 1946: there are many older Chinese who say Japan lost Hong Kong because they desecrated the lions.

Aware of the considerable good fortune attached to the beasts, the Bank reinstated them in front of the new headquarters on 1 June, 1985 – at 5 in the morning. This, it was deemed by the *fung shui* expert employed by the Bank, was the most propitious moment. They were also repositioned by laser so they should be in exactly the same spot and at the same angle to each other and the surrounding mountains as they were in front of the 1935 building. Such is the importance of not disturbing local natural equilibria.

The lions' front paws are burnished gold. This is not from polishing but from the constant passing caress of hands: when you go by Stephen and Stitt, it is said, you must stroke them for luck. Everyone does it – coolies, Filipina maids, yuppies with mobile phones, stooping old men and (be sure of this!) a good many European businessmen. When in Hong Kong . . .

The apparent rear of the Bank is in fact its front. The Bank's address is 1 Queen's Road, the side of the building not facing the harbour but the Peak. The rules of *fung shui* dictate that a bank must not face the water or the money will flow out of the doors:

they also ordain the angle of the free-standing escalators which are set so the sea dragon cannot get into the banking hall in the atrium.

Next door to the HongkongBank is a granite building similar in appearance to the old Bank headquarters only not as wide and four storeys higher. This used to be the Bank of China and, for many years, the loftiest construction in the colony: not to be outdone by the old Bank headquarters being the tallest building east of Suez, and to avoid losing face to the barbarians, the Chinese government went one better. The number 4, however, is the number of death in the Chinese geomancy and many local people would not consider banking there because of the variation in the number of floors.

Opposite the Bank is Beaconsfield House, a bland low building of modern design housing a post office and government offices. The original Beaconsfield Arcade was a three-storey office and shopping block raised by Emmanuel Ralph Belilios, an Indian opium trader who had provided £1,000 for the erection of a statue to Lord Beaconsfield, the prime minister in 1878. Beaconsfield discountenanced the statue so Belilios named his building after him instead.

Turning left past Beaconsfield House is the Hilton Hotel, one of the first of the international chains to set up in Hong Kong and, next to that across Garden Road, is the Bank of China Tower. Seen from any angle, this is an amazing sight. Over seventy floors tall, it was for a few years the highest building in the world outside New York or Chicago. Constructed on a skeleton of steel and coated in silvered glass, is looks like four prismatic crystals standing on end, each triangular in cross-section and of differing heights. The sides are also divided by equilateral triangular silver bars. On the summit are two tall silver parallel prongs, lightning conductor towers which locals refer to as *The Chopsticks*.

Many of the buildings in Hong Kong have local nicknames. Some of these are merely acronyms – for example, the Legislative Council building is known as *Legco* – but others are more meaningful. The Bank is peevishly nicknamed *Battlestar Galactica* by those who do not work for *Wayfoong*; and Jardine House, a forty-plus-storey silver skyscraper on the waterfront in which all the windows are circular portholes, is known in Cantonese as *The House of a Thousand Arseholes*. This does not refer to the windows alone but also to the employees of Jardine, Matheson, one of the original 'noble house' opium and general trading firms and a Hong Kong establishment. In any other country, such a moniker would be based upon hatred for supplying the local populace with an enslaving drug but the name has only existed for a decade or so. Its foundation lies in the fact Jardines was the first local company to allegedly shift its asset base overseas to a safe haven when the Chinese 1997 takeover was declared.

To cross Garden Road from the Hilton to the Bank of China it is best to take the overhead walkway. Central and Wanchai are bisected by dozens of raised pedestrian ways and it is possible to walk from Victoria Hotel to Central Plaza, Wanchai without getting wet in the rain or burned by the sun. The Garden Road crosspaths, however, are roofless and give views of the Bank of China unrivalled by those of any other building in the world. In its glass façade are reflected all the surrounding skyscrapers whilst its chopsticks prick the sky: it is a view of amazing perspective. When I last walked this way I was accosted by a Chinese man of about my own age, dressed in a smart suit and carrying a Gucci briefcase with a mobile phone.

'Do you know,' he began, 'that the sticks on top pass their shadow through the Governor's study window in Government House on certain auspicious days?'

'I did not know that,' I replied, surprised he had spoken to me: the Chinese are not usually so forthcoming with total strangers in the street.

'This will destroy his health and, therefore, the future of Hong Kong. *Or so they think*,' he added emphatically, glancing meaningfully in the direction of the main entrance to the Tower. 'Are you a Hong Kong resident?'

I nodded.

'Then you will know,' he shrugged. ' Look at it! The *fung*

shui is very bad. The main door faces the harbour and the whole building is constructed upon triangular designs. That is very wrong. But then, the architect was I.M. Pei and he is an American–Chinese. And the design was approved by the old men of Beijing – how much do they know of southern Chinese *fung shui*?'

Next to the Bank of China, Cotton Tree Drive rises up the Peak beside which is a copse of trees surrounding another architectural anomaly. This is Flagstaff House. Built between 1844 and 1846, it is the oldest colonial building in Hong Kong and amongst the oldest worldwide. Designed by Murdoch Bruce, the one-time Inspector of Buildings and famous for his sketches of early Hong Kong, it was originally the residence of the general officer commanding the garrison and, when it was built, was known as Headquarters House: all the surrounding area, from the Hilton Hotel to Wanchai and halfway up the Peak, was a military area known as Murray Barracks and Victoria Barracks. It remained the residence of the GOC until 1979 when the government took it over, restored it to its original state and then, most incongruously, turned it into a museum of Chinese tea-ware.

Despite their exquisite workmanship, I cannot get excited about tea-pots but to walk through the building on a quiet afternoon, with few members of the public present, one can sense history moving in the shadows. The building is also said to be haunted by two sentries in nineteenth-century uniform, an officer *circa* 1941 and a Chinese servant of indeterminate period.

Opposite Flagstaff House is the Lippo Centre, a grey glass complex of two identical skyscrapers which, from a distance, look like one of those children's puzzles where sliding pieces have to be fitted in sequence to construct a cube – the child playing with this puzzle has failed for there are bits sticking out at regular intervals, eight- or ten-storey sections suspended in mid-air. I have attended a meeting in a lawyer's office in one of the projecting sections: it is rather like being in the gondola of an airship and just as terrifying. Commissioned originally by Alan Bond it was, I have been told, the flagship building and most consistently profitable part of his extensive business empire.

Eastwards of the trees and the two skyscrapers of the new Supreme Court and the Central Government Offices, is Pacific Place. Hong Kong contains a large number of shopping malls, some of which (such as The Landmark in Central) are spectacular, but nothing touches The Mall at Pacific Place. The entrance is as grand as that of a modernistic palace with huge plate-glass walls, marble floors and fountains. If there is to be a cathedral to Mammon, this is the design to imitate. The mall itself, on two levels, curves for a quarter of a kilometre beneath two office blocks and three hotels – the Conrad, the Marriott and the Island Shangri-La which is lozenge-shaped.

Inside The Mall, the air temperature and humidity controlled, the floors spotless and the trees green (and real), are to be found up-market shops. Here are Benetton and Valentino, Bossini and Lane Crawford (the original Hong Kong department store, now into its second century), the Cotton Collection and Seibu. The latter is a Japanese department store. In 1962, the Japanese Daimaru chain opened a branch in Causeway Bay and, since then, most of the other major firms have also moved in – Sogo and Mitsukoshi, Matsuzakaya and, finally, Seibu. Their prices are high but the quality of their merchandise, much of it sold under franchise, is as good as that to be found in Marks and Spencer of which there is also a branch in the same mall.

The marvel of The Mall, however, lies not in itself – when you've shopped one mall, you've shopped them all – but in the fact that, in less than five minutes' amble, one can go from this opulent environment to that of Spring Garden Lane. Instructions to get there are simple. Leave The Mall by the eastern end, cross the road (under the fly-over), go along the pavement passing several bricked-up entrances into the hillside overhung by trees (and consider that, behind them, is a network of tunnels, galleries and corridors which were the military arsenal and stores in 1865), cross Queens Road East and set off along it, going by sheet metal-working shops, furniture makers, tailors and an assortment of other small shops none of which front on to marble halls but grubby pavements. Buses whip by at breakneck speed. Lorries thunder past. Keep well in. Ignore the narrow and short thoroughfares to your left – Anton, Li Chit, Gresson, Lun Fat and Ship Streets, the latter so named because it was once a slipway for running up ships for caulking: the coastline was less than seventy metres away then. Miss out Swatow, Amoy and Lee Tung Streets but turn into Spring Garden Lane.

It is hard to believe this teeming street was once a quiet residential suburb called Spring Gardens, a row of beautiful colonial houses built along a bund, or waterfront quay, with gardens filled with tropical shrubs and palm trees. The only plants growing here are those in pots and a ficus tree which has tenaciously rooted itself in the roof parapet of an old tenement.

Before the completion of Government House in the October of 1855 on a hillside behind what is now Central, it was here Sir Samuel George Bonham, the third Governor, lived. His official residence was a palatial colonial mansion with the usual deep verandas protected from the sun by bamboo roller blinds. The gardens were formally laid out and fed, as was the house, by a well of clear water which was an offshoot of a burbling spring higher up the mountain where it rose from beneath a rock near to a small temple. Bowring, the fourth Governor, also lived for a time in Spring Gardens before moving to what has been the official Governor's residence ever since.

Hong Kong has many street markets but that of Spring Garden Lane and the surrounding thoroughfares is the most readily accessible for the average tourist: sadly, not many venture this far – culturally, that is. Here can be found the timeless Hong Kong. If you avoid looking up at the high rise modern buildings you could be in any Chinese town in the last two hundred years, allowing for lorries, bicycles, electricity and jeans.

From ten in the morning, for twelve hours, this area teems. It is not a tourist shopping area but one for locals – old women haggling over vegetables, young girls buying clothes, servants purchasing meat and fish, old men obtaining provisions for their songbirds, expatriate European housewives shopping for groceries. There is no racial barrier anywhere in Hong Kong but here it seems obvious by its absence; nor is Spring Garden Lane divided by class for all but the very richest come here. It is, in my view, a microcosm of the ideal human world where everyone talks and trades, laughs and lives together bound by a single code of non-intervention: if London or New York were like this street market, the world would be a better place by far.

Traffic is minimal not because the streets are closed but because no driver dares to venture in without a solid purpose. The wedge of people slows any vehicle to less than walking pace, any cacophonous blaring of horns not sounded in anger but as notification. If the people can make so much noise bartering, talking, trading and taking their time, the machinery feels obliged to exercise a similar right.

The stalls are wide-ranging and often quite large. Some are mounted on small metal wheels which allows them to be pushed against the curb in case of need – the incursion of a foolish lorry, perhaps – but most are permanent structures. None looks as if it would survive collision with a bicycle but I once saw a lorry hit a lingerie stall and it was the stall which won. As for typhoons and tropical downpours, they are unaffected unless something falls on them from a great height, such as one of the hundreds of neon-lit, multi-coloured hoardings which stick out from the buildings to advertise shops, restaurants, barbers, doctors and dentists, tailors and small factories tucked away in the tenements.

All the stalls are laden to spilling with produce: if supplies in one commodity seem to be going well, the stallholder gets on the telephone (often a mobile telephone tucked under the awning or a box of goods) and more are delivered by small lorry, coolie or hand-cart. Every business is provided with electric lights, though supplied from where I cannot say, and the goods are illuminated by bare, bright bulbs. The roof of each stall is wide, to keep the sun off the goods, the rain off the stall and any refuse that might fly down from above from hitting merchandise, merchandiser and customer alike. Most are constructed of beaten tin sheets covered in plastic or canvas tarpaulins.

The vegetable stalls bear piles of Chinese cabbages and spring onions, peas in their pods, lettuces, mange-tout, stringy beans, aubergines and sweet potatoes, bunches of carrots and strings of garlic and baby sweetcorns. Whereas green is the predominant hue of the vegetable stalls, the fruit stalls are a cascade of colour – oranges, lemons, limes, apples, star-fruit, pineapples, bananas, custard apples, pomeloes, grapes, plums, peaches, durian (which taste foul and smell like monkey's excrement), papayas and breadfruit. If it is summer, there are also likely to be lengths of deep mauve-barked sugar cane: the stallholder swipes the bark off with a vicious knife so children and coolies may bite bits off the fibrous cane, chew the sweetness out and spit the masticated pulp on the roadway.

Other stalls sell inexpensive shoes, pots and pans or cheap toys made of garish plastic – panda-shaped, solar-powered calculators which play *Greensleeves* when switched on, battery-driven sun-flowers in pots which jive to any noise stimulus, waddling puppies which bark mechanically, tin airplanes which throw flint-lit sparks out of their jet engines. The clothing stalls are piled high with t-shirts, sweaters, jeans, jumpers, blouses and socks all tumbled by rummaging. And a quick rummage is well worth it. If only the shop-till-you-drop tourists knew of this place! I have bought Emporio Armani and Ralph Lauren polo-shirts, Pierre Cardin and Trussardi socks and a Daniel Hechter jacket at these stalls, all at a fraction of their recommended retail price. Why bother with The Mall at Pacific Place . . .

Not all the vendors own substantial stalls. Wizened old crones squat in gaps between the stalls or on the pavement offering dried fish from carrier bags, the edges folded over to display the goods, or a few pairs of plastic sandals. One wonders how they make a living but they must do so: no Chinese, regardless of sex or age, would waste time in commerce if it was not profitable.

In addition to the stalls are shops. These are tucked away behind the street market as such and yet they are in many

19

ways similar to their potentially mobile competitors. Most are open-fronted and all are just as busy. The meat shops are lit by bare bulbs in red plastic shades. This seems to be a tradition: perhaps the lights tone in with the red hanks of flesh hanging from hooks and dripping on the concrete floors where the blood gathers in puddles to run into the gutter. The range of meat is wide with beef and pork making up the larger carcasses: there is seldom lamb or mutton available, if ever, and I cannot think of a Chinese dish which uses them. Smaller meat consists of rabbits and other indeterminable sources: dog is not legally eaten in Hong Kong – not surprisingly, the canine-loving British have banned it – and is not available in these shops but it can be purchased under the counter in the New Territories. No European, however, will be able to buy it unless he is very well-known to the butcher and trusted not to run for the police or the Royal Hong Kong Society for the Prevention of Cruelty to Animals.

It is an enigma to many Chinese why Europeans will eat meat but draw the line at dog flesh (or cat which is often served with snake). If one knows how the dogs are killed, the attitude might be different. I have eaten dog without regret. The last one to end up in my bowl had lived a normal, happy life wandering the streets of the Chinese city of Wuzhou. It never knew its fate. In the afternoon it was barking and cocking its leg and early in the evening was killed with one mighty blow to the head with a stout pole. It was not raised in a battery farm or intensive-rearing unit and did not suffer transportation to the abattoir where it could smell or hear its fellows going to their death. By comparison, a rasher of Danish bacon is cruelty indeed.

Chinese butchers are not equipped with the technological wonders of their English equivalent, such as electric saws and mechanical slicers, power-driven racks and liquid nitrogen quick freeze driers. Their main tools of the trade are a sharp knife and a chopper. Meat is not dissected into joints or cuts but hacked or slammed into chunks. And almost all the offal is used in some way or another. The shops contain no fly-killing lights, no huge cold-stores and no nattily dressed staff in striped aprons and white trilbys. Insects buzz in the air but seldom settle because the butchery is so busy. Cats and dogs hover in the distance ready for a share of what may fall or what little is discarded. The butchers wear grimy jeans with blood-spattered plastic sheets tied around their waists: they wear no hats and often no shirts or vests, their chests spotted with blood and minute pieces of red tissue. There are no cold-stores to speak of because no Chinese would consider buying food that is not absolutely fresh. If it had to be frozen, it has been dead too long.

The fish shops are much the same as the butchers. Mullet, grouper, shark and parrot fish share the slab with crabs, prawns, squid, octopus and eel. It would be difficult to keep a cow alive until the customer wanted it, but fish are different and the stock of these shops is alive and well in tanks of water overflowing into the street or in rattan baskets with hoses being played permanently upon them. The crabs click with annoyance, their feet and claws bound up with twine. The shrimps doggy-paddle in buckets, their carapaces green as jade or bright pink with black spots. Sea urchins lazily wave their spines at each other and octopuses uncurl and swing their tentacles. The customer chooses his item which is then netted from the tank or basket, dumped on the slab and promptly despatched. I am not sure – and have never found anyone able to tell me – why it is that when the fishmongers gut the fish, they take the heart out separately and put it to one side where it continues to beat or twitch for up to fifteen minutes.

Poultry shops sell not just hens: ducks, quail, partridge, pigeons, geese and pheasants are their stock in trade. Until purchased, they live crammed in crates piled one upon the other, a squawking, clucking, quacking, screeching, twittering, tweeting, scrabbling and pecking chaos. As with the meat and fish, little is wasted. Yet not all the animals in the streets are intended for the chopping block or wok. Close by Spring Garden Lane is an alley where old men sell songbirds.

The keeping of songbirds is a tradition going back in China to before the time of Christ and it is seriously sustained. The birds, which may range from parrots, mynahs and cockatoos down to the smallest of finches, are as cosseted and pampered as a New York dowager's poodle. Their cages are masterpieces of rattan and canework, the night-covers tailor made, the drinking bowls beautifully crafted porcelain and the seed dishes manufactured to the quality of Noritake. Not for the Chinese songbird the plastic mirror, bell and a piece of cuttlefish.

To pass by a cage-bird stall is like having one's ear suddenly filled with the music of rain-forests or pampas. The birds are continually in song, either competing for territories they cannot own or wooing their amours. They flit from perch to bar to cage floor (lined with grit-paper, not yesterday's news), always moving as if seeking to attract not just a mate but also an owner.

Inevitably, the stallholders sell everything one needs for birds, to keep them in health and happiness: pots, dishes, cages and food. Each vendor knows not only his stock but the natural history of each species and can, on occasion, give a passable imitation of any of their stock by whistling or mewing. The bird-food would surprise many a Western fancier. Although a comprehensive variety of seed is on offer, so also are living, pale cream beetle grubs, black crickets, emerald grasshoppers and even sand-brown locusts. They live in metal cages like Victorian meat safes, kept warm with electric lights and fed on greenery. To see a man walking down the street carrying a plastic bag of hopping, flicking insects is a commonplace here. Those who keep ornamental fish, also sold in the neighbourhood, might well go by with a bag containing a thick knot of scarlet blood-worms. As with the humans, the food for their charges has to be bought whilst it is still able to move under its own locomotion.

As with any Oriental street market, Spring Garden Lane also has its fair share of *dai pai dongs*, or cooked food stalls. They can be tiny, little more than a stove and a few stools, or massive affairs with up to fifty tables under a permanent awning, waiters, cooks and a manager: I have seen people queuing for a table at one of the bigger establishments. The food served is as fresh as one can get it: straight from the surrounding shops, through the pan, over the flames and into the bowls.

It is arguable who invented fast food first: I believe it has to be the Chinese. None of the dishes served in a *dai pai dong* takes more than a few minutes to prepare and they may be eaten seated at a table, on a stool, or taken away. What is more, the menu alters according to the time of day. At breakfast, bowls of *congee* or deep fried dough sticks are on offer whereas, by late morning, the fare changes to *dim sum* dumplings, noodles or soup. *Congee*, a form of porridge made with rice, is an acquired taste (I have yet to acquire it: this, turnip cakes and durian fruit are about the only Chinese foodstuffs I cannot bring myself to swallow) but the dumplings are superb. Dumpling is not quite an appropriate name. These are not stodgy suet-and-flour balls such as one might find in a Western stew but delicately shaped balls wrapped in opaque rice flour pastry and stuffed with fish, shrimps, crab or meat with vegetables. Every one is bite-sized and half a dozen make a substantial midday meal, the flavours delicate, the textures complex and the aromas positive aids to salivation. After this, a hamburger is a clumsy, unappetising anti-climax.

There are two other things to watch for in the vicinity of Spring Garden Lane. The first of these are thousand-year-old eggs. In China, everything worth having is a hundred or a thousand years old. It stands to reason. In a society that was culturally and sociologically advanced when Europeans were still struggling to develop languages, age is akin to value. The eggs come in two varieties – *pai dan* and salted eggs. They are preserved and may last several months without refrigeration. Hen's eggs are not used, but those of ducks. For *pai dan*, the eggs are placed in a large urn in a matrix of dampened wood ash, tea leaves and lime. Over about a month, the eggs absorb the flavours and preservative qualities of the mixture. When 'cooked', they are removed, rolled in pale mud mixed with chopped rice straw and seed husks and stored in a pot or just in boxes, one upon the other. They are usually eaten as they are for an *hors d'oeuvre* with pickled ginger, or cut up and added to *congee* or soup. They are quite delicious. They do not smell strongly, as one might expect, of hydrogen sulphide, but the yolks have hardened and the albumen turned a deep sea green, delicate brown or black. Salted eggs are made by covering the eggs with a mixture of burnt rice straw and coarse salt which the whites absorb but the yolks do not. After about a month, the eggs are opened and boiled or steamed to be served with rice. The yolks take on the consistency of cream cheese and are especially used in cakes served at the Moon Festival, when they appear inside buns rather as boiled eggs do in traditional English ham pies.

The last thing to look out for is the one establishment in Spring Garden Lane which only Chinese may enter. A European going through the door would cause consternation unless he was wearing a Royal Hong Kong Police uniform in which case he might engender a sidle for the rear exit by one of two of the clientele. It is not a bordello or an opium divan but a mahjong school. These are not illegal as such, although organised gambling in Hong Kong is contrary to the law unless it is run by the Royal Hong Kong Jockey Club and concerns horse-racing. Many of the mahjong schools are unlicensed and they may be, strictly speaking, illicit but they are not closed down. To shut them would cause rioting, public outcry and worse: it would be like trying to bring a halt to English village cricket, darts in pubs or the friends who play poker in the neighbourhood bar down any American main street. Mahjong is the greatest Chinese pastime there is.

Played with tiles, mahjong has four players. The rules are over a thousand years old and the game – like all games in China – is played for money, with stakes often running into five figure sums. A mahjong school is not a seedy, rundown dive. It is brightly lit with strip lights, clean, white painted walls, the square tables made of polished wood or covered with thick, durable laminates. The chairs are plain but comfortable (for the punters may be sitting in them for hours on end) and each place has an ashtray. Tea is served by waiters – alcohol is seldom on offer: mahjong is a serious business and requires quick wits and a good memory – but usually no food. Passing by a mahjong school, one is always followed by the rattle of the tiles as they are shuffled about on the table by the eight hands of the players or the report of a tile being played. These noises can be loud for the tiles are traditionally made of ivory or bone with bamboo backing although modern, high density plastic imitations are just as raucous. The crack of smashing a tile down is all part of the game's action.

Police interest in these schools can be intense. They are almost all of them owned by organisations with names like The Far East Recreational, Neighbourhood and Martial Arts Social Association or The Southern Chinese Brotherhood Association of Affiliated Cultural Institutes – which is to say, in the Wanchai District in which Spring Garden Lane is situated, one of the Chiu Chow Triad groups who have long held sway in these streets. Although not actual criminal businesses in themselves, mahjong schools are often meeting places for criminals; front organisations. Passing one can give an electric frisson of excitement knowing what lies behind the staggered door, built so no one may look in.

Spring Garden Lane is a long way from the quiet residential area it was in the 1860s and, culturally, as far away from the rest of the world as Barbados is from Boston or Bolton, yet it is only a few minutes' walk from the cool grandeur of Pacific Place and a comfortable stroll from the opulence of the Mandarin.

The Faithful Funicular

On May 28, 1888, an advertisement appeared in the *China Mail*. It read:

The Hongkong High Level
Tramways Corporation
Limited
Opening
THE Public are respectfully informed
that the **PEAK TRAMWAY** will be
OPENED for PUBLIC TRAFFIC on
WEDNESDAY, 30th Instant.
The **CARS** will **RUN** as follows between
ST. JOHN'S PLACE and VICTORIA GAP

Curiously, the fare for going up the mountain was double that for going back down: first class was thirty cents, second twenty cents and third ten. The thirty-seat tramcars were made of teak and mahogany on a steel chassis and wheels, open at the front and rear with only the central (first class) seats being enclosed: Chinese coolies were allowed to travel only in third class and servants permitted only in second if travelling with their missy or master, or accompanying a European child in their charge. No 'natives' travelled in first class at all.

The Peak Tram was the brainchild of a canny Scot, Alexander Findlay Smith, a former employee of the Highland Railways. He had lived in Hong Kong for twenty years as a merchant but a corner of his heart was plainly elsewhere for, in 1881, he successfully petitioned the Governor to allow him to look into the possibility of introducing what he termed revolutionary new methods of passenger transportation. As a result, he entered into partnership with a Phineas Ryrie in 1885 and Hong Kong acquired a funicular railway, the oldest of its sort surviving in the world.

Increasing numbers of people (almost exclusively Europeans) were building residences on what was officially known as the hill station, exchanging the summer heat of the city for the summer mists of the mountain which dulled the sunlight, turned leather shoes green in hours, ruined paintings, warped violins or parquet floors, and demolished the bindings of books inside a week. Sir William Des Voeux, Governor from 1887 to 1891, likened the experience of living in the hill station to being in a damp, gloomy prison in which condensed water ran down the walls to collect in puddles on the polished floorboards and all bed linen had to be stored in a charcoal-fired hot-room until just before use.

In time, the hill station became known as the Peak. The name has stuck but it is a curious one for it does not refer to the highest mountain. This, topped off with radio masts, is known in Chinese as Che Kai Shan (Raising Flag Mountain: *shan* is a mountain or hill) and in English as Victoria Peak. But this is not *the* Peak. The phrase refers to the area below the mountain summit, eastwards from the lower promontory of Mount Austin across Victoria Gap and along a ridge about two kilometres long to Magazine Gap by way of Mount Gough. This wooded chine contains very exclusive residences tucked behind discreet walls along narrow mountain roads shaded by luxuriant trees, built not for sedan automobiles but sedan chairs: this is the land of the taipan and the tremendously rich.

The primary means of access to the mountain was by sedan chair up the Old Peak Road, a tortuous stone pathway in places at an angle of more than 32°. It still exists, overhung by dense foliage and unfrequented save by a select few masochistic foreign devils who jog down it to their offices. The chairs were of a variety of types: the best were four-bearer models with side walls and roofs, the fronts closed either by doors, shutters or curtains of stiffened silk or leather whilst the simplest were two-bearer rattan seats slung between bamboo poles and not unlike an Indian doolie. The former were frequently privately owned and ornately decorated with liveried bearers while the latter were for public hire. The ride up the Peak took just under an hour in a two-bearer chair, the public hire of which cost thirty cents an hour or HK$1.50 for the whole day: a four-bearer public chair cost sixty cents an hour or HK$2 a day.

Not only people but virtually everything else ascended the mountain on foot – domestic supplies, firewood and coal, furniture, cabin trunks, blocks of ice from the store in Ice House Street and personal possessions were suspended from the shoulder-poles of coolies who toiled up the mountain for fifteen cents an hour. Only extraordinarily heavy items (such as pianos and cast-iron bathtubs) went up by mule although a few forebears of today's joggers used to ride up and down on horseback.

Many believed the Peak Tram would put paid to the sedan chair which was already losing popularity in the city to the newly introduced rickshaw but this was not so. Passengers disembarking from the tram at the various stations up the track often had to travel on as far as a mile so the chairs remained, to be joined by rickshaws on the more level roads. The tram authorities even built shelters for the chair bearers and rickshaw pullers who remained in employment until well after the advent of the motor car: the last sedan chair vanished just before the outbreak of war in 1941 and the last rickshaw licence on the Peak expired in the mid-fifties.

Despite the march of progress, the Peak Tram remains essentially unchanged. The bottom terminus is now a twenty-two-storey commercial skyscraper whilst the top station has an oval restaurant balanced over it on piers, architecturally reminiscent of an art deco bidet. The aluminium-bodied cars are much larger, air-conditioned and entirely enclosed, tickets may no longer be purchased on board and the switchman halfway up the mountain has been made redundant by a new set of points, but the track is the same and the location of the stations unaltered. Even the Barker Road shelter looks much as it did in 1954 when, passing through it, I saw Clark Gable filming *Soldier of Fortune* on the platform.

The method of propulsion is basically unaltered and remains delightfully archaic, a survivor of the era of Victorian technology – only the original steam engine was replaced by an electric one in 1924. The system consists of two cars, one ascending as the other descends, with a passing place exactly halfway down the mountain just above May Road. Each car is attached to the end of a one inch diameter steel cable wound round one of a pair of massive drums in the engine house at the top terminus: the turning of the two drums is synchronised by gearing. The cars carry just a brakeman on board whose job is to liaise by a series of bells with the driver in the engine house and hold down a wooden pole which keeps the brakes off. In an emergency – and there has never been one – he lets go of the pole and steel jaws grip a central brake rail bolted to the track bed: the tram will stop in less than ten feet.

I first rode the Peak Tram at the age of seven, my journey a descent: I had gone up the Peak by vehicular road in a dark blue Royal Navy Humber staff car to see the apartment my parents were moving into at Block A, Mount Austin, a building with what must be one of the most spectacular views in the world, for the lounge and bedrooms overlooked Hong Kong harbour and Kowloon (and the hills of China in those pollution-free winter months) whilst the dining room surveyed Lamma Island, the Lema group on the horizon and the sun-danced expanse of the South China Sea.

The tram was open at one end. It was early afternoon, some of the seats in second class occupied by amahs on their way to collect children from school, dressed in white *sam* smocks and black *fu* trousers, their hair scraped back into severe spinster's buns. I chose to ride in the open section and positioned myself on an outside seat. Settling next to an elderly Chinese man in a grey jacket, and grabbing a firm hold of a nearby roof pillar, I found myself being spoken to by a European colonial madam of advancing years, her substantial girth encased in a dress printed with large yellow and red blossoms.

29

'Little boy,' she remarked. 'We do not sit here. We sit inside the cabin.'

I just stared at her, not out of impudence but sheer wonderment. Her permed hair was dyed brown, the colouring growing out at the roots to show grey, her skin bore an over-application of make-up, her fingers were laden with rings and her wrists heavy with bangles. As I was lost for words and made no reply she, interpreting this as either insolence or imbecility, huffed and snorted with righteous indignation. A long ring on an electric bell sounded. She sailed off to the cabin and I gripped the pillar more tightly. My mother, riding inside, knew nothing of this meeting and I decided it best to keep it quiet: the woman looked like a teacher and I was about to start primary school.

The tram began to move, gathering momentum as it edged out of the shade of the terminus, past a red warning notice and onto a bridge section of track. To my right was laid out, at my feet, the buildings of Central, the buff stone blocks of the Hongkong and Shanghai Bank and the Bank of China dominating the city. Beyond was the harbour with cargo ships at anchor, dull grey warships alongside the quays of HMS *Tamar* and, in a heat haze, Kowloon with a white P&O liner berthed at a jetty.

Suddenly, the tram tilted and started to slip downhill. It did not stop at Barker Road but continued on, turning a curve surrounded by impenetrable undergrowth, dense trees hung with creepers and plants bearing huge elephant-eared leaves. Black butterflies the size of swifts flitted in the shadows. Then, in the middle of nowhere, the tram halted. The air was filled, in the void of silence after the rattle of the tram, with the saw and chatter of crickets, the buzz of a million insects. There was no station. My worst fears were being realised: we had broken down and could be stuck here for hours, even days. Glancing into the trees to see if there was some way by which we might escape through the jungle, I saw a snake. It was about three feet long, dark brown with pale brown zig-zag markings.

'He eat wrat, eat moy-see,' said the Chinese man by my side, following my gaze. 'Good to eat for you. Make you st'ong. Make you blood st'ong. No weak.' He touched my arm to test my biceps. 'Ah, no p'oblum. You st'ong now.'

I was not quite sure how to take this approach, having been warned by my mother of letting strange men touch me: in the hotel from which we were moving lived a whisky-breathed European man of dubious reputation. I smiled sheepishly and the old man grinned back, baring a row of nicotine-yellow uneven teeth, in the centre of which glinted a solid gold crown.

The snake vanished into the leaf litter and the tram set off again. Beside the step to my seat, the cable supporting the ascending tram hissed through steel runners and pulley wheels covered in grease: they might have been related to the vanished snake. As I was to discover, it had not broken down. The cable drums work synchronously, both halting when a car stops: as there are more stations in the lower half of the track it follows that when the rising car pulls up at a station, the descending one is necessarily left in the wilds. Over the years, this has caused me to eavesdrop upon a large number of tourist loud-moutheries such as 'Hey! It's gone crook! All out and push!' (Australian tour party) and 'Guess we run outa gas, huh!' (American sailors) not to mention 'Hold tight, everyone! The driver's out on strike/gone for a tea break!' (British sightseers). By their wit, shall you know innocents abroad.

At the halfway point the two trams passed each other, a man in the other car with a camera and a severe case of sunburn taking my picture: then, rattling over the points, it slowed for the May Road station, the steepest part of the journey with the track at an inclination of almost 2 in 1.

The conductor appeared from the cabin section. He was a Chinese in a white uniform with a peaked cap, a ticket punching machine around his waist, next to a leather money pouch. He had a very prominent Adam's apple and wore thick-lensed spectacles which lent him a vaguely professorial appearance. Ignoring me – my mother had paid for my ticket – he collected other passengers' fares. As he did so, he stood at a sharp angle to the floor, the whole world tilted bizarrely. An amah on the platform with a pair of trussed hens and a bundle of green beans hanging from her hand appeared to be defying gravity. On the May Road bridge, a car drove by as if riding along a banked wall. What was more, the world was moving up and down, pitching and yawing. I found myself growing dizzy for the tram was bouncing like a yo-yo on its cable.

'You no 'fwaid,' the old man advised me. 'Wrope strong. No can bwoken.'

Once more, the tram started off, passing under the granite bridge and entering an area of colonial houses with deep verandas lined by kumquat bushes, azaleas and salvias growing in glazed tubs decorated with dragons. Beside the track there was a strip of land in which a man wearing a vest, baggy trousers and a coolie's conical hat was tending rows of geraniums and chrysanthemums in pots, his watering cans suspended from a bamboo pole across his shoulders. After a few more bridges and other station platforms the track levelled, and the car rattled over a bridge above a nullah flowing with fast tumbling water and entered the lower terminus, a four storey building painted cream with apartments on the top two floors.

'You like twam?' the old man enquired, waving his hand about as he spoke.

'I like,' I replied.

My mother came and took my hand.

'You boy cleffer boy,' the old man told her as he lightly brushed his fingers against my hair. 'Be wrich man one day.'

As we walked down Garden Road, I looked back at the terminus: the clock showed a quarter to three but the old man was nowhere to be seen.

'He touched my arm,' I admitted, obeying the instruction to report such incidents. 'On the way down.'

'I expect he did,' came the unanticipated response.

'But he shouldn't . . .' I began.

'It's all right if Chinese do it,' my mother interrupted, 'but don't let Europeans.'

'Why not?'

'Chinese people will touch you because you have blond hair.

Like that old man did. They think if they touch your hair, because it's the colour of gold, they'll be lucky.'

She did not elucidate why Europeans should not follow suit and try for some of the same good fortune but prudence told me not to press the matter. I walked on remembering the snake, the yo-yoing and the tilting, crazy buildings.

For much of my childhood and teenage years, I travelled to school on the tram. It has played a seminal part in my life: I took my first girlfriends out to dates on it, wrote my homework on it, returned apprehensively home on it with atrocious examination results, have ridden on it when the roads were blocked by post-typhoon landslides, have sat on it in the company of Ava Gardner, the Platters and the Ink Spots, Louis Armstrong and Sammy Davis, Junior. Yet I have never forgotten my first ride, the harridan, the kindly old man and the conductor who appeared as an extra playing himself in at least two movies, *The World of Suzie Wong* and *Love is a Many Splendored Thing*.

Remarkably, the Peak Tram has hardly ever shut. Repairs and renovations are carried out at night and the track, which is replaced every twenty years, has never failed, even under Japanese bombardment when it was shelled from a battery in Kowloon: a direct hit on the top terminus failed to halt operations and the shell remains embedded to this day under the main cable drums. The longest period during which the tram failed to run was from Christmas Day 1941 to 5 June, 1942 and this was deliberate. As Hong Kong surrendered, S.F. Chubb, the senior engineer, sabotaged all the electrical wiring in the engine house before being marched off to internment with his family.

When I was a boy, 85 per cent of the passengers were local commuters but today those who live on the Peak go to work in limousines, leaving the tram to trippers and tourists: their servants go to market in taxis. Of the three million passengers who now use the tram annually barely 10 per cent are Peak residents.

What was, as a child, a joyful journey is now reduced to little more than a fairground ride. The tourists begin to queue at the bottom terminus before 9 o'clock, delivered there by tour coach, taxi or a free, open-topped Citibus service from the Star Ferry. Every departure is more or less packed full. The windows are generally kept shut to preserve the air conditioning, the seats are closer together and the brakeman, with whom I used to sit and chat as a child, is now positioned behind a barrier. The cars seldom stop at the intermediate stations, several of which have been tarted up with fake 'Victorian' street-lamps, because there are no amahs carrying poultry and vegetables to alight there. The ride is usually a non-stop jaunt up the mountain from the tourist shops in St John's Building to the tourist shops under the restaurant. The clatter of camera shutters, the cackle of inane comments and the whirl of videocams drown out the cricket song, whilst air pollution from the city traffic has very significantly reduced butterfly numbers. And yet, as recently as the autumn of 1992, I spied a Chinese cobra beside the rails.

At the Peak

Opposite the top terminus of the Peak Tram is a small café: not surprisingly, it is called the Peak Café. A patio under shade trees stands behind a dining room, where butterflies still drift lazily by on iridescent wings, false hornets zip viciously past and birds twitter in the creepers and moss-hung branches. Although the stone building has been renovated in recent years, it retains much of the charm I recall from childhood, sitting there eating ice creams scrounged from American or Australian soldiers *en route* for Korea, homesick men for whom I was a reminder of a kid brother or son left behind in Sausalito or Sydney.

Few know the history of the café which has had a chequered and fascinating past. Originally built in 1901 as a shelter for sedan chair coolies and rickshaw pullers, it was then little more than a stone bungalow with a gentle pitched tiled roof and a fireplace, for the mists can be chill at times and, when a typhoon is in the offing, the wind whips through Victoria Gap, in which the café squats. At the outbreak of war in 1941, the shelter was taken over as a military look-out post. From within yards of its doors, panoramic views of the open sea and the harbour are visible lending it a strategic importance. Several times, Zero fighters bombed and strafed it. With Hong Kong fallen, it became first a police post and then a small restaurant for Japanese junior officers who treated it as a mess. After the war, the franchise of the restaurant was passed to a Chinese woman who became the first non-European to be permitted to operate a business on the exclusively expatriate mountain. She was unceremoniously kicked out in the late eighties when her lease came up for renewal.

Five thoroughfares meet in front of the Peak Café. Mount Austin Road rises sharply directly before it, leading up to apartment blocks, houses and the summit of the Peak whilst, from the left, comes Peak Road, the original motor road up the mountain: tucked away to the right is the Old Peak Road. The last two are Harlech Road and Lugard Road.

Although listed as such, Lugard and Harlech roads are both barely one car wide and closed to public transport: indeed, Lugard Road is incapable of taking the weight of a modern car for at least half its length where it runs across the near vertical north face of Victoria Peak on a viaduct over seventy years old, in its day a marvel of concrete engineering. They meet to the west of the mountain providing what a turn of the century guide book termed *a pleasant circumlocutory perambulation of the hill district*. Whilst Lugard Road is the most favoured by tourists because of the breathtaking vistas it affords, for me, Harlech Road is the wonder.

The best time to walk this way is in the early to mid-morning when the air is cool from the night, the sun not yet severe and the tarmac not yet harshly burning underfoot. Starting between the Peak Café and Mount Austin Road, it sets off through an arched canopy of trees. Gradually, the sounds of tourists and the noise and smell of vehicles fade away until it is hard to imagine Central is less than a kilometre away. The shadows are scattered with butterflies and the leaf litter twitches with lizards.

The slopes of the Peak and adjacent summits are richly sylvan yet this was not always the case. When Hong Kong was first ceded to the British in 1841, the hills were barren and grass-covered with only the gullies carrying stunted trees. Afforestation was carried out as a deliberate policy against landslip. All of Hong Kong's geologically young mountains are prone to movement and high incidents of tropical rainfall only aggravate the situation.

On 19 July, 1926, twenty inches of rain fell in eight hours. During the night, many buildings were damaged, the Peak Tram was uncharacteristically put out of service for a week and a 300-ton boulder slid down on a pumping station, killing four workers. So much mud filled the streets of Hong Kong the decision was made to forest the slopes. The policy was to prove effective but not foolproof: small landslides still occur every rainy season, blocking the occasional road, and a substantial landslide in June 1972 destroyed a block of luxury apartments killing sixty-eight people, nearly a hundred being entombed alive in mud-slips which buried squatter huts at Sau Mau Ping and Kwun Tong.

With the exception of tree-felling in the war for fuel, the policy has continued unabated. Even the massive banyan trees along Harlech Road, hung with tresses of aerial roots and gnarled as sages, are less than a century old, planted intentionally and not the result of natural seeding.

Where trees cannot be planted, or a landslide has occurred in the past, the slope is shorn and covered in concrete which is sprayed onto boulders and earth rather like pebble-dash rendering on a suburban London house. It sets hard and, except for the occasional drainage pipe hole, looks like artificial rock. Sadly, as patches of repaired mountain along Harlech Road show, these pipes are often filled with rubbish which prevents the essential drainage from occurring and stops up potential homes for reptiles and small rodents.

Half a kilometre along the walk, a waterfall tumbles down from a sheer rock face festooned with moss and ferns. This stream, along with all the others on the Peak, feeds down to Pokfulam reservoir which lies in the valley below. Originally there was a pool at the foot of the valley but this was transformed into the existing reservoir in 1864, the first of many Hong Kong reservoirs which, as the population grew, became increasingly important: water was, until the 1980s, a precious commodity in Hong Kong and it was not unknown for it to be rationed. In the early 1960s, I recall one period when the taps only ran for three hours every third day. Baths and buckets were filled, lavatories flushed only when they became as noxious as a nullah and the beaches became crowded with people swimming to get clean.

The valley has another important place in Hong Kong history:

it was here in 1886 that an enterprising Scottish doctor called Patrick Manson, concerned at the standard of milk provided by Chinese dairies (which were mostly just one or two cows milked with scant regard for hygiene), set up one of Hong Kong's most famous and enduring local companies – The Dairy Farm. On the grassy valley sides he maintained a herd of eighty cows which, despite being almost entirely eradicated by rinderpest, was eventually to flourish. The Dairy Farm still provides Hong Kong with milk and milk products, runs a supermarket chain and manufactures its own ice cream, now sadly being beaten out of the market-place by Häagen-Dazs. My memory of the Dairy Farm however, lies not just in milk (enforceably drunk in primary school) but in the popsy men.

In summer no street near a school, no picnic site no matter how remote and no beach was without its popsy man. Riding on a specially adapted bicycle, these vendors carried over the front wheel an oblong aluminium box filled with dry ice and a supply of ice cream tubs and lollipops called popsies, after the Americanism popsicle: under this box was a two-legged stand on which the machine rested when parked for business. Each man wore a white uniform, marked from sweat and contact with the aluminium, and carried a leather money pouch. Behind the saddle was another metal box containing wooden spoons, excess loose change and newspapers in which to wrap his wares if the customer had a long way to walk with his purchases. A popsy, in lemon, orange or sickly pineapple flavours, cost ten cents and came in a thin paper wrapper.

The whole of the Pokfulam valley is now designated a country park and closed to development. Despite its proximity to urban environments, it seethes with wildlife, rarely spied but ever-present. The monkeys that used to live here in abundance are now scarce yet not extinct, being descendants of Hong Kong's original population of Rhesus monkeys. They are not brazen beggars like urban monkeys the world over but are generally shy creatures who do not depend upon human hand-outs for their survival and usually keep away from human settlements and busy roads.

The paucity of primates is made up for by the plenitude of other animals. Two (possibly three) species of civet cat live here. They are nocturnal hunters and hardly ever seen even in the headlamps of a car. Keeping to the deepest forest areas, they are omnivorous, killing rodents and small birds but also feeding on fruit and seeds. Creatures more frequently spied – though still not a common sight – are the muntjak or barking deer. They are delicate, pretty little beasts standing about fifty centimetres to the shoulder, the males sporting short antlers with both sexes having tusk-like upper canine teeth. They gain their name because, in the mating season, the males bark to attract females or establish territories, the noise more like the cough of a fox than the bark of a dog. Porcupines also exist in this valley, occasionally alarming early morning joggers with a rattle of quills in the undergrowth. Thai grey squirrels jump and scamper through the trees. Even the reservoir is not without its residents: the large, soft-shelled mud turtle and the big-headed terrapin live here alongside the common terrapin.

The humans one meets on Harlech Road are as varied as the animals hiding in the trees. At intervals, the urban services have erected poles with discreet notices urging joggers to halt and conduct an exercise. It is not uncommon to meet early morning keep-fit fanatics pausing to breathe deeply, doing a few press-ups and toe-touchings or stepping up and down off a log with t-shirts stuck to their pectorals by sweat, their soggy hair held back by towelling bands. These masochists are the modern equivalent of the other morning exerciser one meets here – the exponent of t'ai chi. Whereas the former has taken to chasing the impossible Western ideal of physical perfection, the latter is after not sleek muscles but tranquillity of mind, harmony of body and soul with the world at large.

In the cool shade of a tree, old men and women stand in solitary peace. The men sometimes roll up their trouser legs, remove their shirts and go through their performance in a vest: the women frequently wear fu trousers. Both sexes have soft slippers on their feet such as Chinese have worn since the time of Christ. In silence, they move through a complex series of unhurried, graceful steps and motions, their arms turning and their wrists twisting, their fingers shaping metaphorical symbols in the air. Their legs rise and fall, stretch and come in, their whole bodies balanced on one foot, their heads looking gently from side to side yet their eyes unseeing. It is as if they are living a frantic dance in extreme slow motion, going through a series of *kung fu* exertions at the speed of a lover's dream. Passers-by may exchange a brief stranger's greeting but no one interrupts these meditating dancers.

Maids walk their charges this way too and, in one form or another, have done so for nearly a century. In the days of Chinese servants, it was common to see baby amahs, their hair scraped severely back to a bun or short cue, chatting and giggling together as they pushed bamboo and wicker-work prams or chairs the wheels and frames of which, being constructed without so much as a metal pin, squeaked and creaked as if seeking to converse with the tree crickets. Their charges were exclusively European children with blond or tousled heads and a command of Cantonese before a fluency in their mother tongues. Nowadays, they have gone, to be replaced by diminutive Filipina maids in brightly coloured dresses and blouses only a few sizes larger than those of the children they mind. Though they also prattle and titter when they meet, sit together on the benches under the trees or walk through the shadows at a child's pace, the children are no longer exclusively European but also Chinese, Japanese and Malaysian.

The tourists who come this way are of a sub-species one can respect. They may carry a camera and dress in the uniform of the holidaymaker abroad, but they are not loud, not brash, not intrusive and their motives are those of curious discovery. Some sport binoculars to watch for birds, some guidebooks and a few of the more enterprising have purchased a government issue 1:20,000 map. They are seeking either the out-of-the-ordinary or a respite from the city, the hubbub of which can be irksome to those not accustomed to it. I seldom walk along Harlech Road without one of these wanderers stopping me to ask a question: as I rarely carry a camera and am never attired as a tripper, they assume me to be a local expatriate.

I remember one bent old man who spoke to me in 1988 at a point where the road widens to include a small area filled with an obstacle course for the keep-fitters. He was English and, I reckoned, in his nineties. Walking with difficulty, he was aided by a stick and his wife who must have been in her late eighties. She wore a tourist flower-print dress but he was dressed in slacks with a crease like a knife and a blazer with a crest on the pocket, the gold braid much tarnished. His shirt was open but he wore a cravat at his throat. His only concession to modernity and comfort was that he was wearing a pair of pristine training shoes rather than polished brogues.

'Excuse me,' he said as I passed them, going in the same direction: I stopped. 'We are looking for the Middlesex stone. Do you know it?'

I replied I did.

'Is it far?' his wife enquired.

'Another two hundred and fifty metres or so,' I answered, adding, 'yards.'

'Right,' said the man. 'Will you lead us there?'

I agreed and we walked slowly on together, passing the steps down to the firing point of a rifle range across a valley ahead of us on a mountain called High West. As I child, I saw ambulance men remove the body of a young woman murdered there by a jilted lover.

The old man was not disposed to talking, his breath coming in bouts. His wife clucked at him, trying to persuade him to turn back.

'It's too far, dear. Much too far. In the hot sun. Much, much too far.'

'Nonsense,' he stammered. 'Nonsense.'

Eventually, we reached a small park with a pavilion and several picnic tables in it surrounded by trees and flowering shrubs.

'It's not as I remember it,' the old man remarked, pausing.

'More bushes. And that,' he nodded in the direction of the park, 'I think was where we mustered.'

I pointed ahead to a boulder up a bank by the path.

'That's the stone,' he exclaimed. 'That's it!'

He hobbled over to it, standing on the path and looking up at it on the bank.

The stone has an inscription upon it which states, bleakly,

25th. Battn
Middlesex Regt.
"Tyndareus"
Feb. 6th. 1917

Throughout my childhood, I had known of the stone but knew nothing of its history nor why it had been placed in this particular spot. In 1981, however, a bronze plate was fixed to the stone which gives its story:

> This stone memorial was erected by Lieutenant Colonel John Ward, Commanding Officer, in memory of those men of the 25th. Battalion, The Middlesex Regiment, who died when the troopship TYNDAREUS struck a German mine off Cape Agulhas, South Africa, on 6th February 1917. The Battalion had embarked in England and were en route for Hong Kong to carry out garrison duties. There is no doubt that the exemplary conduct of all ranks after the accident contributed in considerable measure to the Master's ability to prevent his ship from sinking with further loss of life.
>
> The 1st Battalion of the Regiment subsequently fought with distinction during the defence of Hong Kong – December 1941.

It occurs to me now that the memorial was positioned here as it must be one of the most peaceful places on the island. There is always a breeze blowing, rising from the sea, and in the evenings the long shadows of the setting sun slice through the trees. They must remind the ghosts of home.

The old man stood with his head bowed, his hands together on the knob of his stick. His wife came across to me.

'Thank you so much,' she said. 'It means a lot to him. Friends, you understand. It was his unit, you see . . .' She smiled wanly and, in a near whisper, continued, 'Is it quicker to go back the way we came or carry on round the mountain? His emphysema, you know.'

'The way you came,' I answered and continued on my way but, when I looked back, the old man was resolutely setting off along Lugard Road, his wife quietly reproaching him as one might a fractious boy.

At this point, between High West and Victoria Peak, a number of routes or paths offer different alternatives. Across the park, a narrow path leads to the firing range butts where Japanese and British bullets might be picked out of the stony soil then, almost obliterated from disuse, it carries on down to Pokfulam and the site of the pumping station where the boulder killed the workmen in 1926. Beside this, another much overgrown track runs in a direct line to the summit of High West: this is only for the appropriately shod ultra-fit. Another path, with steps, disappears from Harlech Road up towards the summit of Victoria Peak just below which it joins Governor's Walk, a narrow concrete path which afforded an evening stroll to governors when residing at Mountain Lodge, their Peak residence no longer in existence.

Harlech Road itself continues west along the side of High West, dropping gradually to a ridge where it peters out. Lugard Road curves off to the right to complete the *circumlocutory perambulation* back to the Peak Tram whilst another concrete track called Hatton Road leads off from Harlech Road next to some distinctly noisome public conveniences thankfully hidden by a copse of bamboo.

To make your way along Lugard Road is to undertake one of the most spectacular strolls in the world. Gradually, as the road narrows and hugs the mountainside, turning eastwards once more, the full vista of Hong Kong, the harbour and Kowloon unfurls quite literally at one's feet. For a first-time visitor it can be breathtaking. I have known friends drawn near to tears by it either because of its utter magnificence or from frustration because they cannot get more than a fifth of it in their camera lens at any one time. If the weather is clear, every skyscraper, every vessel in the harbour, every street and lane, every apartment block is laid out directly below the old concrete railings along the roadway. Across the harbour, the whole of Kowloon, the mountains behind and successive ranges stretching off to China are visible. Tiny jet airliners fly across the slopes, tiny ferries ply the waters, tiny cargo ships unload their merchandise into tinier lighters. It is all so seemingly accessible, one might reach down as into a toy village to rearrange a garden, dip a finger in a swimming pool or push a car along just a little bit faster. The sight would beggar even Shakespeare's vocabulary and confound many a landscape painter. It has to be seen, to be experienced, to be heard and smelled and studied to come to terms with it.

The way I usually choose is Hatton Road for it is a little known downhill route all the way from here to Kennedy Town and takes me to another favourite and largely unvisited corner of Hong Kong. The view from here is one which run-of-the-mill tourists do not see. It is a panorama not of the central harbour and city but of the western approaches. In the distance lie the mountains of Lantau and the various western islands of Cheung Chau, Hei Ling Chau, Sunshine Island (where there was once a leper colony, from an inmate of which I bought a set of teak bookends I still own), Peng Chau and the uninhabited Kau Yi Chau. Closer, almost at one's feet for the mountain drops away sharply here, is Green Island where Hong Kong used to have its explosives store and on which there used to live a small snake unique to its four or five acre insular domain. Just in front of Green Island is Mount Davis, the most westerly hill on Hong Kong island and, directly ahead, the factories and tower blocks of Kennedy Town and Sai Ying Pun. Closer, however, is the Hill Above Belcher's and it is here I always go.

Very few people walk down Hatton Road. The grass leans over the pathway while branches reach out to snag at clothing, cleared back only once a year by the urban services department. It was built by the military at the turn of the century and named after a major general. Never intended for public use, it was constructed to give access to a gun battery the remains of which can be seen from the Peak.

Originally, the spur on which the battery was built was covered in pine trees hence its name – Pinewood Battery. Commissioned as a result of the 1898 Committee on Armaments of Certain Stations at Home and Abroad, convened in London, Pinewood was designed to take two six-inch Mark VII guns to cover the western approaches to the harbour. Situated at an altitude of 1,009 feet above sea level, it had a commanding view but there were other batteries in the area: it was built in 1902/3 and declared surplus to requirements in 1906. By 1913, the guns had been removed. In the mid-1920s, with the lessons in aerial warfare learnt in the Great War taken to heart, two three-inch anti-aircraft guns were installed and their mounting platforms remain to this day along with the command post buildings, assorted battery stores and barracks, some underground and approached by weed-strewn slit-trenches. The battery saw action but once. At 08:15 hours on 15 December, 1941, it came under heavy artillery fire from Kowloon. For over four hours, it was pounded, one gun being destroyed, the range-finding equipment wiped out but, amazingly, with only one Indian soldier killed and another injured.

I first walked down to the battery in 1952. It was a shambles with slabs of concrete lying about and huge metal bolts sticking up from the ground. The dug-outs and buildings stank of damp and rotting cloth. I ventured into some of them with a torch. Metal-framed bunks stood rusting against the walls, some of them draped with tatters of military blankets, warped wooden tables and chairs leaned against each other and there were even some remnants of charts or orders pasted to the walls, some in Japanese and some in English. Overhead, cracked Bakelite light sockets hung from the ceilings and the heavy metal doors creaked on their hinges. The place reeked of ghosts and I fled to the sunlight. Several of the buildings, which were painted in uneven brown and green camouflage stripes, had gaping holes blasted through the thick concrete walls and the ground shimmered with shards of glass. By the gun mountings, I searched in vain for cartridge cases but found several pieces of shrapnel and a tarnished military badge with a light cannon on it, the centre of the design being the weapon's spoked wheel.

What drew me into the bushes below the battery I do not know. Kismet, perhaps. But there, in a patch of stunted azaleas, I found a half-buried skeleton. At first, I did not realise what it was: the bones were not white and pristine but green and mottled like old sticks. The rib cage had collapsed, the digits of one hand separated whilst the skull lay on its side, the lower mandible separated from it. In the cranium was a ragged hole. In amongst the fallen azalea leaves were scraps of khaki cloth. I examined these, careful not to touch the bones. They fell apart at my touch. When I returned home, the police were called and the skeleton removed. Subsequent enquiries proved the body to be not a British gunner but a Japanese presumed murdered by local partisans after the 1945 capitulation.

The place is different now. Just before reaching the battery, a path wends up to the left into a narrow gully. Here, under a canopy of dark trees, someone has erected a little shack and set out tables and chairs where old men play mahjong. Their presence is an indication of their avidity for the game and peace: it is a steep uphill walk from the city. Close by is a small, modern wooden shrine of the kind usually found in shops: whether it is intended to placate the evil ghosts of war or protect the spirits of those killed here is unclear. Perhaps its function is to guard the mahjong players.

The battery itself is a picnic site. A small pavilion, a public toilet and a row of stone tables and barbecue grills line the area where once ammunition was unloaded. The command buildings have been whitewashed, yet the other buildings retain their camouflage colours, now fading with years of tropical sunlight, and the blast holes in the walls are shrouded with creepers. In several of the slit-trenches, substantial trees have established themselves. The glass has gone to be replaced with drinks can ring-pulls and the place has been picked bare of shrapnel. Before the command post, a line of pine trees has been planted.

On Hatton Road, below the battery, stands another colonial relic. The boundary of the original city of Victoria was defined by statute and marked with a series of six boundary stones. The third of these stands on the left of the road. It is a granite obelisk about a metre high, incised with the words *City of Victoria 1903*.

The noise of the city, which is somehow muted for the length of Hatton Road, begins to swell at this point. The buzz of crickets and rustle of lizards, the call of unseen birds and the occasional tick of water surrenders over the distance of 250 metres to the thrub of traffic, the hum of machinery, the cacophony of radios and the blare of ships' klaxons.

Uncle Lee's Roast Goose

Alfred my driver bade farewell to his wife, put his mobile phone upon the dashboard and pressed his foot on the accelerator. Our canary yellow Mercedes Benz 190D pulled out from behind a thirty-ton flat-bed Hino truck with dual Hong Kong/Guangzhou registration plates carrying two Maersk Line containers, *en route* for the Kwai Chung cargo terminal: in front of it were four similar lorries, fully laden and travelling at fifty miles an hour. A black Porsche 914 sped up behind us, closing in to our bumper, but Alfred was not fazed by it.

'So many lorries!' Betty exclaimed. My interpreter, she was sitting in the back of the car. 'I don't like to drive out here. It is too dangerous.'

'Do you remember when this coast was quiet?' Alfred asked. 'It took three quarters of an hour to drive to Tuen Mun. Now it takes fifteen minutes unless there is an accident. Less if you speed.' He glanced in the rear view mirror at the Porsche. 'Best not to speed. The police have radar traps on the highway.'

I looked over his shoulder to the sea. Across the Kap Shui Mun sea passage, which has featured on navigational charts since the late fifteenth century, long before Hong Kong itself merited a mention, lay the most easterly hills of Lantau: a little ahead was the small island of Ma Wan.

As a boy, I used to come here to swim at 11½ Mile Beach, now renamed Lido Beach although no lido exists nor ever has: nor, for that matter, were there any facilities save a matshed public convenience constructed of bamboo poles and woven rice straw panels erected over a hole in the ground. The hills around were dotted with the secluded houses of wealthy businessmen; one end of the beach contained two wide pools fed by hill streams, alert with little fish. Where the wavelets broke, the sand was peppered with the holes of thousands of minute, white ghost-crabs. But no longer: the bays are now littered with flotsam, the hillsides a rash of suburban developments, terraced bijou hacienda-ettes and high rise tower blocks clinging to rocky outcrops. No one swims off this shore unless they seek to strengthen their natural immunisation against a wide variety of especially pernicious human ailments.

In Kap Shui Mun at least a dozen cargo vessels were riding at anchor, being refitted. Lighters and barges were clotted at their hulls, each giving off an intermittent oxy-acetylene explosion. Between the vessels, a hydrofoil on its way to Guangzhou was cutting a white scar through the sea, weaving to avoid a grey marine police boat, its deck gun covered by a tarpaulin.

'Are you ready for something to eat?' Alfred enquired as the Porsche ripped by, a young Chinese woman at the wheel. 'I know a good place near here.'

Where the Chinese are concerned, this is a rhetorical question for the answer is expected to be in the affirmative. What is more, the question is seldom posed unless a good restaurant is not more than five minutes away.

'I'm ready,' I confirmed and it was the truth. All I had swallowed that day were a few dozen melon seeds, a dubious bun and a glass of piping hot jasmine tea.

'Good,' Alfred said. I sensed a relief in his voice.

In Cantonese, Betty asked Alfred where he had in mind and, on hearing his answer, said, 'That's very good. A very famous restaurant.'

The fact it was half-past two in the afternoon was of no consequence. A Chinese restaurant usually opens about ten in the morning and stays in business for twelve to fourteen hours. The main rush hours for food are the same as in any restaurant the world over – noon until one-thirty and six to nine-thirty

– but unlike those in most countries, it remains ticking over between times.

At the next junction, Alfred steered the Mercedes off the highway and down into Sham Tseng. This place has been famous for years as being the site of the San Miguel brewery: San Mig is to Hong Kong what Guinness is to Ireland and Budweiser is to the USA – synonymous. I did not recognise the place: when I was last here, the brewery was the only building save a few village houses across a beach. Now it is a thriving small town under the umbrella of the highway which passes across the valley on a viaduct seventy feet high. There is a clinic, a cluster of small factories and a larger area of huts, shacks and low buildings called Sham Tseng San Tsuen, otherwise known as the New Village. We parked the Mercedes in a square of wasteland beside one of the viaduct pillars: a man in a shack asked abruptly where we were going.

'Yue Kee,' said Alfred and the man was appeased.

Main Street, New Village consists of single and two-storey buildings and what might be termed shacks if they were not slightly more substantially built. The actual street is about ten feet wide and strewn with gravel washed down from the viaduct banking, odd bits of paper and wood and several mangy-looking chow dogs asleep on their sides just out of reach of passing car or bicycle wheels. The shops lining the street are general stores selling foodstuffs, pots and pans, light bulbs and Coca Cola.

In this row of buildings stands the Yue Kee Restaurant. From the outside, it is an unprepossessing place opening straight onto the road. To the right of the entrance is a small kitchen equipped with a few open-flame cooking rings, woks and other cooking paraphernalia, whilst to the left is a plywood lectern-style desk with a telephone, a writing pad made of scrap paper and a glass of plastic ball-point pens. The restaurant itself appears to be a single room with half a dozen round tables crammed into it, a staircase rising to the side. At one table, a party of six were finishing their meal, looking up with suppressed surprise at the appearance of a European as they sipped glasses of tea and scratched at their gums with toothpicks politely shaded behind cupped hands.

A waiter wearing a pair of plimsolls, black trousers and an unbuttoned jacket over a string vest directed us to a table and laid three places, dropping the bowls and chopsticks from a height of several inches. The chopsticks were contained in paper envelopes to suggest they were in a state of pristine cleanliness: not that it made any difference for the waiter, no sooner had he put them down, whisked the envelopes off and took them away. Alfred disdained the menu and placed our order. Whilst waiting for it, boiling tea was served in a rice pattern pot and we helped ourselves to a dish of chillied, pickled cabbage in the centre of the round table. All Chinese restaurant tables are round so the diners may reach the food placed in the centre in communal dishes.

The first course was fish, a whole bass served on a bed of vegetables and covered in a brown, sweetish gravy which might have been made of plums. We picked off pieces of the carcass, sucked the flesh from the bones and dropped the cleaned sections of skeleton onto a plate. Next came an oval platter of scallops and celery, steam rising from the colourless sauce.

'How many courses?' I asked.

Experience dictates this polite enquiry: I have sat down to a purportedly 'light' meal which lasted for fourteen courses and two hours.

'Only three,' Betty replied, adding with a hint of anxiety. 'Is this not enough?'

'That's fine,' I said. 'Just right. If I eat too much at this time I get sleepy.'

Fresh bowls were brought and the debris of dishes removed. Then the waiter returned with a wide dish piled high with meat.

'Roast goose, Cantonese style,' Alfred declared. 'This restaurant is the most famous for goose.'

Another dish was placed next to the goose.

'What is it?' I enquired, although I could see two webbed feet sticking out of the contents.

'Goose spare parts,' Betty replied enigmatically.

At the first mouthful, I was reminded of a comment a friend had made to me a few days before. 'It's all very well writing a book about Hong Kong,' he had said, 'but how the hell will you portray the smells of the streets and the taste of the food? You'll have to ask your publisher to provide scratch-pads like perfume adverts . . .'

The goose skin was brown and crisp, none of the flesh containing any of the oily fattiness one finds in European roast goose. The intestines were not at all rubbery, as one might expect, and the liver and gizzard were soft: the feet were chewy but delicious.

'You had the feet before?' Alfred asked.

'Not goose feet,' I replied, 'but I've had ducks' and chickens' feet.'

'These are much better,' Betty stated. 'More flesh and more flavour.'

At the table side appeared a Chinese man. He was quite tall, about fifty years old and of wiry build with a handsome face. His eyes had the deep, thoughtful look of a wise scholar and, on his chin, he wore a straggling little goatee beard like that of a sage in classical Chinese paintings.

'This is Mr Lee,' Alfred introduced us. 'He is the goose cook. He does not own the restaurant but he has worked here for thirty years and is now in charge.'

I shook his hand. It was smooth, cool and strong, the hand not of a manual worker but more of an artist. He passed me a business card upon which was printed in red a smiling goose in a cook's hat standing next to a large urn. In English and Chinese was given the name and address of the restaurant and Mr Lee's name – Lee Sui Hai – after which, in brackets, was printed *Uncle Lee*.

'He is considered to be the best goose cook in Hong Kong,' Betty said, taking up from Alfred's remarks. 'People come from everywhere to eat here. Even from Singapore and Taiwan.'

This was no surprise: the goose was, without exception, the best I had ever eaten and I said so in complimentary but not too glowing terms. It is never done to over-flatter for that may be taken as insincerity.

When Mr Lee spoke, his voice was quiet, almost inaudible

over the sound of the other dining party finally leaving. He thanked me for my kind words and Alfred informed him I was an old Hong Kong resident now returned. This seemed to please Mr Lee all the more: my compliments were not just those of a polite tourism journalist but of an aficionado, a real *gweilo*.

'Mr Lee asks if you would like to see how the geese are made,' Betty translated and we left the table.

What I had assumed to be the restaurant – half a dozen tables in one room – was merely the front. It stretched through a maze of other rooms, across alleyways, next to kitchens, the floors made of uneven tiles or concrete, the chairs piled on the tables and the floors wet from the afternoon mopping session. When running to capacity, the Yue Kee employs eighty staff and seats several hundred customers at once.

We followed Mr Lee down a narrow alley in the centre of which ran an open gutter flowing with lathered dishwashing water. At the end, we turned a corner into a small concrete courtyard bounded by a chain link fence, filled with a number of empty cooking oil drums alongside a lime-green Kawasaki motorbike. Alfred translated Mr Lee's commentary.

'Here the gooses are brought in, killed and plucked. They have their spare parts removed which are stored. Then each goose is blown up with pressurised air and stuffed with herbs. Mr Lee will not tell us what these are. It is his secret. After this, they are put in a cold store.'

Mr Lee snapped the catch on a door like a bank vault to display metal racks of geese lying in sub-zero temperatures. A cold draught spilled over my feet.

'The gooses are not frozen. Just cool. After two days, they come out and are washed inside. All the herbs are thrown away. Then the goose is poured over with a syrup made of honey and other things. The consistency of this is most vital. Too thick and too much sticks, too loose and it flows away.'

We left the cold store and followed in Mr Lee's footsteps down another alleyway. The walls of the restaurant here seemed to be made of corrugated iron and prefabricated sections reminding me of the construction of overseers' offices on building sites. Just to our right was a steep drop.

In my childhood, a stream tumbled out of the mountains at Sham Tseng to run into the sea to the west of the brewery. This stream is no more: now it is a fifty-metre wide nullah about ten metres deep. I could see that the mud and trickle of water in the centre were uniformly black. There were the strong scents of sewage and an unidentifiable industrial chemical competing with each other upon the warm breeze whilst embedded in the ooze were a chromium-plated frame of some sort, a lot of shreds of cloth (or toilet paper) and a dead dog in the final stages of decomposition: from a pipe in the concrete wall in the opposite bank of the nullah poured a steady stream of what could only be accurately described as shit. Projecting over this nullah was a metal veranda with a tin roof under which were hanging at least a hundred geese.

'When the honey is put on,' Alfred continued, 'the gooses are hung here for one day to dry in the wind. This is most important for the crispy skin.'

Reaching up, Mr Lee removed a goose and handed it to me by the metal hook suspending it. It was not as heavy as I expected and the honey glaze was translucent, giving the skin the appearance of the wax one sees running from candles in Roman Catholic churches. It had the same hues as a nun's skin and even felt waxy. Taking the goose from me, Mr Lee carried it into a narrow building which also partly hung over the rim of the nullah.

'Here is the cooking place,' Alfred reported.

Along the side of the building, with barely enough room for one to walk past, were half a dozen of what looked like huge Ali Baba barrels made of iron but black with smoke, grease and oil. Mr Lee, seeing I was wearing a washed silk jacket, warned me to take care. He invited me to mount a step and peer into one of the barrels which was at least two metres high. Within were a number of poles from which the geese were hung: to demonstrate, Mr Lee hung the dried goose *in situ*. In the centre of the barrel a fierce charcoal fire was burning. No smoke was rising but the air was thick with the smell of burning wood. A rim around the edge of the barrel caught the fat which dripped off during the cooking process and was collected in a tin bucket for later use.

'For thirty minutes, the goose cooks,' Alfred said as Mr Lee stopped talking. 'The goose goes the colour of polished wood and very crisp. This is how it is done.'

Mr Lee smiled distantly and led us back to our table. Nearby, two waiters were busy thrusting washed chopsticks into paper envelopes. We sipped at fresh tea, paid our bill and left, the master chef shaking my hand once more, saying he hoped I had found the cooking interesting and that he looked forward to my returning.

'How long has the restaurant been there?' I asked Betty as Alfred paid the car parking attendant and brushed tiny bits of concrete off the Mercedes which had fallen from the viaduct filling most of the sky overhead.

'Just a few years. There was another nearby, but there was a fire. It burned down.'

'How did it happen?'

'I don't know,' she replied. 'Maybe the goose fat caught fire.'

Two thoughts entered my mind as we drove past the brewery and back onto the Tuen Mun Highway. The first was that I had not seen a single fire extinguisher anywhere in the restaurant. The second was a recollection of the old Chinese story about the invention of roast pork, brought about by the burning down of a pig-sty and I wondered if, perhaps, Mr Lee's roast goose began a thousand years ago – for all Chinese legends happened a thousand years ago – with the conflagration of a hen-house, or a restaurant.

Mah Lo Shan

The place has a proper name in Cantonese although I cannot remember it for I have not heard it used in years: in English it is known as Piper's Hill. It is on the Tai Po Road as one leaves Kowloon, opposite a modern car park set into the hillside, contained by an iron railing and some stunted bushes trying hard to survive in the diesel smog and the slipstream of heavy lorries grinding uphill or racing down at breakneck speed.

Taxi and *pak pai* (public service minibus) drivers, not to mention most of the children of Kowloon, know of the place as Mah Lo Shan – Monkey Mountain. This is a somewhat misguided name, for the 'mountain' is actually more of a valley. What it lacks in topographical accuracy, however, it makes up for in monkeys.

The valley is called Wu Tip Kok (known in English as Butterfly Valley), a steep sided near gorge which rises from the cramped factories and fly-overs of Lai Chi Kok by way of a vast terraced Christian cemetery to the Kowloon Reservoir system. About 300 feet deep, Wu Tip Kok is a miracle. Whatever the gradient, it is thickly and luxuriantly covered in a close forest of trees, lianas and creepers, the undergrowth a dense tangle of lantana, bamboo clumps and saw-edged grass that can fray denim. Down the centre of the valley trickles a stream that tumbles over boulders the size of small cars and collects in pools of black water. Into the centre of this sub-tropical jungle passes one road, just a vehicle wide, giving access to a pumping station and an underground service reservoir before petering out at a very rusty, steel military bridge on the far side of which is an immediate wall of bamboo and six-foot-high grass.

No matter what the weather, the valley is always warm and humid, one of the few spots in Kowloon where the sound of crickets kills that of cars. Birds flit weaving and gliding through the cover whilst, in keeping with the valley's name, the air is alive with the dance and jive of butterflies, some as large as small birds and lazy in their flight, others, such as the arboreal *Charaxes*, flying at speed with their wings rustling like burning leaves. Every pool or open patch of sunlight has dragonflies helicoptering over it and the puddles of still water are lined by a shimmer of wings as butterflies and day-flying moths drink. Needless to say, the valley has an abundant reptilian population. The proximity of water, a plethora of insect life and the crowded streets of Lai Chi Kok and Cheung Sha Wan provide all the food a reptile could desire. Chinese cobras and rat snakes are attracted by the rodent population of both forest and factory, pit vipers take amphibians and small birds, kraits prey on their fellow snakes and the insects are taken by skinks and geckos.

This being Hong Kong, the valley is almost as rich in garbage as it is flora and fauna: no part of the valley is without a plastic bag shredded by wind and thorns, a tin can or a discarded bottle, not to mention a derelict car chassis or the remains of a lorry cab. Whereas elsewhere in Hong Kong these constitute eyesores they are somehow acceptable here, the tins rotting discreetly away, the vehicular scrap iron entwined by creepers hung with delicate trumpet-flowers and the bottles inhabited by beetles or tiny lizards. Just as the lower slopes of the valley have been taken over by human squatters, living in shacks constructed of the city's detritus, so here have the animals followed the example.

The valley has an interesting past: it was one of the main routes taken into Kowloon by the invading Japanese and one of the main lines out for escaping prisoners-of-war. Technically in the New Territories, the upper reaches were dammed within a few years of British acquisition in 1898, the main reservoir being the first of any size to be constructed for Kowloon. Across the top of it ran Gin Drinkers' Line, a sort of mini-Maginot Line of bunkers and slit trenches intended to halt any military invasion: it was an abysmal failure, being undermanned, too thinly spread out and inadequately armed. The name, it must be added, was not a comment upon the soldiers controlling it: it began at Gin Drinkers' Bay, a cove north west of Lai Chi Kok, long since reclaimed from the sea and now the site of the Kwai Chung container terminal, the busiest port facility in the world.

Mah Lo Shan is a favourite weekend or evening haunt for Kowloon residents. Ramblers setting off into the hills start their expeditions here. Picnickers purchase their soft drinks from one of two vendors who set up their stalls under the trees by the public convenience, opposite the car park where once there stood a camouflaged pill-box. Lovers heading into the woods above the reservoirs alight at the bus-stop here and account for the erotic decorations that may occasionally be found festooning low-level twigs: they can hardly be blamed for heading for the trees to conduct their dalliances for there is little privacy in tenemental Hong Kong – but they could be expected to take their used prophylactics home. In addition to these, children and old folk, amateur photographers and artists, animal-lovers and haters come here to feed, tease, photograph, sketch and gawk or laugh at the monkeys. Visiting these creatures has been a local pastime since the twenties.

In 1866, a naturalist called Swinhoe recorded that there were monkeys 'on most of the small islands in the bay of Hong Kong'. He classified these as macaques, *Macaca sancti-johannis*, in the same family as the Rhesus Monkey which may still be found from Pakistan to the Yangtse River and wrote of them:

> This rock monkey ... is like a Rhesus with a very short tail ... Dried bodies of this animal split in two are often exhibited from the ceiling in druggists' shops in Canton and Hong Kong; and its bones are used for medicinal purposes.

The Wu Tip Kok monkeys are, however, a mixed bunch.

Some, rather than being St John's macaque (today known as *Macaca mulatta*, the Rhesus macaque), are the crab-eating or long-tailed macaque, *Macaca fascicularis*, descendants of animals released here in 1916. Some may be hybrids: it is hard to tell without a DNA investigation. Certainly, very few are scions of Swinhoe's troops, not one of which survives.

During the Japanese occupation, the forest was felled for timber or fuel and the monkeys scattered. With starvation and even cannibalism rife in Kowloon, vast numbers were trapped and eaten but with post-war reforestation and the return of feeding visitors the population is greater than it ever was. Bands of 150 animals are commonplace.

An hour at Mah Lo Shan is a study in human and animal behaviour. The monkey feeders arrive equipped with plastic bags of fruit and scraps, completely oblivious to the prominent notice which warns the monkeys can be vicious, diseased and are not to be fed at any cost. Traipsing down a narrow concrete path, it is not long before monkeys are spied: if few visitors are about, the animals haunt the public convenience and pester the vendors.

At the first sighting, a crowd gathers (of both varieties of primate) and the bags are opened. The monkeys move in, their pink faces surrounded by ruffs of hair like a nineteenth century sea captain's sideburns, swinging through the trees or loping along the path. Their advance has a military precision about it. The braver ones come forward to snatch offered fruit, bits of biscuit or crusts of bread which they retreat with up a bank or into the lower branches above. Here they feed to the accompaniment of exclamations, shouts, laughs and the whine of camera power-drives. This activity goes on until one of the humans offers a cigarette butt, boiled sweet wrapped in cellophane or film box.

The monkeys are streetwise. They ignore the film box as inedible but they snatch the cigarette butt. If it is lit, they quickly drop it and if it is not they sniff at it, wrinkle their noses at the tobacco and drop it. The boiled sweet they skilfully unwrap and gnaw. This produces paroxysms of laughter and a chorus of *Ay-ahs* and *Diu lei lo mo*s, the Cantonese equivalent of *goodness gracious* and a less decorous version respectively.

While the monkeys scoff their offerings, the humans wolf down packets of roast nuts, polystyrene containers of noodles, ice creams and assorted other goodies. All packaging is discarded into the undergrowth. The monkeys are wise to this, too. They can differentiate between an empty peanut packet and a container with a few noodles sticking to it. They run for the appropriate garbage and squabble over it.

I am always struck by a deep sorrow when I go to Mah Lo Shan. Unlike their truly wild cousins in the far flung nature reserves of the New Territories, these monkeys are semi-urbanised and have lost their dignity. They are like refugees of some terrible disaster depending on charity handouts. If the feeding were to stop, I wonder if they would know enough to feed themselves. Certainly, even the bounties of Wu Tip Kok would not support such a heavy population. Many would starve.

And they are a sorry crew, like urban monkeys anywhere. Streetwise they may be, but they suffer for it. Disease is rampant in them and their coats lack a healthy gloss. Some are patchily bald from a monkey variety of eczema, others have deformities brought on by eating human victuals rather than forest fruits, leaves and insects. Some are blind in one eye. Many dangle a useless limb or are short of an arm or a leg, the result of near or not-so-near misses from passing cars: the Tai Po Road is never without a mangled little corpse in the gutter. Veterinary studies show all have a high lead content in their blood.

I last went to Mah Lo Shan in the spring of 1992. It was nearing twilight and the last of the feeders was there, tossing kumquats from a light blue plastic bag to a big male Rhesus with a scarlet bottom. An old gentleman with close cropped grey hair, he wore gold rimmed spectacles and a Chinese jacket with a high collar unbuttoned at his throat: he had a badly swollen goitre.

'Good evening,' he said, rummaging in his bag for another bitter little fruit. 'Are you come to see the monkeys?'

'Yes,' I replied.

'I have been coming here since 1934, to give them food,' he went on, finding a fruit and throwing it to a monkey who expertly caught it.

I made no immediate response and looked at the monkey. Ironically, it too had a massive swelling on its neck. In the way monkeys do, it avoided my stare and glanced quickly in a sideways shifty fashion at its benefactor. In the bushes above sat six others, scratching themselves or mutually grooming.

'Did you eat monkeys in the war?' I asked.

'No. I am a Buddhist,' he answered, then added with the true pragmatism of a wise man, 'I could not catch them and they were very expensive.'

At that moment, the monkey decided it was either fed up with kumquats or, the twilight deepening, it was time to head for the safety of the trees. It swung round and leaped for a trunk, scampered up it and was gone. The others, seeing its quick flight, assumed an alarm was raised and followed it.

'I will come tomorrow,' the man called out in Cantonese to the disappearing monkeys and, turning to me, said 'Good evening' once more.

I nodded as he screwed up his plastic bag, slinging it into the undergrowth and, as he shuffled up towards the Tai Po Road, I walked slowly down the pathway for a hundred yards or so. I needed a bit of exercise for I had only just, that afternoon, flown in from London: my back was aching and my eyes were tired but not sleepy. Up the valley from Lai Chi Kok blew a warm breeze carrying the smells of buildings and traffic, the ever-present rumble of lorries and the hum of hundreds of factories. When I started to return to the main road, it was nearly night although in Hong Kong this does not imply darkness. Nearing where the monkey had sat, I heard a noise in the bushes. I stopped and peered into the gloom. It was a moment before my eyes adjusted from the glow of the city sky to the shadows.

The first thing I saw was the old man's light blue plastic bag. Then it disappeared, re-appeared and did a dance in mid-air. In China, such a sight might give birth to myths of ghosts and demons.

I edged cautiously forwards. The bag danced again and sort of snortled. It was at that moment I saw them — four fully grown wild boar with a black and brown-striped piglet at their heels. The biggest animal was about three feet high at the shoulder with bristled fur, a short straight tail and curved tusks upon one of which was snagged the bag. The boar shook its head, the bag ripped and broke free and the remaining kumquats spilled out. All five animals started to feed on them for a moment, then they sensed my presence and vanished. Not a branch thrashed. They might have been an hallucination inspired by twelve hours in the hands of British Airways.

Yet I returned the next morning and, sure enough, there were trotter prints on the ground. Not only the monkeys, it seems, have survived both a world war and the advance of concrete.

In the Shafts

China has only ever really had one beast of burden. Horses have been scarce in China because there has never been the wide availability of grass for fodder; this is the reason why China was overrun by the Mongols and the Manchus – they had cavalry. There have been donkeys or asses in China, but these move slowly as do the oxen which have been (and still are) used to draw both carts and ploughs. In northern China and as far south as the Yangtse, camels may be found but these are not plentiful. The main beast of burden has always been man.

Coolies have been the mainstay of China: the Great Wall was built by them, the Grand Canal dug by them. The exhorting films of Communist China show coolies by the tens of thousand happily raising dykes and pouring steel: wherever one travels in China there are men and women toiling under the yoke of the bamboo pole, carting vegetables to market, scrap metal to the foundries and rocks to the tops of the highest mountains. They are the peasant class, exploited throughout history and used to this day despite the extolling virtues which Communism would place upon manual labour. No amount of diatribe or doctrinaire songs about heroic coolies belies the fact they are at the bottom of the social pecking order.

And the lowest of the low, the most abused and the most put upon were always the rickshaw coolies, known as drawers or pullers. Introduced into Hong Kong in 1880 there were, in its heyday, over 5,000 rickshaws in Hong Kong, about three quarters of them in Kowloon where the land was comparatively flat. The island had fewer for not only were many of the roads steep beyond the endurance of even a fit rickshaw puller but there were also 'ladder streets' to contend with, rising up the lower slopes of the Peak in stepped stages impassable to wheeled vehicles.

Contrary to common belief, the rickshaw was not a traditional Chinese mode of transport but a Japanese one exported to China by a European. In Japan, the rickshaw (known as a *jinriksha*) was a delicate and lightweight object but the Hong Kong version was sturdier, more capable of carrying heavier loads and therefore more difficult to pull.

The Hong Kong rickshaw was in essence a two-wheeled seat with a footstep from which a pair of shafts stuck out the front to be joined at the extremity by a cross-bar. They were usually painted scarlet and were obliged to have a licence plate screwed on them in much the fashion of a London hackney carriage. The spoked wheels, at least three feet in diameter and resembling those of a pre-war bicycle, were painted black with solid rubber tyres. In case of rain the seat, which was padded with leather or (later) vinyl, could be covered with a perambulator-type folding hood whilst the passenger's feet and legs could be protected by a flap.

The hire tariff was never expensive. At the turn of the century, a rickshaw cost five cents for a quarter of an hour rising to fifteen cents an hour. By the fifties, this had risen to HK$1 for a quarter of an hour but, in real terms, this was barely an increase.

The rickshaws were sometimes owned by the puller, more often by rickshaw companies which hired them out, raking in a generous cut of the earnings. Whatever the case, the puller was responsible for the machine and lived with it, often in it. Under the seat was a small cupboard in which the puller kept his personal possessions, a rag for cleaning his rickshaw and, on occasion, a simple tool kit such as one receives with a new bicycle. Although there was no formal livery for a rickshaw puller, they all wore an informal uniform consisting of either old military shorts or *fu* trousers with the wide waistband folded over a belt, the legs rolled up to above the knee. Some wore vests but many went bare to the waist save in the coldest of winters when they might wear a thin jacket. Most were barefoot, the skin on their soles as thick as those of a pair of good quality walking boots. The only regular piece of clothing most had in common was their headgear, a small brimmed rattan coolie hat with a low domed crown, the insides lined with newspaper with the outside varnished and sometimes painted with red characters if they were hired pullers.

Riding in a rickshaw was always a peculiar and somewhat unpleasant experience. The seats were seldom comfortable and although the axles in some of them were mounted on minimal leaf springs these had little effect upon sunken manhole covers, drain grilles and tram-lines. When parked, the rickshaw leaned forward so that sitting on the seat was an effort: as soon as the puller positioned himself between the shafts and raised them, the seat rose and tilted so the passenger rode reclining backwards at a semi-regal angle.

Setting off was slow: the puller bunched his pectoral muscles, holding the shafts with arms bent at the elbow and, leaning forward to use his body weight to best advantage, set off with a struggle, the sinews on his neck tight as violin strings and his calf muscles condensed. Once under way, the puller trotted at a medium jog of about ten kilometres an hour, his bent arms moving slightly up and down according to the road surface as if seeking to make up for the deficiencies of the leaf springs. His leg and thigh muscles expanded and contracted rhythmically, his breathing coming hard. If it was summer, the passenger often rode in a slight scent of sweat tinged with a certain indefinable something best described as sweetness. This, of course, was mingled with the ordinary odours of a Hong Kong street and the inevitable taint of diesel fumes.

Braking, especially if this was done in an emergency such as suddenly being cut up by a car or having a pedestrian step into the road, was precarious and must have been agonising. The puller had to lean backwards in the shafts and, with the combined weight of his body, the strength of his arms and the resilience of his legs, bring a load of 150 kilograms of human, cargo and rickshaw to a stop in under ten feet.

The working life expectancy of a rickshaw puller was ten years and their existence was miserable. When working, they had to face the most pain-wracking physical exertion and their lungs were soon weakened by effort, the breathing in of car fumes and the humid, sub-tropical air. Many became tubercular from living almost entirely out of doors: it was not uncommon as recently as the late sixties to see a rickshaw puller asleep between the shafts of his vehicle parked up an alley after dark – as rickshaws carried no lights, they tended not to operate once dusk had fallen except in especial circumstances or brightly lit streets. And they were most of them, as the hint of sweetness about their sweat indicated, narcotics addicts. Unlike modern junkies, however, they did not inject drugs but, as the phrase went, chased dragons.

The first person I ever saw chasing the dragon was a rickshaw puller. I was, I guess, about eight at the time. He was squatting between the shafts of his vehicle under the shade of a tree in Haiphong Road. In one hand he held an oblong of tin cut from a can whilst in the other he had a Zippo lighter either found in a gutter or filched from a sailor. The flame flickered as cars passed by. He heated a small bead of what looked like beeswax on the tin over the lighter flame then, when it was bubbling, he put a roll of paper to his lips and sucked the fumes in. There was no attempt on his part to hide this nefarious activity: in those days, although opium had been illegalised after the war, addicts could register with the government and receive their required supply. Even if he was unregistered, he had little to lose by being arrested and all to gain – a bed, a roof and three square meals a day for the duration of his sentence. If he was fined he could not pay. The police tended to ignore these unfortunates. When the bead had melted away, he leaned back in the shafts of his rickshaw and rested his head on a folded jacket on the footstep below the seat, closing his eyes.

It was always possible to guess how long a man had been a rickshaw puller. If he was new to the business, he was wiry and healthy looking, fit and bronzed. After a few years, he was still fit in appearance but he moved more slowly and his muscles were always taut, even when at rest. By six or seven years, his face was drawn with the physical demands of both work and narcotics. By ten or twelve, he was either dead or past any physical exertion, washed up with a gaunt, skull-like face and arms as thin as a concentration camp inmate's. For the rickshaw puller, life was painful and an early, agonising death inevitable, his only release from it being the poppy's dream.

Today, one is not taken in a rickshaw *on* a ride but *for* a ride in a rickshaw. Long since superseded by lorries, taxies and minibuses, not to mention the MTR, only a dozen or so rickshaws remain, all of them parked in the pedestrian walkway by the Hong Kong Star Ferry pier where they are attended by a number of aged former pullers who dress in loose *sams* and whose only genuine concession to a rickshaw puller's uniform is the hat. They do not accept passengers but prey upon anyone wearing a camera, beckoning to them with down-turned palm, as is the Chinese fashion, inveigling them into the seat, lifting the front bar, having their photo taken with a toothless grin then demanding an exorbitant sum for the privilege. It is best to ignore them for they pester unmercifully, haggle vociferously over the photography fee and are probably the only objectionable encounter a tourist will experience in Hong Kong.

I find this a shameful state of affairs: the old men degrade themselves by such blatant exhibitionism and greed, denigrating the suffering of generations of poor unfortunates who have died penniless, pain– and drug-wracked, in the shafts of probably these very rickshaws.

In the Shadow of the T-Shirt

Known in Cantonese as Chek Chue (Pirate Fortress), the village of Stanley is built on a thin spit of land between the main bulk of Hong Kong and the bulb-shaped Stanley (or Wong Ma Kok) peninsula, deriving its name from Lord Stanley, Secretary of State for the Colonies in 1845. Before the British received Hong Kong in the treaty of Nanking, it was the largest settlement on the island, a fishing village on a sandy bay with an eighteenth century temple dedicated to Tin Hau, and a population of about 2,000. The valleys behind the village, as with those over the whole island, were cultivated by Hakka people who had supplanted the more local Punti population over the previous 200 years. The Hakkas, known as guest folk, were tribes from central China who had been driven south by warlords, drought, famine, persecution and over-population. They had – and still retain – their own customs and dialect.

In some respects, Stanley was the start of British Hong Kong. Some of the very first colonial settlers lived and worked here, not on the north of the island in what is now thought of as Hong Kong and its harbour. An indication of their early settlement lies in the fact that a patch of land was designated as a graveyard here in which there is a tomb dated 1841.

Long before a road reached Stanley, there was a police station there, erected in 1859. It cost £402.16sh. 2d and has served as a police post, army guard-house, harbour master's office, Kempetai (the Japanese Gestapo) and military police station and mortuary.

It still stands today, as a protected building, one of the oldest colonial structures remaining. On the present-day site of St Stephen's College was erected a fort, gun emplacement and small barracks, all made of timber: these were, however, abandoned in less than a decade because the troops suffered badly from malaria and typhoid, not to mention the attentions of the residents of nearby Wong Ma Kok.

This little village on the Stanley peninsula was situated near the top of Che Pau Teng, the hill above Bluff Point, tucked away in a wooded hollow virtually invisible from land and sea: it was so remote that, for many years, it avoided the clutches of even the most zealous tax official. The occupants made their living from a gunpowder mill they operated, selling their product to local pirates with whom they joined on occasional forays. There was also a rumour Wong Ma Kok held a young woman of exquisite beauty but this is no longer ascertainable.

The notorious reputation of the village was well earned. At various times, the residents carried out a number of atrocities: two soldiers coming round the headland in a pay boat were killed and, later, several officers were beheaded on a headland subsequently named Slaughter Point, in full view of their garrison. More famous, however, was another double murder which not only caused the village to be abandoned for some time but also put it firmly on the tax-man's register.

Stationed in Stanley was a certain Captain da Costa (presumably a soldier) who had discovered the whereabouts of the village and, it is said, had fallen in love with the beautiful maiden although this is most likely apocryphal. Be that as it may, da Costa inherited some property in England and, on the day before he was due to set sail, went along the peninsula in the company of a friend. It is likely they were drunk from attending a farewell celebration. Why they went to Wong Ma Kok is unknown but when they did not return the next day a search party was sent out with a local guide. They found the village deserted but there were signs of a fight and a trail of blood leading down to the shore. For the whole day, the rocks were searched in vain but one of the murdered men was found by chance, snagged by a boat-hook in the seaweed. After a manhunt, the village headman was captured and he admitted the two corpses had been weighted and dropped into the sea: he was committed for trial but killed himself in gaol before it began.

Chek Chue, it seems, was an apposite name.

For eighty years, Stanley was a backwater of Hong Kong until, in the twenties, it started to be settled. The round island road and the growth in motor cars made the place accessible and well-to-do Europeans began to build houses on and above the next bay to the fishing village.

Gradually, Stanley grew in size but it remained essentially a village. Pirates still occasionally visited the place until the mid-thirties when two changes occurred to put them off for good. The first was the opening of a top security prison here: no doubt the presence of such a place acted as a firm deterrent reminder of what might befall them. The second was the building of Stanley Fort.

It was decided the British army should take over the Stanley peninsula and so, in 1934, a road was cut along its steep western sides and a barracks built on the south facing slopes of the hill on the peninsula. This necessitated the removal of the remnants of the hamlet of Wong Ma Kok which was considered a just revenge, albeit many decades late. The settlement was by now reduced to half a dozen houses occupied by the descendants of the pirates who lived by fishing and charcoal-making, the latter no doubt with its origins in the gunpowder milling business. When the barracks was completed it consisted of a sports field, parade ground, soldiers' and officers' quarters, a school, a chapel and a mess. Gun emplacements were built and a pier constructed to bring the guns in by sea: some of these are now re-utilised as the foundations for huge satellite communication dishes, the property of Cable & Wireless or Britain's Secret Service. The fort remains, however, still the domain of the army.

The village atmosphere of Stanley remains, too. Despite the coagulation of tourists it remains largely unspoiled. The old *praya*, the road along the beach, exists to this day and is not over-developed although it does contain a few mock bistros and cafés, not to mention an imitation English pub which looks far more incongruous here than a Chinese take-away does in Southampton.

At the end of the *praya*, down a lane overhung by trees, is the real village, comprising of small stone houses, shacks, lean-tos, little tea stalls, *dai pai dongs* and *do fu* vendors lining a not-too-noisome nullah. A few fishing sampans ride the low swell rolling into the bay and the air is filled with the song of cicadas, the chirp of crickets, the clatter of mah-jong tiles and the distant strains of *Canto-pop*, a Chinesified hybrid halfway between the music of Tina Turner and Elton John and classical Cantonese opera. If one is particularly unlucky, this increases in volume to an ear-splitting *ca-thump ca-thump* as the suitcase-sized ghetto-blaster from which the shindig emanates draws closer in the ownership of a party of Chinese youngsters on a hike, picnic or ramble: the youth of China, it seems, likes to travel with a rock festival in its fist. Fortunately, the racket soon fades much as the Doppler effect of a passing train might.

Just across the nullah is the temple dedicated to Tin Hau. The story goes that, in the tenth century, a red light fell upon the hut of a fisherman called Lin in Fukien province. Shortly afterwards his sixth child, a baby girl, was born who, at fifteen, discovered a pair of bronze amulets in a well which gave her prognosticatory skills and the ability to ride on clouds – in other words, go into a trance. One day, she dreamed she saw her father and brothers, who were absent on a fishing trip, in a typhoon-tossed junk: she grabbed the boat by the rigging and pulled it to safe harbour. When they returned, her brothers announced that their father had drowned in a storm but a beautiful girl had walked across the sea and dragged their boat to safety. At the age of twenty-eight, she climbed a mountain with her sisters, boarded a celestial carriage and rode up to heaven. The story of her brothers' rescue was retold by sailors and, in the twelfth century, she was declared a Saintly Saviour and, as the goddess of the sea, the patron of seafarers. Three centuries later, she was given a throne amongst the stars of the Great Bear and, in 1683, having aided the Imperial Fleet in taking the island of Formosa, she was promoted to Tin Hau, Queen of Heaven.

The temple site is the oldest on Hong Kong island. It is thought to have been originally raised about 1767, but the foundation is most probably at least fifty years older: the present building dates from a reconstruction of 1938. Inside, the courtyard fills with sun and incense smoke, the altar standing in its vermilion draperies but not as impressive as one might expect. The tables carry the usual brass urns and joss stick holders, guttering candles and triangular piles of oranges. Red tasselled lanterns hang from the roof, open to the beams. Yet the interest here is not in the religious trappings but in objects to be found to the sides of the main hall.

To the right of the altar are the temple drum and bell purported to have belonged to the infamous pirate Cheung Po-tsai who, from time to time, moored his fleet in the bay and used Stanley as a lookout post. It is said he used both to signal to his junks but that is apocryphal: all temples have bells and drums to communicate with the gods or drive off the devils. The bell, apart from such supposed provenance, is interesting for it was cast in Canton in 1767. Yet to the left of the altar is an altogether more fascinating object.

Hanging high on the wall is what appears to be a very moth-eaten black rug. It is not a carpet or temple tapestry but the skin of a tiger darkened by candle soot and incense smoke. It was shot above the beach just behind the village in 1942 by an Indian, a prison camp guard who had 'gone over' to the Japanese. The hunt for the beast, which had been calling in the surrounding hills and seen on the beach, was headed by a Japanese police commander, Lt Col Hirabayashi. At first, his men tried to net it but to no avail. Eventually, they tracked it down and shot it three times. When killed, it was found to be a small Chinese tiger weighing 240 pounds and standing just three feet high. Speculation was rife it had swum across from the mainland but this was disputed: the truth is that it was a part of a circus menagerie which the owner had released when the Japanese invaded.

The carcass was skinned and divided up for food amongst the Indian and Japanese policemen: tiger is believed to have substantial medicinal properties. A butcher was sent from The Dairy Farm who somewhat inexpertly stuffed it. It was then taken to Government House where it was put on display in the entrance hall as a trophy for the Japanese governor of Hong Kong, General Rensuke Isogai. After the war, it was given to the Stanley villagers who in turn presented it to Tin Hau as a grateful offering for her protection: she had not only saved many of them from drowning but, during the battle for Stanley, they had hidden in the temple which was twice hit by shells which failed to explode.

This battle was one of the bravest (and most futile) engagements in the Pacific theatre of war. The Imperial Japanese Army invaded Hong Kong Island on 18 December 1941, the 229th. Infantry Regiment under Col. Tanaka landing across Lei Yue Mun, pressing south and west. By 22 December they were within a mile of Stanley, held at bay by a company of the Royal Rifles of Canada. By noon on Christmas Eve, they had pushed the Canadians back to a tiny front on the Chung Hom Kok peninsula across Stanley Bay and advanced on Stanley where they met fierce resistance from two companies of the 1st. Middlesex Regiment, remnants of the Canadian units, elements of the Hong Kong Volunteer Defence Force and odds and sods who had made it through the shrinking lines. The IJA lined up heavy field artillery on Stanley Gap Road and opened fire. The defenders had only a few light artillery pieces, some heavy machine guns and ordinary firearms. A heavy machine gun was erected at the junction by the present-day bus terminus and held out for some time but, by Christmas morning, the front line – such as it was – stretched from the prison to St Stephen's beach. At 3 o'clock in the afternoon, Hong Kong surrendered.

In the valley above Stanley is a second, modern temple dedicated to Kwan Yin, the Buddhist Goddess of Mercy. Apart from a six metre high statue of the deity in a pavilion, the place is of little interest save for the view. From here, the shacks of Stanley seem to nestle below modern terraces of expensive houses and apartments – the omnipresent contrast of Hong Kong. To the untrained eye, this is a panorama of want oppressed by wealth but this is a misinterpretation. Go to the parking lot by the Tin Hau temple as people are returning from work: the Mercedes Benz 190s and BMW 325s do not belong to the dwellers of the sumptuous apartments but to shack residents.

In the sixties, I frequently visited Stanley with school friends. The beaches were unspoilt by population or pollution and we used to hold barbecues on the edge of Tai Tam Bay, playing records on a portable phonograph, kicking the sand as we danced or splashing into the sea. It was on that bay I learnt to water-ski, once saw a manta ray gliding like a vast nuclear bomber over the white sand beneath me and was badly stung by a Portuguese man-of-war. After swimming, we would walk in our costumes and shirts to the market, buy Green Spot orange juice in frosted bottles and make our way back along shady lanes with song-birds invisible in the hibiscus bushes.

In Stanley, today, history gives way to high fashion. Since the early eighties, the village has become a world-famous mecca to which even those who visit Hong Kong for only two days *en route* between the flesh-pots of Phuket and the tanning-strips of Bali must pay a call. To them, the village consists not of temples and times past but of a market-place the size of two tennis courts and an alley about 200 metres long with feeder tributaries.

The alleyway is crammed with shops and stalls selling, for the best part, clothing. Ladies' fashions predominate. Silk, I am told by friends' wives, is the best buy with a washed silk blouse selling for the price of a good T-shirt in London or a Red Sox sweatshirt in Boston, a lined silk jacket going for less than half the price of a cheap wool pullover in Paris. Leather coats, skirts and hot pants are other much-sought-after commodities along with cotton dresses, slinky underwear and Nike trainers selling at less than a quarter of their resale price.

However, the professional shopper (which is to say the Hong Kong resident who follows bargain hunting with all the panache and cunning of a greyhound fancier) looks out for designer clothes.

These are sneaked onto the shelves to keep the mystique of Stanley market going, to maintain the reputation of the place and are not blatantly displayed but must be rooted out from the racks of ordinary clothes.

For twelve hours a day, seven days a week, regardless of weather or religious festival (save a direct hit from a typhoon or the first day of Chinese New Year), Stanley market and alleys are jammed with hordes of *Homo touristicus* – be-shorted Australian men carrying six-packs of Fosters following their spouses who are open-mouthed at the merchandise; demure Japanese ladies hung about with cameras; British women dressed in print frocks and floppy hats trailed by bored husbands equipped with travellers' cheques; middle-aged American women armed with wallets of credit cards, and smartly-dressed French tourists (of both sexes) exclaiming about the low prices in hushed, semi-religious tones.

Mingling with them are the other breeds of customer, the wives of British soldiers from the fort, thrusting pushchairs before them and eagle-eyeing each rack with leisured attention or the spouses of expatriate businessmen dressed in jeans and discreet blouses. The latter are the ones to follow for they can see the collar trim of a designer dress at ten paces, camouflaged in a pile of cheap jumpers. Dodging through all these are little, old, bent amahs in traditional *sam* jackets, men bare to the waist carrying baskets of fish or prawns (or Reeboks or belts), children on their way back from school with little animal-shaped haversacks, youths delivering Chinese fast-food lunch-boxes to the store owners who do not leave their premises all day long and, unseen save by the trained eye, pickpockets.

These are the best in Hong Kong, usually working in pairs. I have seen them open a shoulder-hung handbag and sneak out a purse without the owner removing their hand from the flap: on one occasion, I saw an Australian man have his wallet removed from the side pocket of a pair of shorts that were so tight I could see the quite detailed outline of his penis through the material next to the wallet – how he did not feel his money walk I do not know.

Along with the clothes shops come stalls selling junk curios, better quality paintings and one enterprising man has set up a stall in which he will carve your name (in English or the Chinese phonetic equivalent) in a soapstone block whilst you do the rest of your shopping. Leather belt and tie shops sell a vast range of goods (silk ties cost less than £1) and some stalls sell fake designer watches – Rolex, Cartier, Hermes and Gucchi. They look like the real thing until you put a magnifying glass to them: then you see how the vendors escape prosecution – *Gucchi* is printed as *Cucchi, Rolex* is *Rodex, Dunhill* is *Dumhill* and *Cartier* is *Gartier*. I am told there is a watch called a *Herpes* on the market but I've never seen it.

There is only one Stanley stall I patronise. It is next to the taxi rank and run by two old ladies whose English is limited to such phrases as One size fit aawl, Good qualitee, Look see, no must buy and For you, speshul p'ice. They sell shirts: not any shirt but the Australian Outback Red fashion brand – good things other than Foster's lager come out of Australia. They are made of heavy cotton, colourful without being gaudy and seem indestructible. Mine have survived, unscathed, not only washing machines but also African bush laundries – a rock by the river bank.

In a sort of masochistic way, I like Stanley. It is a brash, bustling, entrepreneurial, multi-cultural and –racial microcosm of Hong Kong, yet it has its quiet places, timeless corners. Walking back from the temple, I can eavesdrop on the prattle of young Chinese girls in the tea stalls, the sarcasm of waiters in the restaurants and, if I concentrate, I swear I can hear a tiger calling in the hills. Or perhaps it is just the hum of traffic on the road up the hillside. So long as it is not – and will never be again – the growl of a mortar shell exploding by the bus stop.

Ghosts and Gaolers

Hong Kong's first prison was built above Hollywood Road, between Arbuthnot Road and the appropriately named Old Bailey Street. Known as Victoria Prison, it was first governed by the notorious Major Caine (of 26th Regiment of Infantry), the fledgling colony's first magistrate, justice of the peace, Sheriff and Provost Marshal and, subsequently, Colonial Secretary and Lieutenant-Governor, ruler of Hong Kong in all but name. He and his fellow magistrates were essentially ignorant of both English and Chinese law and, as one of Hong Kong's early newspapers put it, meted out justice according to the judgement which God has been pleased to grant them: in Caine's case, this meant flogging with rattan canes, on occasion without the inconvenience of imprisonment. So severe was his rule of 'law' in the 1850s that questions were asked in the House of Commons, three months' sailing time away. It is hardly surprising Caine became so respected and feared that he had a major Hong Kong road named after him. Regardless of Caine's expediency of flogging then giving summary liberty to his prisoners, the prison was soon filled to bursting: by 1860, extra accommodation was found on a hulk floating in the harbour and on Stonecutters Island.

Despite being heavily shelled in 1941, Victoria Prison still exists, some of the buildings from the 1864 reconstruction remaining – a watchtower, the main building of the accompanying police station and D Hall in which some very illustrious prisoners have been incarcerated over the years including Ho Chi Minh. By 1935, it was so overcrowded the decision was made to build a new prison at Stanley. Completed two years later, it was considered the most modern prison in the Empire and the most impregnable. To this day, it is Hong Kong's maximum security gaol from which only one escape has ever been attempted: one of the prisoners broke both his legs jumping from the wall and the other was picked up limping within half a mile.

There is, however, a certain irony about Stanley prison which makes it almost unique in the annals of incarceration. When it was only four years old it was turned inside out, so to speak. In effect, the gaolers became the gaoled.

At the surrender of Hong Kong to the Japanese, the victors put military prisoners into prison camps which had been barracks: enlisted men were imprisoned in Sham Shui Po, officers in Argyle Street, those Indian troops who did not defect and collaborate in Ma Tau Kok and so on. Yet the Japanese were also faced with non-military prisoners. Although a good number of dependants had fled Hong Kong some months previously, seeking asylum in Australia, India or Britain, there remained a large number of civil servants, bankers and businessmen, many of whom were accompanied by their families. They were all herded into Stanley.

The gaol itself was not large enough so a perimeter fence was erected encompassing the prison officers' quarters and peripheral buildings, requisitioned along with the buildings of nearby St Stephen's College. Until the liberation, this was to be the home of several thousand civilians. Not all were British. The complement included Belgian, French, Dutch and Americans with Eurasians of mixed descent not considered Third Nationals – that is, subjects of neutral countries. Prominent prisoners were kept in the prison proper. The prison officers' quarters and other buildings were used to house men 'of lesser value', women and children.

Life in the prison was harsh. Food was in short supply and substandard, sickness rife and the guards – Koreans and Formosan Chinese as well as Japanese – brutal in the extreme. Prisoners grew vegetables in a plot which is today a children's playground and in pots on the flat roofs of the buildings. From time to time, the

Japanese executed prisoners on St Stephen's Beach either out of spite, retribution or as an example to the rest; people died of illness and fell in love (a number of children were born in the camp); entertainments were contrived and classes arranged for children; the prisoners connived and cheated and undermined and stole from their gaolers with, on occasion, considerable success. A few attempted escape.

My first contact with Stanley prison was through my childhood dentist. He was Mr Sammy Shields who had a practice on the second floor of a low building facing the bus and rickshaw ranks at the Kowloon Star Ferry. Today it is occupied by the multi-storey Star House. During the war, he had been Stanley's prison dentist. Or one of them. I was never quite sure if he did all the dental work single-handed but I wanted to think he did: he was a heroic figure in my mind and remains so to this day.

Visiting him was not as traumatic as it might have been, despite the whirling drive-bands of his whining drill and the foul-tasting mouth-wash he dispensed. All the time he prodded and poked, scratched and tugged and drilled, he spoke of life in Stanley: of roasting rats on shovels over fires of seaweed and dung, of creeping about at night avoiding sentries, of filching food; of extracting teeth without anaesthetic; of discovering penicillin independently of Fleming – he had found out eating mouldy rice cured the boils and sores so many of the malnourished prisoners exhibited. Compared to his macabre tales, having a filling seemed small beer. When he found out my parents were members of the Stanley Prison Officers' Club and I was learning to swim at Tweed Bay, the private club beach below the prison, he regaled me with stories which I am sure were apocryphal and had me very cautious of ever putting my foot down under water: he may have been the greatest incentive to get a boy to float and swim ever known.

I remember once sitting in his chair in late August: I was having my pre-school check-up. As he prepared to fiddle about in my mouth, he passed me an old piece of paper.

'Can you read?' he asked.

I nodded and unfolded it. It was a broadside and I have seen one since so I know how it began: *Allied POWs and civilian internees, these are your instructions, in case there is capitulation of the Japanese forces. 1) You are to remain in your camp area . . .*

'That was dropped from a Flying Fortress over Stanley,' Mr Shields said. 'On this day, in 1945.'

It seemed years ago to me but could have only been seven or eight.

He took the sheet back, put it on his steriliser and handed me a black and white photograph. It showed the corner of a building. The roof was lined with people as were all the windows and the verandas. On the ground was a dense crowd. There were women, children and men in the picture, some of the latter wearing peaked caps and saluting. In the foreground was a flagpole fixed to a lamp-post and, to the left, a priest in a white vestment. From the pole hung a Union Jack.

'Know what that is?' he asked.

I did not.

'That's the flag going up in Stanley camp,' he continued and there were tears in his eyes.

Ever since then, I have wanted to go to that very spot, stand where the photographer stood and look on that view. In the early spring of 1993, I did. And more.

At the express and, I was to discover, exceedingly rare invitation of the prison governor, Senior Superintendent Chan Chun-yan, I was summoned to the main gate at 9.30 in the morning. He had agreed to allow me access to the staff quarters but required, not surprisingly, to meet me first: my bona fides were provided by the government information department. Expecting prisons to be run on near-military timetables, I arrived a few minutes early.

The main gate is about six metres wide and three high, recessed into the massive outer walls of the gaol. A small door to the left was open and I was permitted entry into a large hallway on the far side of which were heavy barred gates giving onto a parade ground. I provided my name, walked through a metal detector and was taken across the parade ground towards a square archway beneath which

I could see several sets of bars and, beyond them, shadowy figures moving. These, I assumed, were convicts.

I had never been in a prison before and, although I am not guilty of anything but the merest misdemeanour (littering, jaywalking, parking without paying the meter), I felt a criminal. It was the adult version of that crawling culpable fear one had in school when the headmaster berated everyone for the sake of castigating one miscreant.

The building on the square archway is the administrative block, the stairs spartan, the floorboards well worn and highly polished; the place smells of furniture wax and dry paper. I was shown into the office of Senior Superintendent Chan, a short and stockily built man with an air of military efficiency wearing a crisply tailored uniform.

'Good morning, Mr Booth. Welcome to Stanley,' he said: he was so urbane he might have been the manager of an hotel welcoming a guest. 'Please, do take a seat.'

The Senior Superintendent's office is very spacious indeed with a large desk, filing cabinets and a big conference table at which I sat. It was surrounded by government issue rattan-seated chairs identical to the dining room furniture I had known at home: my father had been a Hong Kong civil servant. Coffee was served and, for a quarter of an hour, we discussed my memories of Stanley, Mr Shields' stories and the return of several former war-time internees the year before who had signed a prison scrapbook compiled by Mr Chan. Upon the walls hung photographs of the prison and prison officers' gatherings: to one side was a magnetic notice board with the statistics of inmates – the number in each category, the breakdown of offences and such like. The scrapbook was of the sort a proud headmaster would keep of pupils' achievements, the photos like those of successful First XI teams, the notice like a teacher placement chart.

Stanley currently holds over 1,800 prisoners which is well over capacity. Most are Chinese but there are 200 Vietnamese held with assorted other nationalities ranging from Filipino and Korean to Nigerian. And European. Mr Chan was a little cagey on exactly how many *gweilos* he had under his charge – perhaps two dozen was the estimate. About a third of the prisoners were convicted for narcotics-related crimes: armed or violent robbery was the next largest group with a wide assortment thereafter. I noticed approximately three dozen murderers, fewer than half a dozen rapists and one man convicted of incest. Significantly, there were no child abusers. This was of little surprise for child molestation is utterly abhorrent to the Chinese: on the other hand, the low rape/incest figures were a surprise. Hong Kong is incredibly crowded with entire extended families living in just one or two tenement rooms and there is little privacy: I had thought such sexual crimes might be inevitable.

'Perhaps you would like to see this?' Mr Chan said, handing me another book.

The analogy of school remained. The book was a black and red bound hardback exercise book of the sort every child in Hong Kong uses: my A-Level Chemistry notes were written in just such a book. Yet here the analogy ended. I opened it. What I was holding was the execution record. It registered only those persons hanged since the war, or who had died in captivity, of illness or, more frequently, suicide: pre-war and Japanese occupation records are lost.

The first few pages contained names I knew from history lessons – Colonel Noma, head of the Kempetai, Colonel Kanagawa who had controlled the police and the infamously brutal Inouye Kanao, nicknamed Slap Happy by prisoners-of-war, with good cause. After each name appeared other details including the whereabouts of the corpse. After most it simply recorded a burial and a grave number but after the Japanese names (save one, who was a felon rather than a war criminal) it was stated they were buried at sea. The truth was their bodies were taken out into Tai Tam Bay, weighted and sunk.

Mr Chan put on his peaked cap and picked up a short swagger-stick from his desk.

'Now let us look around the prison before you see the staff quarters,' he announced.

Leaving his office, we descended the stairs and turned left towards the first of many sets of double barred doors through which we were to pass. At each stood a correctional officer (as warders are known) with a ring of keys which he jangled as locks snapped open. That sound of the first door closing behind us was one of the most terrifying and depressing sounds I have ever heard.

Inside, the prison was far larger than it appears from the exterior, with wide spaces between many of the buildings, most of which are several floors high and painted white or cream. Despite the space, it was oppressive. There was not a bush or tree to be seen and during the two hours I was in the gaol I neither saw nor heard a single bird. All bars, doors, gates and grilles are painted grey with most of the walls a cream-cum-buff colour. The prisoners all wore dark trousers and brown shirts with padded Chinese-style jackets: the weather was quite cold that day. There were no regulation crew-cuts but all hair was worn short and often cut by an inexpert barber.

'The prisoners work whilst they are here,' the Senior Superintendent explained as we waited for a set of double gates to be opened for us. 'We have a number of workshops where we do all the government printing, make all police or prison officers' uniforms and boots – prisoner uniforms, too – and manufacture all Hong Kong road and traffic signs. And many other items. We cook all the prison food and do the laundry. Last year we had a turnover of . . .' he paused and thought for a moment, '. . .many tens of millions of dollars.'

Even in a top security prison, the Hong Kong dollar ethic survives.

'Are the prisoners paid?' I enquired.

'They receive the minimum wage for their type of job. With some of the money they are allowed to buy biscuits or cigarettes and the rest is put aside for when they are released.'

The doors were opened. At the approach of the Senior Superintendent, all his men stood to attention, saluted and said, 'Good morning, sir!' in English. To me they nodded most genially.

The road sign workshop was as well equipped as a commercial factory with steel cutting machines, chemical bonding units, reflective blue laminates and all the necessary paraphernalia needed to turn out hundreds of signs a week. As we walked through the machines, the prisoners came to attention and also said, 'Good morning, sir,' to the Senior Superintendent in English. For his part, he totally ignored them. A few, to my surprise, greeted me as well. There was a great temptation to reply but I followed my host's example. On many of their faces there was a look of consternation: visitors, I imagine, seldom get beyond the toughened glass screens and telephones of the meeting room by the main gate.

As we made our way through the buildings, Mr Chan told me about the framework of the prison's organisation. There were, he said, no trusties, all prisoners being treated equal regardless of race: the only concessions made were in diet according to religious belief or nationality. All correctional officers were unarmed but carried short truncheons hidden about their persons whilst senior officers had two-way radios. Every building was self-contained and separated by wire fences to contain any riot: there had been one, some twenty years ago, from which, I was told, lessons in prison design had been heeded.

Almost every prisoner I saw was under the age of forty-five, most under thirty-five. Here or there I came upon elderly men who, if they had not been cutting cloth in the tailoring shop (with scissors from which the points had been rounded off, like those for young children) would surely have been hobbling along to the nearest park to play chess with their peers. One moved with a distinct limp and I wondered if this was Ng Sik-ho – Limpy Ho – the most successful heroin manufacturer and dealer of all time who controlled the world trade in No 4 heroin until 1975, when he was sentenced to thirty years.

In the shoe-making department, coming around the end of a leather-cutting machine, I came suddenly face to face with a European prisoner. It was such a shock, I felt words rising instantly to my mouth along the lines of 'Hello! What on earth are *you* doing here?' much as one would say to an atheistic friend discovered in a cathedral. He was about thirty-five years old, taller than me and with greyish hair cut spikily close. His skin was pallid, his hands stained with patent leather boot polish. With sunken, black eyes, he scowled at me and then, seeing with whom I was walking, muttered his good morning and turned his attention to the machine.

'These buildings were not here in the war,' Senior Superintendent Chan remarked as we left the workshops, crossing a wide concrete road, 'but the cell blocks were. These are the original buildings and not much changed since then.'

The building before us was three floors high and painted the colour of buttermilk. Rows of small, identical windows lined the walls, each of them barred. We entered through a door and I found we were on a ground floor landing. The walls on either side were lined with heavy grey doors in which there was a grilled window and a hatch near the ground for food. It was utterly quiet.

'The prisoners are all at work,' Mr Chan explained, then turned his attention to the first cell. 'These doors are post-war. The original ones were solid, with just a spy-hole in them but most of these have been replaced. Would you like to see in a cell?'

He assumed this was a rhetorical question and the officer by our side unlocked a door, swinging it wide on huge hinges. I stepped into the cell. It was about one and a half metres wide and two and a half deep with a ceiling height of about three and a half metres. Near the ceiling was a barred window. Two plastic beds stood against the walls, the only bedding a rolled up duvet. In the corners by the door were two corner shelf units upon which were several Chinese comic books and a cigarette packet. By the foot of one bed was a pair of plastic buckets with lids, one pillar-box red and the other brilliant yellow: they provided a garish, happy contrast.

'The yellow is for fresh water, the red is for the calls of nature,' Mr Chan explained.

'Where are their private possessions?' I asked.

Mr Chan, pointing under the beds to two plastic boxes the size of milk crates, said bluntly, 'Here. They are allowed no radios, no televisions or papers. No pictures can be put on the walls although a few pin up pictures of girls without clothing . . .' He smiled distantly. 'We turn a blind eye to this.'

'This cell . . .' I began, but Senior Superintendent Chan was thinking ahead of me.

'This cell held British prisoners-of-war,' he said. 'All this block.'

I made no reply. Looking up at the tiny barred window and the grey door, I tried to imagine what is must have been like for Sir Mark Young, Governor of Hong Kong for only three months before he had to surrender it to the enemy, for his Colonial Secretary, F.C. Gimson who had arrived in Hong Kong to take up his post on the night before the Japanese attacked, for Sir Vandeleur Grayburn, head of the Hongkong and Shanghai Bank who died in here of meningitis brought on by ill-treatment, for the thirty-two men and one woman – British, Indian and Chinese alike – executed in October 1943. And I recalled one of the inscriptions which had been written during the war in charcoal on the walls. It went:

D.W. WATERTON
ARRESTED STANLEY CAMP JULY 7TH. 1943
COURT-MARTIALLED OCT 19TH 43 AND
CONDEMNED DEATH
NO DEFENCE
EXECUTED DATE CALENDER STOPS

The scratched calendar stops on 29 October.

I had never expected to be so lucky, if that is the appropriate word, as to see one of these cells, never mind get in it. As I stepped out, and the officer closed the door with a dull and terrible thud, it came home to me what the internees' imprisonment must have meant: they were not here because they had committed a crime but because they had held the wrong passport. And, unlike the present occupants, they expected and indeed received little experience of justice.

After the cell block, I was shown the kitchens, a red tiled

recreation room (just tables and chairs), a classroom where some prisoners were being taught advanced mathematics for their London City and Guilds examinations. The Senior Superintendent was keen to show me that inmates had won the bronze medal for the whole world thrice in recent years. Just when I thought my tour was over, we passed an exercise yard – a wire cage the size of a tennis court with two prisoners standing morosely in it – and entered another, three-storey building with windows like ventilator covers. The ground floor contained a double row of different cells. The doors were not solid but iron grilles from floor to lintel. There was one prisoner to a cell and a number of correctional officers standing around: at one end of the floor was a television set broadcasting a Cantonese opera but only two or three cells could see it.

As we entered, the officers snapped to attention and an order barked out. The prisoners came to the grilles of their cells and stood stiffly upright. As the Senior Superintendent looked at them they positively shouted out their good morning greeting.

'This,' Mr Chan said, waving his swagger-stick at the cells, 'is Death Row. All these men are condemned to death.'

The death sentence has never been repealed in Hong Kong.

'Today, however, death sentences are commuted to life. No one has been executed since 1965 although an official executioner was on the payroll until well into the eighties.'

I looked at the prisoners. They were all murderers awaiting their reprieve.

'The gallows is upstairs,' Mr Chan continued. 'It is closed now behind a board but it is all still there – the trap-door, the rope.'

'What,' I wondered aloud as we returned to the administrative building, 'will happen to these men after 1997 and the Chinese takeover?'

Senior Superintendent Chan smiled but volunteered no reply.

After the cells, I would not have been surprised if the staff quarters had been an anti-climax, but they were not. With Correctional Officers Lau and Lee, I was shown the Tweed Bay hospital block, the leprosarium (in which leprous civilian prisoners were held with PoWs), the row of garages that had been the prisoners' kitchens and the married staff quarters buildings. Little had changed at all. There are parts of Hong Kong which are utterly unrecognisable but these little private roads and low buildings looked almost exactly as they did in the war.

Strolling through the grounds, I asked Mr Lee if the prison was haunted. I think he was pleased someone was taking an other than rehabilitational interest in his prison for he was keen to talk. The prison is haunted, he assured me, by ghosts only seen at night when there is a minimum guard presence: one is seen to flit along the perimeter wall, another is heard in the cells. By day, a little European boy may be spied in the playground (once the vegetable patch), watching the modern, living children play and an elderly European man may be sometimes seen walking in the dusk around the quarters.

I did not need to be told when we reached the spot depicted in Sammy Shields' photograph. The building is unaltered save for the addition of a few air conditioners mounted under the windows. I stood where the photographer had been and took my own photo. The lamp-post is still there, renovated. On the top balcony of the building behind a cross chow-dog barked at me. Had he been there half a century before, he would have been fattening for the pot.

As I was about to thank Messrs. Lee and Lau, I discovered my tour was still not yet over. We took a car and drove into St Stephen's College. Many of the buildings are post-war but the central block still stands and we walked along the corridor where the Japanese had bayoneted wounded soldiers and doctors, had repeatedly raped and then murdered three British and four Chinese nurses on Christmas morning 1941.

I could not stay in the corridor and watched for a door by which to escape into the sunshine: suddenly, a bell rang and the passage filled with laughing, talking, smartly uniformed children changing class. I wondered if they knew.

We strolled on through the college, passed the bungalows in which prisoners had lived: Bungalow C was accidentally bombed by the US air force and the occupants killed. It is now rebuilt but very haunted: I was told the resident teacher living there gets angry when his house is approached so we did not draw near. On the end of the low ridge on which the college is built, we stopped by a tennis court. This was where the prisoners had been mustered on the first day of captivity and it was here, under a large tree, the last machine-gun post to fall in the battle of Hong Kong was manned. I looked in the dirt for shrapnel but found only a sloughed snake-skin.

Back in the car, we drove out of the college and down to Stanley Bay.

'One more thing,' Mr Lee said as we left the car in a cul de sac. 'No one knows this.'

'Not even many of our fellow officers.' Mr Lau smiled.

We set off along a concrete path, past some British soldiers on holiday setting up a ski-boat, past canoes and surfboards piled on the beach. I knew where we were going, but did not let on so as not to spoil Messrs. Lau and Lee's surprise.

St Stephen's Beach is a narrow strip of sand a hundred metres or so long and ten wide at low tide. On it is a small marine club building – a diving club, I think: I paid it no attention. This was the beach where the Japanese executed Waterton and his comrades-in-death by decapitation with a sword, unceremoniously dumping the bodies in a mass grave. I had seen it before and did not want to see this place again and was about to turn back when Mr Lee beckoned.

'This way,' he called. 'You know of the beach but not this.'

In a little steep-sided valley behind the clubhouse was a small, neatly tended allotment. Banana trees grew in clumps, rows of beans or lettuces pushing through the soil. On a concrete path was a used tin barbecue.

'The man who owns this land,' Mr Lee began, 'lived here in the war. When the prisoners arrived, one of them asked permission to go onto these hills –' he waved his hands at the trees, massive boulders and dense scrub-strewn slopes around the valley '– to collect the dead. The Japanese agreed. When they reached here, the man who grows these plants said he knew where all the bodies were and guided the burial party. On the first day of freedom the prisoner, who was a senior government official, came immediately here and gave this land, which belonged to the government, to the farmer. He owns it now. Come!'

We passed the barbecue and reached the end of the cultivated area. Here the scrub began, thick and dense. To penetrate it would need a machete. Just inside the tangle of lianas and lantana, I saw a rusty chain-link fence with a yellow notice on it forbidding entry in English and Chinese.

'You know this?' Mr Lau asked.

I did not.

'It is where the hanged are buried. All overgrown now. So long since the last execution, many people forget this place.'

'Do the relatives of the dead not come here to make offerings?' I enquired. The Chinese, even those who are Christians, will not forget to pay their respects to their ancestors once a year on the Festival of Ching Ming.

'Never,' Mr Lee replied. 'We have never had a request. It would be allowed, but ... They do not come because of the shame.'

Half an hour later, I sat in the Oriental Café, my favourite little restaurant in Stanley. Over the top of my Tsing Tao beer and a plate of cold king prawns and chillies, I could see the beach and, behind it, the impenetrable undergrowth. Outside, four Australian tourists were talking: the men were discussing cricket and the women clothes they had bought.

I considered what the ghosts might think of it all.

Din Che

Hong Kong has arguably the most advanced, comprehensive and efficient public transport system in the world: it also has one of the oldest forms of mechanised transport still in operation. In Cantonese, this is the *din che* or electric car: in English, it is the tram.

The system runs on a thirteen-kilometre double track network along the north shore of Hong Kong island from Kennedy Town in the west to Shau Kei Wan in the east with a single track, a three-kilometre spur off to Happy Valley. It was opened in 1904 by the wife of the Director of Public Works whose small son travelled in the inaugural tram car ringing the bell which was the means of warning pedestrians out of the way. The first tramcars were single-deck vehicles painted scarlet, but by 1912, some of them had seats added on the roof surrounded by a railing. This top level accommodation was a boon in the hot weather but passengers were drenched when it rained and it was not unknown for them to be accidentally pelted with rubbish tossed out of windows whilst passing through built-up areas.

The tramway system was the pride of the colony and regarded with such esteem that in 1909 the Governor, Lord Lugard, took the Viceroy of Canton in an especially decorated pair of trams to Quarry Bay to show him the Taikoo docks and shipyard under construction. The Viceroy was utterly captivated by the journey which was probably the first he had ever made on land not propelled by human toil. He privately stated on returning to

China that the tram was far more interesting than the ship repair facilities.

Since their inception, the trams have run continuously with breaks in their service only because of a public boycott when the company refused to accept Chinese minted silver coins, the first few months of the Japanese occupation and at the height of the very worst typhoons. They survived not only these calamities but also a number of moves to make them redundant and an assortment of other currency devaluations, bank collapses and the public bombing campaigns of 1967, spurred on by the Cultural Revolution.

Twenty-six single-deck tram-cars were originally built but, by 1918, the system was expanded to eighty. Running on steel rails sunk into the metalling of the road, they each contained an electric motor receiving its power via a pick-up pole from overhead cables which restricted them to a speed not in excess of thirty kilometres per hour. Their construction was of wood mounted on a iron chassis which remained constant until 1991 when all the trams were re-bodied with metal, the old-fashioned wooden slatted seats being replaced by moulded plastic ones.

Other modernisations have taken place in recent years. The tinny warning bell has been replaced by a hooter-like instrument, the reason being that the bell was no longer clearly heard in the hubbub of traffic. The trams, once painted red and later green, are now multi-coloured, each one a moving hoarding for a single advertisement. The management of Hongkong Tramways Ltd hit on a brilliantly simple advertising gimmick: instead of mounting a number of advertisements on every tram, they opted to paint each one in accordance with an individual advertiser's demand. This has resulted in trams painted to look like transistor radios or washing machines, the windows where the speakers or control panel might be; others are intertwined with dragons or painted in the same livery as a Cathay Pacific 747.

Despite these garish paint-jobs, riding on a Hong Kong tram is to step back into the genteel era of leisurely travel, quaint and slow, rattling and swaying, comfortable (now the slatted seating has disappeared) and idiosyncratically Victorian – except when crowded to bursting in rush hour. The fares are also Victorian: there is a fixed charge per journey, be that one stop or the entire length of the system – it is HK$1, about ten pence.

To take a tram one has to know the ropes. Boarding is at the rear and alighting at the front, the fare is paid on getting off by dropping the right money into a box by the driver's elbow: there are no conductors or tickets. Tram stops are usually islands in the middle of the road under a concrete shelter *but not always so*: some are merely white and green signs on the pavement so would-be passengers have to step off the curb to signal the driver to stop. In traffic, this can verge on the suicidal but vehicles must halt if a tram is at an island-less stop. It takes about one and a half hours to ride the track from Kennedy Town to Shau Kei Wan and it is an utterly fascinating journey through the whole of urban Hong Kong yet few tourists undertake it: it is also a voyage through Hong Kong history. Despite the fact over a third of a million people travel by tram every day, the journey can be not only relaxing but also not crowded out of rush hour.

Starting in Kennedy Town, right alongside the colony's biggest abattoir, the tram sets off through the oldest part of urban Hong Kong, an area still containing low-rise buildings thirty or more years old with arcaded pavements and grimy concrete façades, little shops and companies trading in goods from China, factories making a vast assortment of objects from metal crate-banding clips to the frames of coolies' trolleys. Kennedy Town is in the area of Belcher's Bay, an inlet long since reclaimed from the sea. And it was here, it is thought, the first British landing party set foot on the newly acquired colony.

One might have expected the cove to be named Elliot Bay. It was Capt Charles Elliot, RN who gained Hong Kong for the crown. The son of a former governor of Madras, Chief Superintendent of Trade and Her Majesty's Plenipotentiary in China, Elliot oversaw the cession of Hong Kong under the Treaty of Nanking. It was but a part of the deal which ensured peace between Britain and China: the remainder included China paying reparation of $21,000,000, opening the ports of Canton, Amoy, Ningpo and others to British commerce, releasing all prisoners, proclaiming an amnesty and ceding Hong Kong.

And so it was that, on 20 January, 1841, Hong Kong became a British colony, formal possession being taken five days later with Elliot, aboard HMS *Wellesley*, not anchoring in Hong Kong harbour until 2 February.

Contrary to myth, it was not Elliot who first set foot in British Hong Kong but Capt Edward Belcher, master of HMS *Sulphur* after which Sulphur Channel, between Kennedy Town and Green Island, is named. Belcher landed on 25 January, at a quarter past eight in the morning. With a group of officers and men, he made his way to a little rocky outcrop (which he called Possession Mount, now the corner of Hollywood Road and Possession Street) where Her Majesty's health was drunk and three cheers hollered. Even then, the Union Jack was not raised. That ceremony was conducted at the same place the following day by Commodore J.G. Bremer, a relation of Prince Albert. All the ships in the harbour – naval vessels and merchantmen – fired a Royal Salute.

Elliot's gaining of the new colony did not go down well in London: Palmerston, the Foreign Secretary, dismissed the chances of 'a barren island with hardly a house upon it' becoming 'a mart of trade' and Elliot was recalled and castigated. His career was to essentially stagnate and he was appointed chargé d'affaires to the Republic of Texas. (His Chinese opposite number, Ki-shen, who had given Hong Kong away, was similarly berated and ended up in a minor post in Tibet.) None of the thoroughfares or buildings, mountains or bays, straits or passes were to bear Elliot's name. Only one small part of Robinson Road carries his name into history – Elliot Crescent – and that is of a comparatively modern origin.

Passing along Kennedy Town Praya, soon to be cut off from the sea by land reclamation, the track swings right and enters Des Voeux Road West. The buildings start to rise more sharply here, are newer and taller but, at street level, this is still very much the mercantile Hong Kong of old with small shops and freight forwarding businesses rubbing shoulders. For many years, this district of Sai Ying Pun was the dockside of Hong Kong. It was here not only junks berthed but also steamers from abroad, backing into wooden jetties to unload.

Sir William Des Voeux was Governor from October 1886 to December 1891. Already an old man of dubious health, with two other colonial gubernatorial posts under his belt, he was not a success, being more of an indecisive caretaker than an active agent who spent a substantial part of each winter duck shooting a thousand miles north on the Yangtse River. He did oversee Queen Victoria's Golden Jubilee, the opening of the Peak Tram, the foundation of the Chinese chamber of commerce and it was he who commissioned the statue of Her Majesty for Statue Square but one has the sense these achievements were made in spite of rather than because of him.

At the beginning of Des Voeux Road Central, skyscraper country begins in earnest. The tram passes the twin black and red-banded towers over the Macau Ferry terminal, clatters past Soonvar House, the home of the all-powerful Independent Commission Against Corruption (ICAC) which cleaned up the Royal Hong Kong Police in the seventies and is now acting against corruption in government offices, the legal and business communities. Officers' powers are swingeing: they may demand bank statements of suspects and their entire families, raid premises with the efficacy but not involvement of the police, confiscate property and prosecute with impunity.

Throughout Central the trams clack and shudder past forty or more storey buildings, architectural fantasies when the tracks were laid. To watch a tram swaying over a set of track joins beside one of these structural miracles is to have encapsulated the essence of Hong Kong – the old and new. Where the track turns from Des Voeux Road into Queen's Road is the place for a photograph: in one frame can be trapped the Bank of China, a tram, a sylvan park, a flyover footbridge and the domed, nineteenth century Legco building. Historically, the spot is even more interesting: where the prismatic Bank of China stands was once Murray Barracks, the Hilton not only on the former parade ground but also the site of the Colonial Church, Hong Kong's first Christian house of worship, built in 1841 out of bamboo poles to which were sewn walls of palm, banana and bamboo leaf mats. Not 300 metres from here was the site of the world's first gas street lighting (erected in 1865: four of the lights remain converted to electricity) as well as the ice house where blocks of ice, shipped from Alaska in sawdust and straw, were landed to be stored: just beyond it was the site of the first Hong Kong Club founded in 1846 and specifically excluding in its constitution the membership of 'shopkeepers, Chinese, Indians, women and other undesirables.'

Queen's Road, which for a distance between Central and Wanchai becomes Queensway, was Hong Kong's first thoroughfare and, inevitably, named after Victoria. Originally, it was a wide path along the shore linking the few little houses and hamlets occupying the coastline but, by November, 1841, a fair section of it had been transformed and was lined with Chinese houses, a market, the Commercial Inn and a building called the Birdcage which became the first dispensary.

On the tram shuffles, past Pacific Place and its hotel complex, to the start of Hennessy Road where it swerves into Johnston Road in the heart of Wanchai, later swinging back onto Hennessy Road.

Many believe Johnston Road was named after A.R. Johnston who was Charles Elliot's deputy and therefore one of Hong Kong's very first colonial administrators, but this is a fallacy. It is actually named after Sir Reginald Johnston, one-time governor of the British enclave of Wei Hai Wei who subsequently became Professor of Chinese Literature at the University of London: he is, however, far more famous as the personal tutor to Pu Yi, the last emperor of China, from 1919–22.

Hennessy Road gets its name from Sir John Pope Hennessy, Governor from 1877 to 1883. A temperamental and brooding Irishman, he was posted to Hong Kong from the Windward Islands to become an unmitigated disaster. The European residents took against him in no uncertain terms. Invitations to Government House were snubbed, Hennessy was booed and hissed in the street and some pointedly crossed the road to avoid him. His trouble was that he was too liberal, a humanist far ahead of his time and a man who would brook no racialism in a place which then, for all intents and purposes, operated a system of admittedly benign but nevertheless positive apartheid. In short, he took the side of the Chinese, banning the branding and flogging of criminals (save for violent crimes), criticising restrictions of Chinese building in the town, speaking out against the night-pass system whereby Chinese were more or less kept under curfew and, worst of all in the eyes of his fellow countrymen, he invited prominent Chinese to dine or take sundowners and tea at Government House. The British saw this as racial subversion and complained to London: a report stated the problems in Hong Kong arose from the Governor's observation that 'long residence among Chinese, & familiarity with the Chinese character, has led the residents of Hong Kong to believe that a Chinaman is not to be dealt with as an Englishman or even as an Indian or a Malay might be. [Hennessy] thinks this inhuman, and determines to set to work vigorously to reform what he believes to be a grave abuse. But, having no political wisdom, he proceeds in such a manner as to alienate from him all public sympathy . . .'

At least, European sympathy was lost: the Chinese were not so much against him. A month after he came into office, the first Chinese barrister to be admitted to the English Bar set up a law practice and, three years later, was appointed the first Chinese to the Legislative Council. Secular education was introduced to government schools giving Chinese the chance to avoid Christian religious instruction if they so wished. Hennessy refused, against his humanitarian conscience, to act against the *mu tsai* system (of buying and selling young girls for servants or as concubines) which he regarded as a Chinese cultural matter despite the fact the British Chief Justice wanted it outlawed. What further alienated him from his European subjects was the scandal of his wife's affair with Hong Kong's leading Queen's Counsel and his accusation of immoral practices against the Registrar-General. And yet he did much good: the first typhoon shelter for junks was suggested by him, he massively expanded the education service and he established the meteorological observatory in Kowloon but his overriding success, seen with the hindsight of history, lies in his liberal racial attitudes which set a stamp on Hong Kong which has never suffered, as did so many British colonies, from racial division, distrust and detestation.

It is an irony which never escapes me that Hennessy Road ran for a long time through the red light area of Hong Kong, the 'Chinese quarter' as it was known for a time and I often wonder if the road was so named out of spite. Every other thoroughfare named after a prominent nineteenth century European runs along a far more salubrious route.

The length of Hennessy Road used by the trams was the scene of heavy street fighting in the week before Christmas 1941. A number of trams were overturned at and between the junctions with Morrison Hill Road and Percival Street, partly to prevent the Japanese from using them to gain access to Happy Valley, for these are the turn-off points for the spur line round the race course, and partly to provide barricades. Today, the track is overlooked not by Japanese snipers but massive Japanese department stores.

Causeway Road in Causeway Bay, the next urban district on the tram route, cuts through between Victoria Park and a sports ground complex before veering north into King's Road, North Point: the king was Edward VII. It is hard to imagine, as the tram rocks by a bus terminus and MTR station to enter more high-rise buildings, that this was once the shore line. Fifty metres from the track is a seventeenth century Tin Hau temple, one of the earliest on the island: on a still day, the scent of the incense drifts as far as the passing trams.

For the next four kilometres, the rails run along King's Road, between the towering residential blocks of North Point, the most densely populated place on earth, on to Quarry Bay and Taikoo Shing where the Viceroy of Canton alighted and where there once stood Hong Kong's sugar refinery and dry docks which, in their day, could handle the biggest merchant vessels afloat.

Although almost every structure in this area is less than a quarter of a century old, it seems utterly and timelessly Chinese.

In through the tram windows comes not the tang of incense but the perfumes of cooking food, spices, concrete dust, diesel fumes, herbs, the not-too-distant seashore, and the luxuriant greenery of the mountains rising sharply behind the buildings. Overhead pass rank upon rank of colourful shop signs, advertising hoardings and laundry suspending out of windows to dry on poles.

Eventually, the tram lines reach Shau Kei Wan and bend in a loop around a small circle to start on the return journey. Shau Kei Wan is a residential and industrial area now but, in 1841, it was the second largest settlement on the island with a population of 1200, the shore of its bay lined by the slipways of boat-builders who manufactured junks here until at least the middle of the present century. A story based in the village concerns one Tsang Koon-man who settled there early in the nineteenth century and was the person to start quarrying in nearby Quarry Bay. With the coming of the British, the quarry prospered to such an extent he was able to build the walled village of Tsang Tai Uk for the Tsang clan which stands to this day, in true Hong Kong style, close to a large flyover in the Sha Tin valley.

Above Shau Kei Wan is a hill, the site of Lei Yue Mun Fort. As the strait of Lei Yue Mun was the main entrance to Hong Kong harbour, it was defended from 1845 when a wooden barracks was erected there only to be quickly abandoned because of malaria and dysentery. In the 1880s, however, the site was revitalised, the Victoria Redoubt being constructed. It was a warren of tunnels, passages, ammunition and command bunkers dug into the hill with six-inch gun emplacements encompassed by a drawbridge over a dry moat. More batteries were added at Pak Sha Wan, at the foot of the hill. Once more, in the 1930s, the fortress was increased in size with more barracks and stores being added.

The whole enterprise was pointless. Britain being a maritime power, it was expected that any attack would be sea-borne so most Hong Kong batteries faced the ocean: understandably, the invading Japanese attacked over land, under the angle of the guns or out of their arc of fire. Shau Kei Wan, close to one of the landing points for the invaders at Sai Wan, was the scene of fierce fighting, many of the local Chinese population being killed. Later in the war, it was a hive of partisan activity from whence escapers, saboteurs and both Nationalist and Communist guerrillas were smuggled by sampan to and from the mainland. The inhabitants of Shau Kei Wan, therefore, have a certain just pride.

Strategically useless, guns were not Shau Kei Wan's only military blunder. Close to the fort, at sea level, is a man-made cavern of which most Hong Kong residents are ignorant. This was excavated at the turn of the century to house a Brennan Torpedo Unit. The weapon, one of Britain's most secret, was a land-based, cable-guided torpedo with a range of two kilometres. It was launched from a ramp and operated by pulling on two wires, with the aid of a pair of high-powered steam winches, in much the same way as one controls a two-line kite. The 'pilot' could tell where the weapon was because it had a flag projecting from its back above the surface, his steering assisted by a look-out in the fortress above reporting down by telephone. It was never used in action.

One need not take the tram back to Central. Two minutes' walk from the turn-round is an MTR station situated, more or less, where the Japanese landed and the partisan fighters departed. From here, the subterranean train passes either towards the skyscrapers of Hong Kong or under Lei Yue Mun to the new industrial areas of the 1990s – Yau Tong, Cha Kwo Ling and Kwun Tong. Separated only by a street and a small municipal recreation area of trees and stone benches beneath an overpass, are working examples of the most antiquated and most modern tracked transport systems in the world. And, as they would have to in Hong Kong, they both make a gargantuan operating profit.

Pimms and Curry Puffs

Expatriates live well in Hong Kong but they are, in general, expected to work longer, harder hours than their contemporaries in London or New York, shoulder heavier burdens of responsibility and accept they may be dismissed as readily as they may be hired. Despite the insecurity of 1997 and the exodus of apprehensive professional and highly-skilled workers ahead of this date, Hong Kong companies are still able to attract and employ good quality expatriates. Recession in Europe and the USA has made Hong Kong a much-sought-after employment destination; yet the acronym *FILTH* (failed in London, tried Hongkong), coined in years of economic stability, is still somewhat prevalent. It is, however, inaccurate not just because of the quality demanded by companies but also because there are fewer and fewer British firms operating in Hong Kong. British trading superiority in China has waned dramatically in the last thirty years so that now there are fewer British working in commerce than there are French and German: the Americans make up by far the largest expatriate community.

In exchange for the heavy demands and expectations in the workplace, expatriates are afforded perks few could expect anywhere else in the world. Membership of and subscription to social clubs (where a joining fee may easily exceed US$50,000) is paid for as a matter of course, accommodation in luxury apartments (rent as much as US$10,000 per month) is common and generous allowances are made for servants, health care and the education of children either in Hong Kong or in boarding schools back home, not to mention high value air ticket provision for long weekends away in the resorts of Indonesia or Taiwan in addition to end-of-contract or home leave flights.

Yet the perk the majority would be most loathe to surrender is 'the boat' and an invitation to a day out on 'our boat' does not refer to an afternoon in a blustery English Channel bouncing about in a fifteen-foot cabin cruiser with a hand-pumped lavatory and a hissing butane gas ring.

Most multi-national companies have at least one 'boat': the Hongkong Bank has a fleet, of which some are designed vaguely along the lines of classical Chinese junks (without masts or sails, with powerful marine diesels) whilst others are floating gin palaces of chromium and teak. Needless to say, they are hardly 'boats' at all but luxurious fun craft up to sixty feet long (on occasion bigger) equipped with swimming platforms at the stern, ski-boat and skis, offshore radar, depth sonar, radiophone links and, for those which venture farther afield, satellite navigation and self-steering. A few companies have craft which look so fantastic they might be the invention of science fiction writers – the vessel owned by the company that manufactures *Matchbox* toy cars is one of the most astonishingly beautiful craft I have ever seen. When I last caught sight of her, she was moving slowly past Donald Trump's luxury yacht and eclipsed it.

Boat parties come in three varieties. First, there is the evening, mid-week party which involves a leisurely journey through the harbour to a nearby bay, usually on the north side of Lamma island: the sight of Hong Kong harbour at night is unforgettable with thousands of neon signs, the illuminated skyscrapers and the black mass of the Peak dotted with house and street lights behind, hanging in the sky and reflected in the sea. These events are usually connected with business, guests being visiting contacts or people in need of being impressed. Second is the Saturday afternoon party. All Hong Kong offices work until one o'clock on Saturdays so an afternoon on a boat after a morning's slaving over the fax or Apple Mac is a welcome diversion. It is not unknown for be-suited expatriate men to arrive at a pier to board their boat carrying a briefcase and a laptop computer plus a beach bag with a change of clothing in it. These afternoon jaunts entail sailing to the south coast bays of Lamma or Lantau islands. The third party is the all-day Sunday treat which can travel much farther afield, round to Port Shelter or Rocky Harbour, out to the Po Toi island group or the Ninepin Islands. Rarely, a weekend may be dedicated to a trip which could take vessels as far as Mirs Bay and Ping Chau, the nearest island in the east to China, but these are not common trips and there was a time, in the fifties and sixties, when such an undertaking ended in a diplomatic incident when the boat's owner inadvertently sailed into Communist waters to find himself facing the belligerent end of a gunboat.

I know of few better ways to spend a Sunday than going out on a boat. I first did it at the age of six and I still do it, given the chance. These days, I invariably go at the invitation of Tony and Ulli Frazer, an old and close friend and his wife. He works for the Bank which is a fortunate coincidence, for the Bank boats are, in my opinion, the *crème de la crème*.

Boats arrive at Blake Pier in Central from their moorings to pick up the day's passengers: at certain times, the water around the pier is a traffic jam of high-powered luxury craft edging forwards to the steps, revving and throttling up their engines to hold station in the queue but against the tide. The pier is an L-shaped concrete and steel structure about two hundred metres long. The spine of the L is a public jetty on one side and a mooring for what is left of the wallah-wallah boat fleet on the other whilst the foot is the pier for the hovercraft to Tuen Mun and the high-speed hydrofoil service to Discovery Bay.

The original Blake Pier stood at least 300 metres nearer the Peak, on the inland side of what is today Connaught Road. It was then known as Pedder Wharf, named after Lt William Pedder who had arrived in Hong Kong in 1841 and was the first harbour-master, but it was renamed Blake Pier after Sir Henry Blake, the Governor at the turn of the century, to much public annoyance: Pedder is still remembered however, by Pedder Street, the road which ran down to his jetty.

The present pier is barely twenty-five years old but is still a romantic spot for a good many important moments of Hong Kong's history took place on or before its precursor. Lord Kitchener landed here in 1909, the Prince of Wales, later King Edward VIII, in 1922 and General Rensuke Isogai in 1942: indeed, all Hong Kong governors landed here until Queen's Pier was built in honour of Elizabeth II. Blake Pier or Pedder Wharf have survived innumerable typhoons, being bombed and shelled and hit by merchant vessels in the days when sea-going ships moored directly on Connaught Road.

The majority of the Bank boats are those constructed in a style unique to Hong Kong. The wooden hull is built like a Chinese sailing junk with a high straight stern and a lower but rising bow protected on either side by a outriding board. It is quite broad of beam and does not taper greatly to fore or aft. Where a junk has a clear deck, however, a Bank boat has a superstructure with a bridge amidships and a wide, large afterdeck under a roof. Forward of the bridge is a series of cabins, the roof of which is a sun deck and, by the bows, a gently sloping foredeck contains anchors, ropes and chains. Although they do not ride low in the water and do not have a large keel, they are surprisingly stable and, whilst they may pitch and roll in the wake of a faster, more powerful vessel, they quickly settle again to an even state. They are not capable of great speed which seems somehow more appropriate for the Bank: it is better to be sedate and quick rather than flashy and fast if you are in the banking business. If these craft were Bank officials, they would be dark-suited corporate finance managers rather than messengers or PR hustlers.

Each boat carries a Chinese crew: one is never sure how many of these there are for they are as discreet as Victorian servants, hiding away somewhere until called upon. The coxswain is in charge. He knows Hong Kong waters and their hazards better than his passengers know the affairs of their most dubious financial clients. At his command is a working knowledge not just of currents and underwater rocks, wrecks and reefs but also how to steer through the water traffic of the busiest harbour in the world, avoid fishing nets, where to go for the best swimming and water ski-ing, the pollution levels in various bays, what the weather is doing on one island or another (for the weather in the harbour may be very different from that on an island not five miles away) and which beaches have open restaurants, bars or a peaceful lack thereof. To aid him, he has inshore radar and depth sonar but his most important instruments are his eyes and his wits.

Food and drink is brought on board the boat from the Bank mess. Stewards in old-fashioned white jackets and black trousers carry it to Blake Pier and load it there. As traditional as their uniforms is the fare they carry: beer, gin and tonics, whiskies and sodas, Pimms and soft drinks with curry puffs, several varieties of curry, rice (cooked on board in a rice cooker) and small chow. This phrase covers two types of food. First, it is the nibbles accompanying drinks – peanuts and cashews, lobster crackers, gherkins, potato crisps and a range of savoury Chinese objects, of some of which I have yet to discover the ingredients: even the stewards are ignorant of the contents. Second, it covers a variety of side dishes to be sprinkled over curry – desiccated coconut, crisp-fried onions, unsalted nuts, sliced cucumber, mango chutneys, poppadums, diced tomato and chopped boiled egg. Dessert is fresh tropical fruit salad with coffee.

Once cast off from Blake Pier, the day becomes a hedonistic blur. In the first half-hour, the harbour sights slide by to a conversation about the Japanese stock market, the week's movement of the US dollar to which the Hong Kong is pegged, the condition of such and such a corporation or multi-national, the state of shares in this and that. Wives and girlfriends chat. Gradually, as the boat sails past Green Island, the engine changing note against the currents in Sulphur Channel, the conversation and mood changes: the world of finance and futures, of cash and commodities fades as the skyscrapers dissolve in the haze of sun and traffic fumes. It is now people tell jokes – not smutty bar-room jokes or coarse raucous jokes, not esoteric banking jokes but Hong Kong jokes . . .

. . . like the one about the three architects who die and go to heaven – one is Japanese, one British, one Hong Kong Chinese. St Peter welcomes them but sees from his clipboard that heaven only has room for one architect. The three exchange glances: who's to go in? St Peter waves his hand at the Pearly Gates. 'As you can see,' he says, 'these need a bit of renovation – so I'll tell you what. You each tender for the work and the one who gets the job gets into heaven.' The three stand aside and whip out their calculators. Ahead of the other two, the Japanese jumps forward. 'I have a tender!' he exclaims. 'Six thousand dollars.' 'How does that break down?' asks St Peter. The Japanese replies, 'Two thousand architect's fee, two thousand labour, two thousand materials.' St Peter nods and the British architect steps up. 'My tender,' he declares, 'is $9000.' St Peter looks quizzical: there's a place in heaven at stake. 'My breakdown,' the British architect goes on, 'is $3000 fee, $3000 labour, $3000 materials – all good British quality,' he adds. 'British workmanship, British materials . . .' St Peter thanks him. The Hong Kong Chinese is still busy with his calculator. 'Are you ready?' St Peter asks at last. 'Yes, yes! Ready!' the Hong Kong Chinese responds. 'My tender is $12,000.' 'Twelve!' St Peter replies. 'Did you hear the other two tenders?' 'Oh, yes!' says the Chinese. 'So how do you break this sum down?' asks an incredulous St Peter. 'Easy!' comes the answer. '$3000 to you, $3000 to me and we sub-contract to the Japanese.'

Arriving at a bay on one of the outlying islands, lunch is served followed by coffee. The conversation changes once more. The jokes still hover about but the subject moves to tentative comments about house prices in Britain or America, mortgage rates and the future: as with every expatriate the world over, thoughts turn in quiet moments to home, to the potential insecurity of the years to come. Some talk of their holidays in Hawaii or Mexico, touring Europe or on safari in Africa but there is a wistfulness in the air, a knowledge to which no one wants to admit, that the good times must end one day, the bubble sure to burst.

Food settled, some swim off the boat in a dark blue sea as warm as a bath. A few others might take to the ski-boat and zip across the bay, avoiding other luxury boats that will almost assuredly have arrived. The remainder of the party laze in the sun making small talk. The coxswain stays at his post, relaxing in his tall seat reading a newspaper. The stewards pass about topping up glasses or replenishing bowls of nuts and gherkins.

At such moments, I like to go ashore, hitching a lift in the ski-boat and walk along the beach. The hot wind stirs in the bushes and undergrowth, silent hints of birds gliding through the shadows and on the sand, if the coxswain has been wise in his choice of bay, will lie a flotsam not of trash but of seaweed and coconut husks, lengths of sea-bleached wood and dogfish egg-pouches. In the shallows, minute fish dart in squadrons.

Sitting on the beach looking out at the boat, the skiers and the horizon, it seems as if the good times really have lasted for ever and will never end.

Stepping the Imaginary Line

Our black unmarked saloon turned into the yard of the police station to halt beside several dark blue Landrovers. The Chinese police constable who was the duty driver nimbly got out and opened the door for John, a (very) senior officer in the Royal Hong Kong Police. Another constable, his khaki summer uniform starched and creased, his black Sam Browne belt shining in the sunlight, opened my door.

'Good afternoon, sir,' he said as he saluted me, which I found a little nonplussing. 'Welcome to Sha Tau Kok.'

A European inspector in a peaked cap lined with silver braid walked out of the deep shadows cast by the afternoon sun and saluted my companion. We all shook hands.

'I suppose you're ready for this?' John asked.

I nodded. Sha Tau Kok is a place that remains, even today, in the imagination of most Hong Kong residents. Unless one is in the police or the British army, or a local village resident, entry is virtually forbidden: it is, as was pointed out to me, easier to get into the grounds of Buckingham Palace than into the environs of this border town – after all, an intruder had successfully entered the palace and explored as far as the Queen's bedroom before being apprehended. No restricted person had made it into Sha Tau Kok without a permit and those are extremely hard to come by.

Sha Tau Kok is at the north-eastern tip of Hong Kong, where the Communist border meets the sea. It is a small town with a population of perhaps 3000 – on the Hong Kong side: on the Chinese side, there is a similar, mirror population.

'Tienanmen Square's made them a bit jumpy,' the inspector in charge remarked, 'but not really more than usual. No major problems . . .'

Knowing that the region across the border from Hong Kong is today classified a Free Economic Zone by the Communist authorities, and somewhat relaxed in its attitude towards Westerners, their capitalist ways and the heady corruption of consumerism, I asked if Sha Tau Kok was not really now a bit of an anachronism, a tame place compared to how it had been.

'No,' the inspector said. 'Not really. It's still a bit of a prickly spot . . .'

We left the station yard, surrounded by barbed wire and watch-towers, and strolled across a wide concrete area which might have been a market-place on an off-day. Ahead were two parallel rows of houses divided by a narrow street.

'It was here our lot got hammered,' he commented.

That was during the upheaval of the Cultural Revolution when cross-border relationships were somewhat strained. The People's Liberation Army had opened fire on a British army patrol in the streets of Sha Tau Kok, killing a number of soldiers. The open concrete space had then been buildings: they were later razed to the ground on the Hong Kong side to provide an easier field of fire. Looking ahead, I suddenly saw – in the gap between the buildings ahead of us – a machine-gun post at first floor level. The inspector saw my line of sight.

I must have looked uneasy.

'That's where the strafing fire came from,' he remarked. 'It's still manned by them. No machine guns now. Just a watchtower these days.'

Sha Tau Kok is unique because, since the Berlin Wall was pick-axed, this is the last touchy spot on a Communist border anywhere in the world bar Korea: the Bamboo Curtain passes right through the village. This may not sound like a unique situation: the West/East German border ran through many villages, not to mention Berlin. Yet in Sha Tau Kok there is no visible border: there are no concrete posts, no floodlit no-man's-land or ditches, no razor wire or trip-lines, no minefields, no checkpoint gates, no walls smothered with peacenik graffiti. The border is an imperceptible demarcation running down the centre of the village street.

We arrived at the street. It was, for all intents and purposes, a normal Chinese village street. People thronged about: a coolie went by with a woven bamboo basket of subdued chickens, several women chatted outside a rice shop, a youth pushed by with a bicycle upon the pannier of which balanced several enamel buckets, a mangy-looking dog sauntered from the sunshine into the shadows and was hissed at by a cat on top of a pile of rattan chairs. Several children ran by, laughing. From the shops came the babble of chatter, the raucous cacophony of Cantonese opera blaring from a transistor and the tooth-jarring screech of a machine sharpening something metallic. It flashed across my mind it might be honing a bayonet.

I looked for the halfway line. There was no marking painted on the ground. A number of pedestrians crossed from one side to the other with impunity: local residents, with the required permit, may saunter internationally, but I could not – nor could the policemen with me.

'The border's invisible, as you can see,' John remarked. 'Runs from bollard to bollard. Take care you don't cross over the invisible line. We don't want to ask Beijing if we can have you back.'

He was only half-joking.

Every fifty yards or so, there is an innocuous concrete stump in the road. It might have been a naked keep-left sign or one of those obstacles city authorities put up to pedestrianise a precinct. Yet these blocks separate not feet from wheels but nation from nation, religion from religion and dogma from doctrine.

A People's Liberation Army soldier approached us. This was the closest I had ever been to a member of the armed forces of Ronald Reagan's Evil Empire. He looked rather innocuous and short-sighted. I guessed he was a corporal or the like, but his olive-khaki uniform had the impression of a major general about it – gold braid epaulettes, sleeve rings, more scrambled egg on the cap peak than that to which the police inspector could lay claim. He was carrying, slung over his shoulder, a Chinese version of an AK47. With the trained eye of a local, he walked straight towards us and stopped at the force field of the invisible border. The police inspector saluted him: he saluted back.

'*Goo' ahtfahnung*,' the PLA soldier said.

The inspector returned this greeting in Cantonese and they chatted for a moment or two. During this conversation, neither man touched or moved nearer to each other: they were only three feet apart but they might have been three miles for all the contact they could dare to make. Every now and then, the PLA glanced in my direction and grimaced. Eventually, he saluted once more, grinned expansively at me and moved off on his patrol.

'He wanted to know who you were,' I was told as we set off in the opposite direction. 'Your hair's a bit – ' the inspector searched for a polite phrase to describe my collar-length cut ' – too writerish for him.'

'What did you say?'

'I told him you were my brother-in-law, visiting me on the job. I said you were a famous movie actor. He was most impressed.'

Twenty years ago, this normal rural Chinese street was a battlefield down which no one moved. Not even a Red moggie would cross over to visit a Capitalist lady cat in season. The shop fronts were heavily boarded or bricked up and the alleyways leading into the street rammed shut with sandbags and soldiery. This was then a front line.

Insults were exchanged either by loud-hailer (the Communist troops) or by cupped mouth (the British squaddies). Occasionally gunfire was to be heard echoing in the street leading up to the massacre of British soldiers. No lights were shown and no cigarettes smoked. It was a strange, dim, foreboding world, a little Chinese tinder-box which could have sparked World War Three if something had gone wrong. It was a Chinese Cuban Crisis waiting to happen, the stuff of spy novels and real-life political thrillers.

We reached the end of the street and were obliged to go

down an alleyway. A street barber was busy in a doorway cutting an old man's hair. A stiff onshore breeze blew through the alleyway, little tufts of the old man's shorn crop drifting into Communist China.

At the end of the alley, we arrived in a Hong Kong side street running parallel to the main thoroughfare. Down this we made our way, past a butcher's shop, a tailor's and a man weaving rattan seats. Suddenly, we came out into sunlight and, ahead of us, stretched a jetty. No vessels were moored alongside, although steps led down to the water. Off the jetty, however, a large number of fishing junks and sampans were riding at anchor in Hong Kong waters. Nothing was afloat in the Chinese sea.

We set off along the jetty, halting at the end, the inspector stepping across it.

'I am now in China,' he said quite matter-of-factly.

I joined him.

It did not feel different. Yet I had, for just a few moments, gone over.

Suddenly, a white egret appeared out of the sky, flew low over the water, rose in altitude at the jetty, soared over our heads and was lost amidst the armada of fishing vessels, not one built to a design less than three centuries old. Close to the jetty, catching the sun on their fins, swam a school of little dark green and silver fishes. The whole scene seemed timeless, beyond the tentacular reach of politics and the stupidities of men.

On our way back to the police station, I was guided once more down an alleyway leading to the border. At the end, we stopped. Ahead of us was a stone-lined nullah flowing with a light trickle of sewage. On the far bank, not twenty feet away, was a road and a modern three-storey block of apartments which looked exactly like those in any Hong Kong middle-class suburb. Before it was parked a Datsun van. It looked like any delivery van in Hong Kong, yet it had a Guangzhou number-plate. In the centre of this mundane view was a concrete border stump against which was leaning an old, black bicycle.

'Looks so innocent, doesn't it?' the inspector commented.

'Isn't it?' I asked.

Perhaps this was a listening post or an anti-personnel mine, cunningly disguised as a clapped-out bike. I smiled to myself at the ludicrosity of this thought and remembered Evelyn Waugh's exploding goat in his novel *Men At Arms*: this, I considered, was an opportunity missed by John Le Carré in his *The Honourable Schoolboy*.

'About a month or so ago,' the inspector related, 'the PLA nipped across here one night and grabbed a man from our end of the alley. Whether he was thinking of doing a flit over there or not we can't tell. But they knew him and they had him marked.'

I must have looked puzzled.

'An old man,' John explained, 'one from the old days, before '49. He was a member of the KMT – Kuomintang – Chiang Kai-shek's lot – Nationalists . . .'

'Must have been in his sixties,' the inspector went on. 'At least. Anyway, they felt his collar and hauled him over the nullah.'

'Where is he now?' I enquired.

'Who knows? Dead, probably. They've long memories over there.'

I looked again at the bicycle and it didn't seem funny any more.

Chip Shop

Fifty metres from the Fuk Wa Street exit of the MTR is a snake shop and restaurant. It is an unpretentious establishment much like any of the others of its ilk to be found in Hong Kong: it has a few tables for diners, a façade carrying a board painted with a striking cobra, tiled floors and it opens onto the pavement. The menu lies for the most part immobile in glass tanks at the front.

Snake is eaten not only for its taste but also for its medicinal properties. The flesh is said to strengthen the blood in cold weather, the blood may be drunk to heal lethargies and lassitudes and the bile is mixed with a wine like port as a cure for rheumatism, headaches and as a general pick-me-up: like so many folk remedies the world over, it is also said to rejuvenate the male genitalia. Almost any snake may be used, but some are deemed more efficacious than others – the more poisonous, it seems, the better.

When snake is ordered, the customer chooses his reptile which is then brought to the table-side and killed. The snake executioner slides a razor-sharp thin blade the length of the snake's belly, the organs and intestines falling to the tiled floor – tiles are more easily swabbed than boards – only the gall bladder retained. The blood is collected in a bowl. This done, the snake's skin is ringed just behind the neck and, with a deft movement, is torn off inside-out down the creature's length to be dumped with the guts. For those without the courage to try it, the flesh has a soft, delicate taste which is quite unique, the blood tastes of iron and rust and the bile wine has a sharp cut to it but is quite refreshing. It may be purchased in most wine dealers and health shops and is very cheap indeed unless you require one of the rarer vintages which contains the whole snake (or lizard – they too have their culinary uses) pickled in the bottle.

I frequent Fuk Wa Street on a regular basis but not for the snakes although, on one occasion, I came very close to them.

The snake shop has a front man, a sort-of whipper-in of customers and promoter extraordinaire of the beneficial properties of reptiles and his employer's stock in particular. In his early thirties, this man positions himself across the street from the shop at a point where there is a no parking zone. Many of the surrounding streets becoming markets from late afternoon onwards; it is a good pitch for there are always crowds of people milling around and, just a street away, there is a major *pak pai* and bus terminus.

On the curb, the man places several sacks and a low steel mesh cage in which are samples of the shop stock. Dressed only in a pair of grubby trousers (besmirched, no doubt, by snake blood, bile and bodily juices) and grimy sneakers, the man proceeds to take snakes from the sacks or cage, display them, wrap them around himself, cause them to strike at him and generally do what any showman does – show off. He picks all the snakes up with an iron rod, the end of which is bent into an L-shape, and wears a glove only for the biggest of the pythons which can administer a nasty if non-venomous bite. His stock usually consists of a constrictor, a few brown rat snakes and a cobra. Banded kraits are common in snake restaurants but the showman rarely has one: they are immensely venomous and, although they are usually docile and rarely bite, he obviously does not wish to risk it.

Although Europeans are a common sight in Fuk Wa Street, they are not cast in the usual tourist mould and do not bother to pause and watch the display. I, however, do. I am interested in seeing what snakes the shop has imported and, besides, the man's act is a part of the Hong Kong I have known and loved all my life.

An aside here: Hong Kong imports so many snakes, mostly from China and Thailand, that the stocks in the wilds are dropping to exceedingly low numbers. This is dangerous not only for the snake world but also the human one for snakes serve a vital purpose in eradicating vermin (particularly rodents) and where the snakes have been exported in vast quantities, the rat population has exploded. The long-term effect of this on rice and wheat stocks, not to mention the risk of widespread bubonic plague which has re-emerged in Indo-China in recent years, has yet to be assessed.

The showman is also a smart-arse, ready to mock anyone he sees might be a butt of his wit. He occasionally moves forward quickly, a snake at arm's length, so the audience gathered to watch his display steps rapidly backwards: a blaring of car horns greets such a move and the showman laughs and chides the crowd for being afraid. Several years ago, I was the object of his derision.

The current snake on display was a rat snake, a metre and a half long, decorated with alternate pale white and black bands and a pallid cream underbelly. The species, very common in Hong Kong, is a constrictor which kills its prey of rodents, frogs and birds by biting onto it and crushing it against a rock or hard ground. It is a fang-less snake: this said, it is also readily annoyed and strikes at the slightest movement so it makes an ideal tool for the showman. He knows it can do no harm other than give a hard bite, but his audience doesn't.

After a few lunges at onlookers and sarcastic remarks about their lack of bravery, the man suddenly turned on me and thrust the snake out. I did not step back. I was damned if I was going to lose face to him. Besides, I know a rat snake when I see one. My immobility annoyed him and, stepping towards me, he suggested in mime I might take the snake. I nodded and reached out, putting my left hand halfway down the creature's belly with the intention of placing my right over the showman's hand at the snake's neck. He, however, saw his chance and let go of it as I grasped its belly. The snake fell, jerked to a stop in mid-air and started to strike at me. Having handled snakes before, I merely held it out at arm's

length, ran my right hand up its body and gripped it firmly round
the throat. This accomplished, and the snake prevented from
striking, I wrapped its coils round my arm. It tightened on me
but made no effort to squeeze. Now it was my turn. I stepped
forward, paraded the reptile to the throng – now much larger at
the sight of a *gweilo* with a snake – stroked its head and looked
closely into its bead eye. I wondered if I might kiss it as Indian
snake-charmers do to their fang-drawn cobras. No harm would
have come to me from the snake but I was more concerned with
where it had been . . .

The showman came forward. He wanted his snake back and
was quite plainly annoyed. He had lost face in no uncertain
measure and two old men in the crowd were taking the mickey
out of him, pointing from me to the showman and back again
and laughing fit to bust. With his right hand, he beckoned to me
to return the snake.

'You giff me one snake,' I replied in pidgin English: my spoken
Cantonese doesn't go as far as discussing the merits of reptiles with
a crowd of would-be customers but I did decide to pass comment
on the creature's culinary value. '*Ho she*,' I went on. '*Ho sik*.'

The crowd laughed loudly: this was a *gweilo* with at least a
bit of Cantonese and not a tourist as, I suspect, the showman had
assumed.

He shook his head and said quite tersely that he had not
given me the snake, merely passed it over as I was so interested
in it. I shook the snake a few times, to get it well and truly riled,
then gave it back to its owner in the same fashion he had passed
it to me.

Whenever I return to Fuk Wa Street, in the Sham Shui Po
district of Kowloon, the showman remembers me: I can tell by
his glance, his avoidance of my eye and the fact that he does not
hand his wares over.

Sham Shui Po is what friends refer to as darkest Hong Kong.
It is a thriving area of tenements, factories, markets and traffic.
The streets are constructed on an American-style grid pattern and
lie directly under the flight path for Kai Tak, aircraft passing

overhead at about one hundred and fifty metres. There is hardly anything here to interest the ordinary tourist but there is one building that a certain type of tourist, local expatriate and Chinese resident makes for in droves.

It is the Golden Shopping Arcade.

The casual observer might not be criticised for thinking it sells the best of Swedish or Japanese pornography for those who go there are almost exclusively male. Such a misconception might be further enhanced by the fact a nearby street has become infamous in recent years for its arrant whores, most of them Filipinas, Thais and Vietnamese who stand in alleys and doorways wearing the barest essentials for immodest decency.

This, however, is not the case, for the Golden Shopping Arcade is not a strip club or a whorehouse but a computer centre. With a difference.

The building is an unprepossessing-looking place with two storeys of shops below what I assume are offices, small factories or residential apartments. Once, they were ordinary commercial units but, eight years or so ago, the computer brigade moved in so that now there is not a single business present handling any other sort of merchandise.

All the shops – some of them little bigger than a large broom cupboard – line narrow, low-ceilinged corridors with cheap neon lights and bare concrete floors. I would guess there are about 150 businesses in the building, all of them at the cutting edge of computer technology.

Hardware is available in staggering abundance: desktops and laptops, minis and towers, sound cards and video-cards, CD-ROM drives and umpteen gigabyte hard disks, keyboards and joysticks, mouses and trackballs, 24-pins and inkjets. There is nothing that is not here. Equipment arrives sometimes before the main dealers receive it and frequently months ahead of dealers in Europe or the USA. What is more, it is all on sale at discounted prices and, due to the tax-free nature of Hong Kong trade, can result in a considerable saving for overseas visitors even if they still declare the items purchased to customs authorities in their home countries.

Not only whole computers may be purchased but so also may constituent parts. Circuit boards, hard cards of every sort and even individual microchips including those by such famous brand leaders as Intel, AMD and Toshiba are all obtainable over the counter and on demand at knock-down prices. When there was a world-wide micro-chip famine in 1988/89 even the rarest of chips were readily on show here at a discount.

Carrying a desktop computer onto a flight to Dallas is not easy and even a hard card or chip may be damaged by the X-ray or magnetic bomb-searching equipment used by airline security. Software, however, is another matter. The Golden Shopping Arcade is famous (or infamous, depending on the point of view) for computer software. Much of it is legit. but a good deal of it is pirated.

Almost every shop has rack upon rack of computer pro-grammes on offer. Some are displayed in their manufacturer-designed packaging, others in cellophane or printed envelopes, yet more still in plastic diskette boxes. Rows of entertainment software include games unheard-of in Europe or North America. Every shape and form of alien may be zapped in these, every conceivable type of spacecraft flown. Some of the games are not so flippant being airline flight simulators and business games but some are mindless mechanical exercises in which one has to stop small mobile creatures from impaling themselves on stakes or falling into an abyss: others are distinctly naughty, such as *Strip Poker*.

Games programmes are not what most punters visit the arcade for: most visit to see the business software. Some of this is pirated but some of it is present in pre-release Beta-versions. In other words, the programmes are the manufacturer's trial run editions and although they may have bugs in them − faults to the uninitiated − they are a fair indication of what is soon to appear on the market and arouse intense interest amongst the micro-chip *cognoscenti*.

Pirated software is what most people purchase, the pirating done on site. The system works like this: the customer chooses a software programme from the packaging or the manual on display and may, if required, see the programme running on a desktop computer. Once the decision to buy is made, the shop owner either takes a set of manufacturer's master disks and copies them on a PC behind the counter or, if he is somewhat more canny or the programmes are not available in the shop, will send a mobile phone message whereby a copy is made in a nearby building and the disks brought over. This is a precaution that was common a few years ago, after the police raided the arcade a few times at the insistence of the big multi-national software houses, but is less frequent now. The copied disks are placed in plastic boxes and handed over for a very low sum indeed. A manual is no problem either: some shops specialise not in the software but pirated manuals printed from the originals in Taiwan or China. They, too, cost a fraction of the original.

To mix a metaphor, the pirate vendors are no cowboys. They are all young whizz-kids with infinite computer knowledge and considerable skills. Some of these stallholders or employees arrive in the late afternoon for work still wearing their school uniforms. Copy protection systems are not a problem for them but a challenge to be overcome. Programming in various languages is a skill most have acquired. Computers and software are in their blood – so much so that one young man I know, on taking a Western name to go with his Chinese family name, chose to call himself Fortran: Fortran is a programming language.

The authorities seldom swoop on the Golden Shopping Arcade these days. They know they are on to a loser. If the shops are closed down, they only re-open somewhere else days later. As a good few of them are also owned or sponsored by Triad crime syndicates, the culprits' fines are soon paid. As for the multi-national firms, I wonder if they have not decided the Golden Shopping Arcade, internationally famous throughout the network of hackers and programmers, chip-freaks and alien-chasers, is working to their advantage. I know of at least a dozen people who have wandered through the crowded corridors, elbowed their way to the front of crowds to study new games and business packages and bought a few pirated copies which, having studied them in depth and realised they are what is needed, have promptly ordered the real thing from the bona fide manufacturer.

In the region of Fuk Wa Street, there are both kinds of Chinese showman – the one with an art a thousand years old and one that's barely a thousand days into existence.

Rats, 'roaches and
Wartcher Beechews

Every night, the waterfront before Hong Kong City Hall offers one of the most spectacular urban panoramas on earth. Across a mile or so of water, the huge neon advertisement signs on Ocean Terminal, the illuminated sweeping walls of the concert hall and the myriad windows of the Kowloon waterfront hotels shimmer in the heat of the sub-tropical evening, coruscating upon the sea. Behind them, like a stage curtain, the Kowloon hills stand blackly and, if the evening is clear, the moving lights of an arriving aircraft cut across them, lowering to disappear seemingly into the buildings.

Turn around, and the skyscrapers crowd in, tens of thousands of lights in thousands of windows. On top of the HongkongBank are the bright, distinctive red and white triangles of the company's logo. Along the edge of the roof, the Mandarin Hotel has its name in discreet lights: on the other hand, the nearby Furama Hotel emblazons its name in garish green, contrasting with its conservative neighbour. The Bank of China looms high into the sky, lit by a million candle power spotlamps which project the shadows of the chopsticks onto the clouds. Over to the right is the tower of Central Plaza decorated with vertical yellow neon stripes and looking like a giant Wurlitzer, the blaze of lights that is the Hong Kong Arts Centre and the newest convention centre.

The area between the City Hall complex – main library, concert hall and theatre – and Queen's Pier is closed to through traffic. It is pedestrianised, with stone benches, small shrubs in pots according to the season and a line of low trees, the ground tastefully paved with flagstones. Queen's Pier stands halfway between the Star Ferry and the main gate to *HMS Tamar*, the headquarters of the British Forces in Hong Kong – but not for much longer: the White Ensign has come down and the dockyard, once the farthest British naval base east of Suez, is to join its surroundings and become skyscrapered. It is not a pier as such but a tidy quay with flights of landing steps under a nondescript concrete roof and has been, in modern times, the official landing point for visiting dignitaries and newly arrived governors who step off their launch here to mount a podium in their gubernatorial plumed helmet which Sir David Wilson, the penultimate governor, is reputed to have called his 'chicken hat' and which the present governor, Christopher Patten, declined to don.

The promenade is seldom busy unless there is an important show being staged in the City Hall. Most evenings, people stroll leisurely along it, young lovers hand-in-hand, sailors heading for a night on the town, businessmen clutching their cases as they await a rendezvous. A few people sit on the benches and, once in a while, a taxi might go by to drop someone off at the pier to catch a private boat.

On the last occasion I was to meet a friend at the Star Ferry, to go for an evening drink – 'the Ferry' is the most common of Hong Kong meeting places, much as Piccadilly Circus was during the war – I arrived a little early and strolled along to Queen's Pier. A splendid three-masted yacht was moored alongside, beautiful young women in evening gowns gingerly stepping onto her shifting gangplank, the accompanying men smart as emperor penguins in tuxedos. From fifty paces, diamonds glittered momentarily in the lights of the pier.

Seated on one of the benches, I watched the view which I have known and seen mutate for most of my life, observing Hong Kong's meritocracy boarding its vessel. After a few minutes, however, I realised I was myself in turn being observed. By a large, sleek and quite brazen rat.

It was perched at the other end of the bench, not two metres from me. Not caring a jot about my presence, it was grooming, rubbing its face with its front paws in that endearing way rodents have. I guessed it was about twenty-five centimetres long excluding its tail which hung over the side of the bench. Lacking the creamy belly of the ship rat, or the grey belly of the Chinese buff-breasted rat, I assumed it to be one of Hong Kong's most populous animals – the ubiquitous brown rat.

To see what happened, I moved my arm and shifted my briefcase, ready to leap to my feet if the creature attacked. It did not. It halted its toilet, gave me a quick glance, sniffed the air then carried on preening. An elegant couple walked by on their way to the three-master, the woman dressed in a green silk gown with emerald accessories to match. The rat did not budge. It had obviously learnt that men in vests with brooms might kill it but men dressed in dinner jackets posed no threat. Nor did men with briefcases.

After several minutes the rat, having cleaned itself and taken the air, slid fluidly off the bench and ran, head down, towards Queen's Pier. At the edge of the quay, it halted and was then gone. I walked to the spot. On the water bobbed a thick wedge of flotsam. Leaning over, I noticed a sewer outlet just above the tide line. The rat was sitting in it. At my appearance, it dived out of sight.

Rats are common in Hong Kong. This is no criticism. They are just as prevalent in London, Lisbon and Los Angeles. The Urban Services Department wage a continual war on them, trapping and poisoning them in their thousands: they do considerable damage in buildings where they gnaw power cables, honeycomb cavity walls and can even wake residents with their fights: yet they do little damage to the health of the human population. This, however, was not always the case.

In January 1893 – just as in January 1993 – Hong Kong suffered a bitterly cold spell. For three days, the Peak was ice-bound. When the weather turned, it was noticed several Chinese had died of 'a pestilential fever accompanied by sores and contusions'. Bubonic plague had arrived in Hong Kong. By 1 May, 150 people had perished: by 15 May, the death toll had risen to 450 and was climbing sharply. The Chinese population accepted the outbreak stoically but Sir William Robinson, the Governor, and his government went into a state of near panic. The Sanitary Board tabled and immediately passed bye-laws ordering the cleaning and disinfecting of plague areas, the provision of extra fever hospital places, the compulsory removal of infected victims, the eviction of healthy people from infected buildings and, in one instance, the forcible burning to the ground of a tenement coolie boarding house. Three hundred Indian and British troops were seconded to help out but when five of them fell to the plague, they were withdrawn.

The local Chinese took umbrage at what they saw were infringements of their rights: they objected to health visits in their houses, not to mention mandatory eviction. Posters appeared in the streets of Canton warning people against visiting Hong Kong adding that the plague was invented by the foreign devils whose doctors gouged out children's eyes to make a cure. Another worry for the government was that many families were keeping their dead in coffins awaiting a propitious date for the funeral – no Chinese is buried on an inauspicious day – and victims who were poor were being left in the streets: on just one day in June, 109 corpses were gathered in by the health authorities. Large areas of the Chinese quarters were roped off, 3,000 people evicted with no alternative provision and a glassworks and as-yet-to-be-opened pig depot became fever hospitals or, more accurately, waiting-rooms on the way to eternity.

The outbreak did not die down until the autumn by which time 2,500 had died and 80,000 had fled the colony. Hong Kong being declared an infected port, business was severely disrupted – and that is not acceptable in Hong Kong.

By 1898, when bubonic plague returned with a vengeance killing 1,175 that year with another 1,428 the next year and 1,434 in 1900, it was known that rats were the vector. Once more, citizens fled and business was threatened. Sir Henry Blake, the new Governor, opened battle against rodents. Houses were rat-proofed, traps were issued. Each rat's tail delivered to the health authorities earned two cents. In 1900, 43,000 rats' tails were surrendered. Needless to say, a large number of these had been imported from Kwangtung Province: never underestimate the entrepreneurial skills of the Chinese.

Yet the plague was beaten and, although minor outbreaks or isolated cases were to appear as late as the early fifties, it was never again a scourge except during the war when social conditions deteriorated under the Japanese occupation. The rats, however, remain, an important part of the local fauna, providing food for snakes on the periphery of the urban areas and sport or sustenance for the tens of thousands of feral cats that roam Hong Kong.

One frequently sees them: in the same week as my meeting with the city gent of a rat at Queen's Pier, I saw one in a live trap being drowned by gleeful children, one in a storm drain feeding on discarded food, one (dead) in a gutter, one scampering like hell through slow-moving evening traffic in Mong Kok and, to my surprise, one running pell-mell across the top of a urinal in a restaurant I often visit as I stood there relieving myself.

The presence of rats may upset a squeamish tourist but does not bother me at all: there are rats in my English garden. What sends shivers down my back are cockroaches. Just as airline pilots know they are in Hong Kong from the smell so I know I am home – truly home – when I see my first cockroach.

These are not the little shams you get in London, squashed with a thumbnail or flattened by a tissue. These are giant cockroaches – *Periplaneta americana*, the American cockroach: as the name implies, these are the biggest, the slickest, the most polished of their kind. Four centimetres long, they shine the colour of waxed mahogany, their six hairy legs ever active and their whipping antennæ never still. They can run as fast as a man jogs and, worst of all, they fly. I have seen cats back away from them and Tina, an Alsatian dog my parents used to own, assiduously avoided them. In the insect world, they are the armoured brigade in their assault on humans. I have hit them repeatedly with woven bamboo fly swats only to have them get up and start running again, have batted them down in mid-flight only to have them slam on the floor and scurry for cover. Despite their size, they can slip into (or out of) a closed matchbox and, when they are finally squished, they exude a creamy gunge that smears and sticks to any surface.

There can be few worse experiences than waking in the middle of the night in need of a glass of water, going to the kitchen and snapping on the light to be confronted by a dozen of these insect behemoths patrolling the floor and work surfaces where, during the day, everything seems as clean as an operating theatre. As soon as the light is on, they head for safety. This might be below the draining board, down the plug-hole or under your instep. The braver specimens take to the wing and head for the window or the door. To be hit by one in mid-flight is an appalling experience: the impact is quite hard – a small bird would feel like this – and, as soon as the flight is arrested, the insect drops into the folds of your clothing, seeking shelter there. I would rather have a snake drop down my front than a cockroach.

They eat anything from the merest breadcrumb to books, from a near invisible smudge of food on a table top to a leather wallet. The most fastidious housewife, amah or Filipina maid can do little to counteract the cockroach other than keep the home as clean as possible with all sugar, bread, flour, rice – or almost anything else – in tough plastic containers. Even the inside of a fridge is not safe: I have discovered cockroaches in every compartment but the ice-box, slowed down by the cold but nevertheless still going about their business. The only effective defence again them are cockroach traps, cardboard tubes containing poison which are placed against skirting boards. The cockroach heads for them as safe haven when disturbed or enters them when running round the edge of rooms: like mice, they avoid wide open spaces. Once the poison is on them, they either breath it in through their spiracles or ingest it and are goners. In the morning, the corpses are swept up and thrown into the garbage bin where, no doubt, they provide nourishment for their fellows.

Not all insects that invade the house are to be similarly spurned and one in particular, the common large water beetle, has a special place in the hearts of both local Chinese and myself. As the name implies, it is large for its sort, about three centimetres long with a black shiny carapace lined by a delicate light brown or yellow stripe. The hind legs are oar-shaped and curved to aid in fast diving and swimming.

I first met this creature in the second week of September 1952, introduced to it by Halvie, the bell-boy of the Fourseas Hotel where I lived. I never knew his Chinese name: he was affectionately called Halvie by the European women residents as a diminutive of Half-pint. This was particularly apt as he was squat, firmly built and wore a white uniform with a matching pork-pie hat. His command of English was not good: neither was my Cantonese.

'You wan' look-see bik wartcher beechew?' he asked of me one morning.

Curious, I nodded. We were intermittent friends: I was eight years old and he was about twelve.

From a small Shippams potted meat jar in his pocket, he produced one of the water beetles. Around its hind legs was tied a three metre length of cotton.

'You see. He go,' Halvie announced and commenced to swing the insect slowly round his head by the thread, lengthening it as it spun.

Suddenly, it took to flight. Halvie paid out the cotton and walked quickly down the sloping drive of the hotel, the beetle flying ahead of him like a little motorised kite. At last, he stopped walking and the insect, reaching the end of its tether, stopped dead in mid-air and fell to the ground, vibrating its wings to prevent a damaging crash landing.

I begged Halvie to sell me his living toy. I offered as much as twenty cents but he was reluctant to sell.

'You get you wung,' he said and returned the insect to its jar.

'How?' I implored but he was silent.

Ching, our roomboy, let me in on the secret and, that evening, I went into the street at about half-past seven. Swarms of beetles were gyrating around the street lights: every September, the local population takes to the wing to find new ponds and mates. At intervals, one or two would fly into the light with a metallic thud and fall dazed to the pavement where the hotel porter collected them up in an enamel bucket. He showed me how to judge which were uninjured: if their wings showed from under their carapaces then they were damaged and of no use to me.

Back in my room, I duly tied lengths of cotton to their swimming legs and, the next morning, was able to join Halvie with whom, between his opening taxi doors and carrying luggage, I had beetle flying sessions. This innocent activity came to an abrupt halt when Mr Peng, the kindly but stern manager, caught the bell-boy failing in his duties.

My beetles packed in individual State Express 555 cigarette tins with the lids perforated, I headed for the flat hotel roof to fly and exercise my insect stable. Under the main hotel staircase was a cubby-hole in which the porter stayed, brewing tea over a single ring for the office staff and waiting to be called to unblock drains or fix door locks. As I passed by, he beckoned to me.

'You wan' beechew?'

'I have some,' I answered proudly and produced my tins.

'I got,' he replied and again beckoned to me to enter his cubby-hole. I went in.

An old steel saucepan on the ring was filled with boiling beetles, the air filled with a delicate tang I had never smelled before in any of the multifarious scents and odours of the streets.

'*Ho sik*,' the porter said, a glint in his eye. With a pair of wooden chopsticks, he stirred his witches' brew and, lifting a beetle out, put in on a plate, waving his hand over it to cool it. Then he motioned to his mouth and pointed at me.

I had lived long enough in Hong Kong to understand the implications of losing face so I nodded and accepted the beetle. The porter showed me how, with my thumbnail, to peel back the wing-case, tear off the wings, legs and head and chew on the beetle, sucking the meat out.

It was gritty and tasted like shellfish, a certain marine flavour I attributed to it being a water beetle. Parts of the thorax wedged between my teeth and the porter handed me a plastic container of toothpicks from the hotel dining room. By a mixture of pidgin English, sign language and Cantonese, he explained I was not to swallow the shelly bits but to spit them out into the waste basket by his feet. I did this.

For about an hour, the porter and I consumed the contents of the saucepan. When he was briefly called away on an errand, I kept the pan simmering. From time to time, other members of the hotel staff called in, took away a few beetles and grinned at me. The result of this repast was not so much as a stomach ache and my estimation in the eyes of the Chinese room-boys rose to dizzying heights. From then on, I was presented with all sorts of delicacies some of which I ate and instantly spat out but others for which I have a taste remaining to the present.

For those who wish to try the same cuisine, the common large water beetle is called *Cybister tripunctatus*. It may be found in ponds throughout Europe, including the British Isles and, for all I know, in North America, too. In England, it is called, I believe, the great diving beetle. The recipe is thus – place live in cold water overnight; change the water for fresh and bring slowly to the boil, scooping off any scum that may form. Simmer for about twenty minutes. Add a little salt to taste. Serve without sauce or garnish.

Quite delicious.

Facing the Tiger's Mouth

About five miles off the most westerly point of mainland Hong Kong, Lan Kok Tsui (known in English as Black Point), stands Lingding Island. It is about three kilometres long and a kilometre wide at its broadest point. A twin-peaked mountain covered in scrub and trees rises very sharply to 330 metres and although its southern, ocean-facing shore is more or less featureless, its northern edge contains two bays. It is very sparsely populated indeed and, being more or less in the centre of the Pearl River estuary, is in Chinese territorial waters, yet it has played a vital part in the history of Hong Kong and been a source of particular interest, or fear, for all those who have lived along the western coast of the New Territories.

This area, then part of the Sun On District of Kwangtung Province, was well-known long before the rest of Hong Kong. Lingding Island first appears on a Chinese navigational map dated 1425, pre-dating the arrival of the first Europeans, the Portuguese who, contrary to common belief, did not settle first in Macau but in the New Territories at Tuen Mun, known in English as Castle Peak. They landed in 1514, building a fort, manufacturing ammunition with Chinese gunpowder expertise and generally lording it over the heathen natives whom they found barbaric and resistant to Catholicism. In 1521, after taking the law into their own hands and executing a few intransigent Chinese, they were forcibly driven out. But for diplomatic arrogance, religious zeal and xenophobic self-righteousness, vibrant Hong Kong might have become a Portuguese colony instead of sleepy neighbouring Macau. No archaeological evidence remains of this brief clash of cultures: Tuen Mun today is a satellite city of more than 350,000 served by a state-of-the-art light railway network and housed in tower blocks up to forty storeys high. Extensive reclamation of the sea has created a new headland called Butterfly Point (although there are virtually no blossoms there to encourage the hardiest of butterflies) and the site of one of Hong Kong's primary power stations.

The trading success of the British in China was based upon opium. The introspective Chinese were not eager to do business with the outside world, but the British were desperate to expand their maritime influence so they addicted the Chinese nation to opium grown and refined in India. This shameless venture is unsurpassed in human history save, perhaps, by the slave trade. Huge fortunes were amassed by merchants who brought opium into China and took out silver, tea, silk and any other commodity they found they could sell in the West. Of course, the Chinese authorities tried to stamp out the trade. The first edict against opium was published in 1729 and forty-seven others followed of which twenty-two were issued personally by the emperor but to no avail. By 1767, 65,000 kilograms of opium were being imported annually. By 1800, trade in and consequently consumption of the drug had trebled.

In 1820, foreign opium clippers were driven out of Canton but there was nowhere for them to go: Hong Kong was not yet a British possession and the Portuguese did not want them in Macau. It was then Lingding Island came into its own. The opium traders established a depot on the north, leeward shore and business carried on as before: in 1836, the annual import of raw opium was 1.8 million kilograms. Suppression of the trade was impossible for addiction was rife throughout Chinese society and corruption was as endemic in China then as it is now.

With the acquisition of Hong Kong in 1841, the British no longer had a use for Lingding Island and it was abandoned. Only in the summer of 1899 did it enter into Hong Kong history once more when the colonial Volunteers occupied Shenzhen for a few months in order to impress upon belligerent local people the fact the New Territories were now leased to Britain. The force ejected the Chinese customs officials who temporarily transferred to Lingding. The Imperial Japanese Navy established a temporary naval station on the island in 1942 but deserted it in 1944 for lack of manpower.

Not only Lingding appears on those early maps: so does the tiny, uninhabited island of Lung Kwu Chau half a mile to the south-west of Black Point and the settlement of Lung Kwu situated in a bay beside the promontory. Little more than a gathering of hamlets, it has a few groups of traditional stone houses with accompanying bamboo groves, an insignificant temple and, sprouting from the crevice of a huge boulder, a banyan tree of venerable age considered to have magical properties, just inland from a beach and a swamp of stunted mangroves alive with mudskippers. There were once rice and vegetable paddyfields but these were abandoned twenty years ago when the young men and women of the village gave up the hoe and plough for the textile loom and plastic vacuum moulding machine. Nevertheless, a road (of sorts) wound round the shoreline below Castle Peak to terminate just short of Black Point. The road was built by the military in the late thirties and improved upon by the Japanese but, apart from that, modernity had passed by Lung Kwu.

North of Lung Kwu, on the other side of Black Point, is the even smaller settlement of Yung Long. Even at its heyday, it consisted of only a dozen or so houses beside some fields of sandy, gravelly soil from which the inhabitants scratched a meagre crop of beans, cabbage and sweet potatoes. There was, until the turn of the century, a small temple little more than a large shrine dedicated to the goddess of heaven and the protector of seafarers, but it has long since vanished. The long beach, broken in two places by streams coming down from the steep hills behind, afforded a place upon which to bring sampans and the bay has always been protected by Black Point in all but the direct hit of a tropical storm or typhoon. Those people who did not grow crops were fisher-folk – except for one family, the Chengs.

The only surviving building at Yung Long is their family home. It is about a hundred years old although it is positioned on the site of a previous structure dating back at least to the early eighteenth century. It was erected by the present owner's grandfather and is a cross between a minuscule castle, a godown and a traditional village house. Raised on an oblong foundation, the front facing the sea is like a squat tower with two floors and a battlement pierced by two slits and two round holes: on this tower roof is an additional brick shed under a tiled roof. To the rear of the tower, the building is single storeyed and consists primarily of a large barn-like storehouse. All the windows are covered by steel shutters painted green with very small, thick glass panes in them. To the front of the building, at ground level only, has been added a large wooden lean-to with a set of wide doors under a traditional tiled roof whilst to one side are a few outhouses once pigsties and chicken coups. Between the building and the beach, a distance of not more than twenty metres, is a courtyard shaded by trees, surrounded by a wire fence and entered through a square arched, stone gateway in which there is no gate in the accepted sense but five carved vertical tree trunks which slot into holes in the lintel and others in the architrave.

Within, the building is hardly touched by time: electricity, despite the power station being only a kilometre or two away, only reached Yung Long in the late 1980s and the only source of fresh water to this day remains a spring up the hillside. Heating is done by collecting driftwood off the beach. The interior is dark, peaceful and cool, even when the sun is at its height. The wooden staircase into the tower, which contains the family living quarters, is polished by generations of hands and slippers, the barn vast, musty and dry under heavy, ancient cross-beams. The floors are flagged and the main (and only) door into the building is of ancient Chinese design but covered with a heavy steel sliding grid.

Like the gateway into the courtyard from the pathway, the door is of especial interest: there are few like it left in Hong Kong.

It does not operate as Western doors do, swinging open on hinges. Instead, it is constructed of half a dozen thick planks which stand vertically in a groove cut in the stone step. They are independent of each other and may be locked in place by a wooden slider mounted over the door: for reinforcement, a bar may be dropped across the inside as well. In this way, the door may be either just one plank open (allowing a thin person to slip inside) or wider, simply by the removal of more of the planks. Not being suspended on hinges with a single lock mechanism, it is considerably stronger than a conventional door.

The owner, Mr Cheng, is in his eighties: so is his wife. He has lived all his life in the house and his wife all the years of her marriage, coming to reside with her husband's family on their wedding day as was the accepted practice. Neither of them look their age, they are self-sufficient and independent, kind and generous.

When I last visited them, they were both sitting on stools in the lean-to part of the house. It was a cold and grey day, only a week after Hong Kong had experienced its first frost for forty years. Mr Cheng was wearing a padded *sam* jacket in blue silk and matching *fu* trousers. As it was not the right season, they were not expecting visitors: for some years now, they have made their living by selling soft drinks and beers, snacks and sweetmeats to hikers and picnickers. In the courtyard were piled benches and wobbly tables with some cut-down oil drums to act as barbecue fires. Their cross-Chow mongrel lay in the dirt, its collar loose about its neck and its spine arched by rickets. Nearby lay a bowl of boiled rice: most Chinese village dogs suffer in this way because of their diet.

It was only my second visit to Yung Long. I had gone there first the previous year in the company of a friend, bought a beer, passed the time of day and travelled on, yet Mr Cheng remembered me.

'How are you?' he said in English, bowing slightly and shaking my hand in both of his. His wife smiled and opened a can of 7-Up which she took from a battered refrigerator.

For years, Yung Long has been inaccessible save by foot or boat. Until last year, to reach there meant a two hour walk from Tuen Mun or the use of a private launch. Now, the whole of the coast from Castle Peak to the Chinese border is 'under development' and a wide, fast through road has been put in, the contractors having cut dirt access roads between the sea and the hills making Yung Long accessible, if with difficulty. I had returned to hear Mr Cheng's story. He had touched upon it at my first visit, but his English is not fluent and my Cantonese insufficient for sustained conversation. This time I had Betty with me to act as translator.

We sat in the lean-to. A cold wind began to blow through cracks in the wooden wall and the dog got up, circled tightly around and lowered itself into a snug ball. When Mr Cheng was ready, he began the tale of his life, pausing only so Betty could catch up with her interpreting.

He was born in the house which, in those days, was surrounded by other houses around the bay but they have disappeared into rubble. The people who lived in Yung Long were farmers and fishermen, many of whom also grew mulberry bushes and raised silk worms which they sent up to Canton. In those days, the Pearl River was a busy and important fishing ground and the fishermen were always in need of supplies so the Cheng family established a chandlery, his father and uncle using the building as a trading post for the fishermen. They sold food, fresh water, ropes, nets and all the fittings needed by any vessel from a sampan to a full-size junk. All the provisions were kept in the godown and most had to be brought over the mountain from Tuen Mun or round the peninsula by boat.

The family made a good living and, from time to time, bought the catches of fishermen which they sold at market. They were not rich but well off and needed for nothing. Mr Cheng was educated in Kowloon where he stayed, only returning for holidays or festivals: it was there he learned English. One day, when he was a little boy – he is not sure of the exact year but he can remember the event – pirates raided Yung Long, their main target being the

Chengs. There was a gunfight at the house and Mr Cheng's uncle was kidnapped and held to ransom.

In those days, pirates were a common hazard. They raided junks, sacked and looted coastal villages and even struck with some success at inshore ferries and ocean-going vessels. On one occasion, they had the audacity and temerity to commandeer a ferry sailing across Hong Kong harbour. Their *modus operandi* were not only stealing and killing but also kidnapping, ransom payments forming an important part of their income.

I asked Mr Cheng who the pirate was who had taken his uncle, but he did not know: subsequent research makes me think it was most likely that the pirate band belonged either to a particularly ruthless pirate called Wong Kiu or a woman buccaneer, Lai Choi-san, known as the Queen of Pirates. Both were very active in the Pearl Estuary throughout the twenties and relied upon kidnapping for hard currency income.

When Mr Cheng's uncle was taken, the family received a ransom demand for 4000 *taels* (or Chinese 'ounces') of silver. At the time, this was worth the equivalent of about HK$2 million. By realising assets, borrowing money from relatives and other sources, the ransom was raised and paid: the money was also recovered although Mr Cheng does not say how. Quite possibly, there was a swift action of retribution against the pirates once Uncle Cheng was safe.

Where, I asked, had the pirates come from? Mr Cheng waved his hand in the general direction of the sea.

'Nei Lin Tin Chau,' he said quietly. Lingding Island.

After the kidnap, Mr Cheng's father asked the Hong Kong government for help in combating pirates. Royal Navy patrols were stepped up in the area and the government paid to have the steel shutters put on all the windows, making the building impregnable. At the same time, they installed the sliding steel grille across the door, issuing the family with rifles and a limited supply of ammunition.

The family were not attacked again and returned to their chandlery business which continued to flourish until the Japanese invasion. Times were hard during the occupation. Fishing tailed off and the population of Hong Kong more than halved. By 1944, there was no food and people were starving. Japanese soldiers were stationed in Yung Long and had an anti-aircraft gun battery mounted on Black Point: the Chengs' house was used as an ammunition store and billet.

Mr Cheng pointed to a number painted above the steel grille, put there by the Japanese who numbered all the houses around the bay. Leaving his stool by the door, he went into the house, returning and handing to me a heavy bullet about six centimetres long. It was a Japanese AA cannon shell. There are, Mr Cheng informed me, sitting down once more, a lot of these about the bay. When the Japanese departed, they left their ordnance just lying around and the villagers cleared it away, dumping it in the sea from a sampan.

After the war, the provisioning of fishing boats tailed off. As vessels were fitted out with motors, travelling to Tuen Mun or Hong Kong became easy and there was no longer any need for an isolated chandlers. Faced with this change of circumstance, the Cheng family turned their hand to farming, growing vegetables which they sold in Nim Wan, an hour's walk away. In time, this business also became obsolete as market gardens became more commonplace and vegetables were imported from overseas or China. What was more, Mr Cheng was getting old. The late seventies, however, saw a new business opportunity. People started to walk in the countryside, seeking a release from urban living and Mr Cheng and his wife developed their home as a rest and refreshment halt on the day long hike round the Castle Peak peninsula.

This life story is not untypical. There are thousands of New Territories families who have similarly adapted to changing times, seen the way the wind of change was blowing and bent with it, searching out opportunities and exploiting niches. This tenacity and resourcefulness is what has made the Chinese so successful throughout the world.

Where much of the New Territories are concerned today, this

wind of change has proved to be more of a typhoon of ruination. Forty years ago, when I was a child, driving through this hinterland between Hong Kong and China was to journey back through the centuries. Duck farmers walked along the roads, holding up what traffic there was with their flocks controlled by ten-metre-long bamboo switches, coolies loped by under the weight of roast pigs – entire carcasses, from snout to tail, as glazed and polished as light mahogany – and old women shifted knee-deep in paddyfields as they planted out emerald rice seedlings one by one. Buffaloes plodded before ploughs or lay ruminating under trees. Pools of carp, ponds of lotus plants and groves of mulberry bushes for the raising of silkworms were around every corner.

All that has gone but not just in the cause of progress: it is not a matter of the old woman being replaced by a rice drilling machine or the buffalo by the tractor. Nor have the paddyfields and market gardens returned to nature. And they have not necessarily been built upon. They have instead been raped: nowhere in the industrialised world can there be a worse violation of the earth mother. What I knew as farms and hamlets are now vast scrap-yards for thousands upon thousands of derelict cars or lorries, dumps for all kind and condition of recyclable trash from aluminium cans and bottles to paper and plastic.

Yet the biggest eyesores of all are the cargo container stock-piles. These huge metal boxes are piled twelve high like the bizarre building blocks of some filthy giant's child. They cover areas in some cases of twenty hectares or more, divided only by lanes of mud and oil churned up by cranes and forty-ton articulated lorries.

Although there are still some duck, goose and fish farms in existence, for the majority of local villagers and one-time small market gardeners, the cash crop is no longer rice or cabbages, water chestnuts or lychees but lines of rusting steel boxes awaiting the end of the world recession or the next container ship to leave Kwai Chung. Such is the all-pervading influence of these grotesque boxes that, in some places, they have not only suborned the old fields but even the old houses. Not far from Mr Cheng's home, a number of these monstrosities, surplus to the requirement of international trade, have had windows oxy-acetylened into their sides and air conditioners appended to them to become cheap domiciles. In a grotesque mockery of the past, they are festooned with creepers and surrounded by minuscule plots of vegetables as if the history and old ways of China are trying in vain to reassert themselves.

To find an unspoilt piece of countryside now one has to either visit the militarised zone along the border, which is closed to all but local pass-carrying residents, or travel to the farthest reaches of eastern Hong Kong where mountains, shallow seas and rip tides have held the present century at bay. For a while, at least.

Mr Cheng stood up once more and we went out into the courtyard. Overhanging the courtyard, a small bird was wheeping plaintively in one of the trees and the wind hissed on the sand. In the distance, close to Black Point, I could see the vague hint of Lingding Island.

Mr Cheng pointed to a number of young Chinese men working in what had been a vegetable patch when I first visited Yung Long.

'They are digging,' he remarked in a rather offhand tone.

I enquired why and was told through Betty they were archaeologists looking into what might be found there: as the coast has featured in maps for six hundred years and is on the mouth of one of China's great rivers, I should imagine they might be onto something worthwhile.

At my request, and in keeping with the practice of so many Chinese these days, Mr Cheng and I then had our photograph taken together.

On the beach were two bamboo poles with yellow flags flying from them: if they had been triangular, they might have been festival banners, but they were square. I asked what they were for.

They were surveyors' markers, Mr Cheng told me.

The whole of Yung Long was doomed, he continued. Within a few weeks, the entire valley was to be razed. All the trees would be felled and burned, the hills cut into, the beach dug up and the bay filled for a distance of 400 metres from the present shoreline. The whole of the area is to be a deepwater quay, an industrial complex and a new natural gas-fired power station. That, Mr Cheng went on, was why the new road had been built. His home was to be demolished and he and his wife were being re-housed in a tower block in Tuen Mun. The government had not yet moved them out because they were still haggling over the compensation sum: the government was trying to sell him short.

'What price can you put on this?' I asked and Betty translated.

Mr Cheng shrugged and replied, 'No money.'

Already, the government have readied for his departure. The bones of his ancestors which have rested in ossaries on the hillside above the house for at least one and a half centuries have been moved. The valley has been evaluated and assessed, portioned in to industrial plots upon some master plan in a government office in the skyscrapers of Central. The archaeologists are conducting what is in effect a rescue dig, to find out what they can before the huge Komatsu earthmovers drive in.

Mr Cheng touched a huge frangipani tree by the gate.

'My g'and-farfer,' he said in English, mimicking digging and planting.

'I collect plants from my travels,' I said so he took up a spade leaning against the wire fence and lopped off two boughs from which I sliced three cuttings, placing them in my camera bag.

Mr Cheng spoke to Betty, his back to me and, when he stopped, I saw tears in her eyes. She is a young and pretty Chinese girl in her twenties, a city girl unaware of such hidden corners of Hong Kong.

'He says,' she half-whispered, 'that now at least his grandfather's tree will live.'

Then, quite suddenly, Mr Cheng took hold of my hand and pressed something into it. I wondered if it was another frangipani cutting but it was the Japanese bullet.

'You take,' he said. 'You take.'

And I did.

We bade farewell to Mr and Mrs Cheng then, Betty and I walking out through the ancient gate and up the path to our car. The archaeologists appeared to be finding nothing: I could see no different occupation layers in their trenches, just a continuous stratum of sandy soil.

As we reached the rough track above Yung Long, we stopped the car and I looked back. Little seemed to have changed for centuries. Lingding Island was more visible now and the trees of the valley hid the archaeologists and surveyors' flags. If a Portuguese galleon, a Jardine & Matheson opium clipper or a pirate junk had sailed into sight just then, I should not have been surprised. Instead, around the headland of Black Point there gradually came into view a large, grey dredger.

Hunting for Mr Dior

'OK. Good p'ice for you. First sale today. For you, no' $400. *T'wee fifty*. Because you my first customer. I only jus' opun my shop. Jus' now. OK. You buy. No more bargain. T'wee fifty ve'y good p'ice. I take cash, trafeller cheque. Can do credit card. You got Veesa? Mastercard? American Express? No problum. I can take it.'

So goes the typical sales spiel. No matter that the shop has been open for more than an hour, has already turned over HK$38,000 and the customer only came in to browse. Hong Kong shop owners are the most persuasive and guileful yet least bullying and objectionable in the world. One has the feeling that if they sold time-share properties in Spain there would be no room left for the Spanish.

Against such salesmanship, shopping in Hong Kong is an almost professional activity, an art acquired by experience. At least half of the tourists who spill from jets at Kai Tak tend not to regard the place as a slice of the mystic Orient but as a vast shopping mall and, deservedly, they are likely on occasion to get taken. A fact which fails to astonish me is that something like 80 per cent of all Hong Kong tourists stay for under fifty hours: Hong Kong, despite an avid and ultra-efficient tourist association, is regarded not as a holiday destination in itself but as a stopover en route to Australia or on the way back from Beijing and the Terracotta Army.

Nowhere in the world is shopping such engrossing, amusing, serious fun. The most rabid anti-shopper soon falls under the spell of it for, in Hong Kong, one can buy virtually *anything* – uncut gemstones, massage machines, hi-tech gizmos of all sorts (sun-tan measuring wrist gauges with burning alarm, calorie-counters for office workers, fountain pen with internal radio), pornography (mild or hot), 999.9 fine gold, heroin, grated rhino horn and tiger's penis, Chinese antiquities, traditional Chinese coffins, Japanese cars quite unavailable in Europe, dried sea-horses, decorated ink-blocks, Royal Doulton china, Waterford crystal, mink coats and take-away *sushi*. It is just a matter of knowing the right place and there are whole books dedicated to the subject.

To visitors, the advantage is that all consumer goods are completely tax-free: there is no sales tax on any item except alcohol and that is not exorbitant. Savings are such that Japanese tourists buy Seiko watches and Canon cameras in Hong Kong because they can be half the price they are in Osaka: British tourists can purchase Van Heusen shirts at a similar saving on the price they would pay for them in Taunton, five miles from the factory. Only those who would purchase a car in Hong Kong would discover a hefty tax levied on it for cars are so burdened in order to discourage people from buying them and putting them on the road: if every vehicle in Hong Kong was to be driven at once, there would be insufficient road area to accommodate them all. This tax ploy is, however, a failure.

Some shops are worth visiting because they are attractions unto themselves. Herbal medicine stores never fail to draw attention. Before one sees the door, one smells its presence. The air is alert with a curious fusion of scents, smells, perfumes and tart odours not one of which is recognisable to the Occidental olfactory system. The walls are lined with ranks of wooden drawers containing an exhaustive range of obscure herbs, spices and what might best be described as dried bits of animal matter whilst cabinets display the velveteen antlers and tongues of deer, bears' glands, bowls of snake-skin, dishes of discarded insect carapaces and fossils. The latter carry such labels as *dragon's teeth* or *dragon's bones* and are a fascinating source of material for the amateur palæontologist: I have bought several woolly rhinoceros and mammoth teeth in these shops, not to mention the vertebra of a dinosaur and a length of copralite which, I was assured, was *extinc' liza'd shit*.

Although these shops sell prepared medicines, some of which are exceedingly efficacious and some pure panacea, they are mostly used by patients of traditional Chinese medicine doctors who make up individual prescriptions to be filled out by the pharmacist. Darting from counter to drawer, he gathers together the necessary ingredients according to the prescription which is frequently a long, convoluted document filled with many characters. One cure may consist of more than fifty different dried herbs, roots, barks, leaves, flowers, fruits and animal products according to the metabolism, complexion and stature of the customer not to mention their specific ailment. Also on offer is a vast range of different ginsengs, from the most expensive wild varieties from north-eastern China down to the cheap white ginseng cultivated in America in addition to such things as crushed pearls which are said to improve a lady's skin. Everything is measured out either by the rough guesswork associated with cookery (a pinch of this, a spoonful of that) or with a pair of Chinese scales the design of which is over two millennia old. Called a *ching*, it usually takes the form of a thin rod of wood marked off with inset brass or bone gradations and suspended from the fulcrum by a loop of cord. The goods to be weighed are placed in a small pan whilst a brass weight is slid up and down the rod until a balance is achieved. All medicines, like many other loose products in Chinese shops and markets, are sold in traditional measures. The system is centuries old, the units being the picul (or *tam*) equal to 60.478 kilogrammes, the catty (*kan*: hundredth of a picul), the tael (*leung*: sixteenth of a catty), the mace (*tsin*: tenth of a tael) and the candareen (*fan*: hundredth of a catty). Gold is sold by the tael, mace and candareen troy units with a tael troy being the equivalent of 37.429 grammes.

The gold dealers are as fascinating as the dragon's teeth vendors. Their shop windows are displays of the most tasteless wealth available. For the Chinese, gold is the best investment and even the poorest coolie might be seen to wear a gold chain about his neck: when I was a child, it was common to see a coolie with a gold crowned tooth or two which had been fitted not only to cover a cavity but to give status and, upon death, to pay for a funeral.

Whereas a European usually buys nine, fourteen, eighteen or (less commonly) twenty-two carat gold in the form of jewellery which has been amalgamed with other metals, a Chinese will only purchase either *Chuk Kam* (about 22.5 carat) or twenty-four carat (or fine) gold – that is, utterly pure gold. And although many buy their gold in the form of bullion, which is not illegal in Hong Kong as it is in most countries, the majority obtain it made into an artefact of some sort even though their purchase is made by weight.

Each gold dealer advertises the cost of his stock on a board or digital display in his window. Two prices are given, buying and selling, for the shop will purchase as well as purvey gold. The door of his premises will have an automatic lock on it, the window glass is laminated, double-strength and blast-proof and, on occasion, an armed guard is present carrying a shotgun.

Until 1988, this was a sufficient deterrent but, in recent years, the robbery of gold dealers has become popular amongst disaffected Communist Chinese soldiers who have crossed the border armed with high-velocity Chinese-made assault rifles, grenades and side-arms and blown their way into their chosen targets, killing and maiming passers-by in the process. The guard's shotgun is utterly useless against high-velocity military weapons and the gangs strike so quickly the police are usually powerless to apprehend them, despite being adequately armed themselves. The gangs choose to attack at the height of rush- or lunch-hour when the streets are crowded, the ensuing chaos of a raid affording good cover and the traffic so thick as to be a hindrance to police mobility.

The value of the gold is what the thieves are after – or else they have remarkably poor taste for the artefacts in the windows are, by and large, gaudy and vulgar in the extreme to Europeans. Packs of thick blocks embossed like playing cards, ornate dragons with emerald eyes, cased statues of assorted gods (especially the God of Wealth), the Four Winds or Seasons tiles from a mah-jong set, lion dogs with ruby eyes, horses with diamond eyes, junks in full sail or sampans with amahs rowing them, rickshaws and coolies, even realistic scale models of Ferraris and Porsches, all made of twenty-four carat gold. Gold comes in four main colours – white (mixed with platinum), red (mixed with copper), green (mixed with silver) and gold, the colour of the purest form. When in this state, gold looks cheap, the garish colour of fake costume jewellery or chocolate wrapping foil and so appear all the items in a gold dealer's window.

Few tourists enter the gold shops: for some, to simply own twenty-four carat gold at home is illegal. Apart from curios and the usual tourist trash – wall-mounted fans and fake coolie hats, T-shirts, cheap porcelain statues of anonymous goddesses and soapstone ashtrays – they seem to go for pocket mini-computers, Walk-, Disc– and Videomans, high-powered transistor radios, jewellery, state-of-the-art cameras and wrist-watches.

The purchase of such items requires a certain delicate and well-honed expertise. A good many shops, especially in Tsim Sha Tsui, specialise in selling such consumer items but the rule of *caveat emptor* was never more valid than here. It is not that the goods are shoddy: one may count on them being the newest model, in full working order and straight from the manufacturer. Nor will the guarantee be dud or the item of inferior specification. I have never known a shop refuse to replace without question an item that was in even the slightest way sub-standard. The buyer must be wary not of the goods but of the sales patter and the price.

It is expected in a good many places in Hong Kong that the customer haggles for a bargain. This is not done in the department stores or those shops primarily catering for residents. Some shops do not entertain a paltering patron and which shop is which takes a bit of local knowledge. City Chain watch shops, for example, are not open to argument over terms. The price is set (often with a side tag expressing 30 per cent discounts on the stock) and that is that. Yet bargaining is common practice in street markets, at stalls and in the tourist traps. He who does not dicker gets done.

Take wrist-watches, for which I have an abiding penchant and of which I can state, without a smidgen of modesty, I am an expert shopper. Buying a watch is not simply a matter of going into a shop, asking to see a watch, trying it on and buying it at the labelled price as one would in most Western cities. That is not only foolhardy but no fun: for shopping for anything in Hong Kong is, above all, fun. Yet the process requires an inside knowledge of the game.

Entry into any shop in Hong Kong is a tacit agreement to join battle with the shop staff yet not in the sense one would in London trying to find someone to serve you who is not engaged on the phone, talking about football or boyfriends, or in Paris where the staff are the rudest in the world and studiously ignore the shopper with the panache of a film star. Here it a locking of polite antlers. They are determined to make a sale and you are determined to get the best price – or not buy.

The war of attrition, good manners, pathos and power-playing goes like this:

'Goo' morning, sir! How are you today? Wha' can I do for you?'

It is essential to know your goods otherwise you are at an immediate disadvantage and likely to be sold something you did not want and had not even considered. I have seen tourists enter a shop and ask to see video-cameras yet leave having bought an electronic organiser.

'Good morning. I want a watch – titanium strap, chronometer, stopwatch, waterproof.'

'Okay, we got plenty. Please, sit down. How much you wan' to spen'? You like a Coke, sof' d'ink?''

This former question is to be avoided: it is a pit trap. If you state an amount, you'll wind up paying it. If you accept the drink, you'll have to stay longer and become more susceptible. Sitting down is not a problem: you can easily stand up and leave.

'No, thank you. I'll see the watches first.'

The watches start to appear, drawn from display cabinets or glass-topped counters. They are laid out in front of you. You may try them on. The first to appear are the cheapest for one seldom buys the first item shown. These are followed by the mid-range watches.

'This watch Citizen. Make by Seiko, Seiko inside. Good quality. Face enamel. Got the date, one hundred' second sweep hand. Watch waterp'oof to ten atmosphere. Good for diving, swimming. Any time can wear.' The shopkeeper taps the face with his fingernail. 'C'ystal glass. Ve'y st'ong. Battery last five year. You like?'

'Maybe.'

This is a sign you are unsure. He then produces a better one.

'How 'bout genuine Seiko? Also face enamel but better. Roman number. Ve'y stylish. This a new model, just come in. Waterp'oof for fifteen atmosphere. Gold on strap better quality. Not fade.' He rubs it with his finger as if to prove the point. 'No rub off. World-wide guarantee. But more expensive.'

You compare the watches, adding to them any others that might be produced. The shopkeeper maintains a patter throughout, shifting the watches about on the counter like a fairground shark operating a shell game.

'Maybe you wan' to see more?' This question is rhetorical: you are going to see them. 'I show you this one . . .' A Rolex, Audemars Pigeot or other similar Rolls-Royce of a watch is brought out and laid down with all the gentleness of an antiques auctioneer handling Venetian glass. 'Also a new model. Jus' come in. Titanium steel but the gold is eighteen ca'at.' He weighs the watch in his hand. 'Ve'y heavy. Ve'y good quality but maybe too expensive for you.'

'Yes,' you reply but the die is cast. The Rolls-Royce watch looks fantastic and unless you are careful you are now hooked to buy the one that looks most like it but which will be the most expensive of the lesser makes. More patter is made about the others, the film star's watch being put away like a sin best not indulged in. Besides, it has served its purpose. The addict has been fed.

Eventually, the question of cost arises. At this point, the shopkeeper will look at his label on one of the watches. This carries a price that is plain to see. Say HK$4,500. Next to the price, however, are either a few tiny Chinese characters or a code.

'This one $4500 but, for you, $4000.'

The antlers of commerce clash. There are three bands of price for watches in Hong Kong. Band A is for Japanese tourists: they are quietly despised for Japan has been China's enemy for centuries and this animosity goes deep into the Chinese consciousness. To rip off a Japanese is one of life's common little pleasures. Anyone else who is stupidly gullible also falls into this band but without any ulterior motive other than that of profit. Band B is for the general tourist or unsuspecting expatriate whilst band C is for locals. The mark-up on the latter is anything from 20 to 60 per cent: a sale to a gullible Japanese, therefore, can heftily hike up profits.

You hum a bit.

'Four thousand . . .'

You pick up several of the watches and enquire after their prices as if juggling one against the other. It is at this juncture you must commit yourself. Either you are going to buy one of these watches or you are going to look elsewhere. To prolong matters now will get nobody anywhere. For the sake of example, you go for the Citizen Quartz Titanium.

'How much is the Citizen?'

The shopkeeper is ready now. This is the one he might sell. He studies the label.

'This one $3,500. But for you . . .'

He pulls a desktop calculator across the counter into which he ostentatiously punches 3500, taps a few more keys, knocks down a percentage figure, taps the total key and turns the calculator around so you might see it. The liquid crystal display reads 2950.

'Speschul p'ice. Good discoun'.'

You consider this, finger a few of the other watches then say, '$2,100.'

This is as ludicrous a low figure as the original $3,500 was a high one. You know it. The shopkeeper knows it. What is more the shopkeeper knows you know it and you know he knows you know it, too.

'This too much,' the shopkeeper replies disarmingly, his face seeking your sympathy. 'If I sell for this, I get no p'ofit. Citizen a goo' watch. Goo' quality.' He picks it up, taps the glass once more, undoes the strap. 'You try on again.'

You put it on your wrist and admire it. This is the one you want. For sure. But not at $2,950.

'Look ve'y good on you. Got plenty style,' the shopkeeper remarks as if the watch was bespoke. 'Latest fashun. Titanium steel.'

You finish admiring it and take it off, place it back on the counter and start to finger one of the cheaper specimens. After a few moments, the shopkeeper turns to his calculator and hits the keys again. The price drops to $2,750. It is at this point the war of attrition starts to hot up and a degree of bluff is called for on both your part and the shopkeeper's. You wince infinitesimally at the new price and hover about the other, cheaper watches. You may revert to looking at one of the more expensive watches again and go through the calculator ritual with one of them but always return to the Citizen.

A number of gambits – or all of them – may be now brought into play: the Citizen is the watch you like but you think you've seen it for $2,450 down the street; it is a *nice* watch but maybe you'll give it a miss because of the price; $2,750 is more than you are willing to pay; finally, you start to rise and say you'll think about it and come back. This, the shopkeeper knows, is a downright lie. The chances of you returning are less than those of a green sun rising. The calculator clicks again.

'OK. $2,600. My bes' p'ice.'

This is the point at which the tourist surrenders and reaches for his plastic, traveller's cheques or wallet. For the expatriate, there is one last stratagem.

'*Ayah!*' you say, smiling self-deprecatingly. '*Yee chin lok baak man-ah?'* This requires a hint of incredulity followed by another gentle smile and a disarming, '*Yau mo gaw chor ah.*' This roughly translates as 'Good Lord! $2,600? What kind of a dolt do you take me for?'

The fleeting look on the shopkeeper's face is a delight to behold. You have just blown his entire artillery battalion off the field of combat. He grins and remarks, in Cantonese, that you speak the language well. The reply should be in English, a denial of a knowledge of Cantonese: unless you speak it well, it is now important to get out of it fast. Your ignorance could be his cavalry coming to the rescue.

A friendly conversation follows about how long you've stayed in Hong Kong, where you live and so on. Finally, attention returns to the watch and you suggest $2,550 which sum is accepted without further ado. If, however, $2,600 is held firmly to, then you must be aware this probably is a genuine bottom price and you should pay it.

The method never fails but requires that expertise of knowing the ritual, having the innate sense of cognisance as to how far to push the shopkeeper so as not to unduly dent his profit margin but, on the other hand, not be suckered like a chump. The last occasion on which I purchased a watch, I brought it down from the marked price of HK$5,250 to HK$2,950, a reduction of 43 per cent. The shopper's maxim, it's not what you spend but what you save that counts, is never more appropriate than in Hong Kong.

Yet this is not the most exciting shopping. The really thrilling sort does not involve a war of attrition, a chess game of manners and feints, but a hunt. And, like any hunt, one must be familiar with the ground, know the quarry and have an eye for it at a distance.

My wife buys designer clothes with an expertise learned whilst apprenticed to Ulli, a consummate and brilliantly effective *shoppuese* who can spot a silk dress of immaculate pedigree at thirty feet in a shop crammed to the ceiling with tat, tourists, milling Chinese bargain-watchers and expatriate adepts.

There are three basic skills involved. The first is Mapping

the Jungle. Unless you are mega-rich, designer clothes are not purchased in shops with mannequins in the widow looking like Sunset Boulevard wannabees. The keen, poor shopper visits street markets like Stanley or Spring Garden Lane – and outlets.

The outlet is a curious object of which there are two sorts, the factory outlet and the ordinary outlet. Both sell clothes which are 'extra to requirement'. A large foreign buyer (say Sears) orders so many hundreds of a certain dress but the manufacturer makes an extra percentage to cover faulty workmanship or extra demand: the buyer, on the other hand, may reduce their order during manufacture. The result is the over-run. The factory outlet sells these almost exclusively, the other sells these and faulty items. The fault, however, may be the wrong style of button, a wider than required hem or a tiny section of double stitching none of which intrinsically affect the quality of the garments.

Finding factory outlets takes you well off the tourist path, an adventure for many even if they are armed with one of the guides to outlet buying. They are often manufacturing units in industrial areas where the streets are lined with lorries, the gutters filled with the remains of the drivers' lunches and the pavements littered with packaging, boxes and plastic binding tape. No shoppers or office-workers jostle you here but bare-chested stevedores or coolies carting crates to the waiting trucks. Their backs and arms may be decorated by Triad society tattoos but they have pagers and mobile phones tucked in their belts.

Land being at a premium in Hong Kong, factories are set up in industrial tenements, each of twenty floors a different firm. The hunter has to know not only which building to visit but also which floor. This is no mean feat for the entrances are often small and frequently not named in English. You go up in a lift with a bale of material and the outlet is not a shop but a corridor or anteroom with concrete floors, bare neon lights and a woman behind an old desk with a glass of tea. The clothes on offer hang from galvanised metal racks on squeaky wheels. From behind a wall comes the whir of sewing machines or the whine of computerised cutting tables. When an item is chosen, the old woman takes the money or credit card and that is that. There are makeshift fitting rooms but seldom any other facilities yet this shortcoming is made up for by the bargains and savings available which can be massive – for example, a Diane Freis dress for HK$1,000 which, four miles away in a shop would cost HK$3,000 and six thousand miles away in London would be pegged at HK$5,000.

Ordinary outlets are different. They are not in industrial zones but skyscrapers. Here the knack is knowing how to read a building directory. The outlet address might be Room 2048, Chow Ping Building, Queen's Road West. Finding the building it not difficult but I have seen tourists walk away because they think they cannot hope to find Room 2048. In fact, this is simple. The first two numbers are the floor so 2048 is Room 48 on the twentieth level.

The outlet is usually a spartan affair. The door looks just like any other on the same floor which it may share with an export company, a shipping firm and a chemical products agent. The floors are probably covered in wooden tiles or threadbare carpets and there may well be fitting spaces behind sun-bleached curtains, but that it the extent of any lip service to luxury.

The second skill is Spotting the Hanger. Outlets and market stalls are crammed tight with stock but some items are not good buys and a lot of time can be wasted sorting through the dross. The expert hunter can judge an item by a shoulder or collar, by the hem of a skirt or a cuff. The technique is akin to that of an archaeologist who sees a fragment of pot sticking out of the ground and knows instinctively that beneath it lies a first-century amphora. At a blink, the trained eye can tell rayon from pure silk, linen from polyester mix. My wife, when under tutelage, bought a raw silk Pierre Cardin suit in a stall in Stanley for less than £25.

Number three: Checking the Goods. Some items may be damaged. If the racks are too tightly packed, clothes may be torn by eager fingering and tugging, buttons ripped free by snagging and material stretched. Marks that will not launder out have to be watched for and care taken not to purchase silk which has hung too long in the sunlight and faded on one side. Another thing to be wary of is the use of different rolls of cloth to make one garment, the colour qualities being slightly disparate.

The next and last hunter's trick is Knowing Labels. The designers have a deal with most outlets and stalls that sell their over-runs. No item may be put on the racks with the original label intact. The stall or outlet owner therefore disfigures the labels. This may be done simply by running a felt marker over it (beware the marker has not touched the fabric of the item) or, more frequently, by cutting either a section out of it or removing it save for the edges. It pays, therefore, to be able to interpret what is left of the label to know the design origin of the item.

Although most of the clothes are women's, some outlets cater for men as well and I have myself taken a few lessons in the art of clothes hunting. My instructresses have been Ulli, my wife and May, the wife of another close friend. Between them, they have chided, encouraged and pointed at distant racks. This has resulted in my discovering where to buy Yves St Laurent shirts at £10 each (an outlet on the umpteenth floor) and an assortment of silk, linen and cotton jackets (not one costing over £25) designed and made by established international couturiers. One of these, a pale cream silk and cotton double-breasted blazer is the envy of Terry, May's husband, who has on innumerable occasions sought another like it in the same little outlet-cum-shop three floors up in a tenement in Kimberley Road. He has never found its like. That, too, is a part of the game: you have to be in the right place at the right time.

The peak of my hunting career, however, was the bagging of the ultimate trophy. It is a grey, pure silk dressing gown made by Christian Dior. I found it, with a little help from May, on a rack at the rear of a very chaotic shop in Sai Yeung Choi Street, Mong Kok. It was slightly grimy from having hung in a warehouse for a while, but it was otherwise perfect. The CD in the crest on the pocket was picked out in silver and, incredibly, the magic label was intact. It cost just over £5.

Tart's Tonic

Thirty years ago, on the corner of Luard Road and Hennessy Road in Wanchai, there stood the Liberty Bar. The entrance was hung with a curtain of plastic beads and the windows – for it had originally been designed as a shop – were filled in with concrete blocks over which plaster had been smoothed and painted scarlet with imperial yellow footings. Beside the door, at pavement level, was a tiny wooden shrine not much bigger than a shoe-box dedicated to Ts'oi Pak Shing Kwan, one of the gods of wealth. Before a little coloured woodblock of the deity there was always a minuscule bowl of rice wine filled with dirt from passing feet and a few glowing joss sticks the ash of which was never swept away, forming a grey mud around the bowl when it rained.

Inside, the place was fairly spartan. There was a small bar counter to one side behind which stood ranks of bottles on shelves: every conceivable alcoholic taste could be catered for, ranging from Jack Daniel's bourbon through White Label whisky, Pusser's rum and Gordon's gin to Japanese saké and Chinese *sam seh chiew* (three snake wine) the bottle of which contained a two-foot long reptile bleached into anonymity by the spirit in which it was embalmed. In an icebox were stored bottles of beer and Coke whilst under the counter was where the glasses and cash box were kept. Above the bar was suspended a violet strip light which turned everything white into the most delicate shade of iridescent lilac, the hue of the shirts worn by George Chakiris in *West Side Story*.

Along the wall opposite the bar were half a dozen cubicles containing a table surrounded by a bench upholstered with dark red fake leather, a small light of insignificant wattage illuminating the interior. The floor was made of polished boards and the ceiling, walls and bar painted in a colour so dark it was indiscernible even when the door curtain was pushed aside and brilliant sunlight momentarily invaded the place. There were a few chairs and tables scattered around the walls, cheap wooden pieces with hard plastic surfaces and protruding nails which snagged clothing and skin with equal impunity.

The only other major piece of furniture was a jukebox. This was a genuine American monstrosity. Had it been a car, it would have been a Cadillac or a Studebaker. It was decorated with chrome strips, fins and stars: the record selection gear was housed under a toughened glass dome and the choice buttons glimmered like rows of candles in an Orthodox cathedral. All the other lights in the machine – red, blue, gold, green and white behind plastic panels – winked without any sense of synchronicity at all. The slot took ten cent coins and played forty-fives or, rarely, EPs.

The Liberty Bar was owned by a Chinese man called George. In his mid to late thirties, he was quite plump with the blanched skin of a man who works in the entertainment industry and seldom has the opportunity to get out in the sun. Invariably dressed in a white (and therefore iridescent lilac) shirt and black trousers with a heavy stainless steel Rado watch on his wrist, he was always cheerful, never short-tempered and, on occasion, could be generous to both his staff and clientele.

As a general rule, the bar opened at about six in the evening and closed around one o'clock the following morning: over the weekends, it could remain open until well after sun up. Hours of business were governed by the availability of military personnel: British squaddies or tars usually had to be back in barracks or on board ship by midnight, the last American navy liberty boat departing the pier in Fenwick Street just before that hour.

George dispensed more than booze and beers. The Liberty Bar, like all the similar establishments in surrounding streets, was also the front-of-house for a thriving brothel. The bar-girls were all in thrall to George. They were without exception Chinese, aged between sixteen and twenty-two and frequently very pretty indeed. In those days, the 'tradition of service' which encompassed concubinage still vaguely lingered in the oriental subconscious and, although the girls were invariably looked down upon by their peers not on the game, they were nevertheless not ostracised. Although a few took to wearing tight skirts or jeans, at least half frequently wore traditional *cheong sam* dresses in silk or brocade with a slit up the thigh which could be extended to the waist by an artfully concealed zip. Most of them kept their hair long, below the shoulder and although they used make-up this was never excessive as is usually associated with whores or harlots the world over. What was more, they all spoke at least fluent pidgin English and one of the twenty-something-year-olds had more than a passing smattering of colonial French, presumably picked up in Indochina.

By comparison with whores in other Far Eastern ports, Hong Kong bar-girls were exceptionally 'clean' and more or less obliged to be health checked every month or so, their clean bill consisting of a white card which they could show to would-be clients on demand. British sailors were advised to ask to see these and the incidence of venereal diseases amongst British service personnel was consequently low as a result. Even the pestilential, antibiotic-resistant strains carried out of Vietnam in the 1960s by the American military – nicknamed *Vietnam Rose* and *Saigon Sally* – were comparatively rare. These were virulent strains of known diseases (suggested by some to be the source from which AIDS mutated) fostered by American servicemen who, before hitting a port or a weekend on the town, overdosed themselves on 'lifesavers', high-strength antibiotics so named because they looked like the popular *Lifesaver* candy. Ironically, these took lives in the long run by fortifying the diseases against other combative drugs.

Bar business centred on three sources of income: one was drink and peanuts in their shells sold in small paper bags, another was tart's tonic (as George called it) and the last was, of course, sex.

The price of drinks was marginally higher than in hotel cocktail lounges but not exorbitant. Above a certain floor price a scam angle was added, the cost fluctuating according to the apparent wealth of the client: when the US Navy was in port, the cost of beer or whisky rose by at least 25 per cent except for regular and recognised customers for whom it remained more or less constant. Similarly, the price of the bar-girls' favours also vacillated.

The girls could be hired at one of three rates. The quick-time was a quarter of an hour and restricted to a one-off act of fornication which was as efficiently commercial, and about as thorough, as having a car attended to in a garage – metaphorically, the tank was filled and the windscreen cleaned but that was about the sum of it. The next was longer and lasted between half an hour and an hour. The client received a modicum of attention, some loving conversation and as much sexual activity as he could muster while the meter was running. Long-time meant the rest of the night. Prices varied from about HK$50 (at a rate then of about HK$14:£1 or HK$8:US$1) for a quickie to HK$300 for the premium service. British soldiers and sailors, whose weekly salaries amounted to little more than HK$100 could obtain either a hand job or a *very* quick one indeed either in the alley at the back of the bar, up a tenement staircase or, on occasion, in the cubicles in the bar: this service cost HK$25.

Tart's tonic was an altogether different scam.

Known by other somewhat cruder names, George called his brew tart's tonic. It was served either in a whisky glass or a sherry schooner and consisted of cold tea or flat Coca Cola mixed with a hint of either rice wine or cheap sherry. Some bars served just cold tea but George disdained this: he was conscious of the fact that, if a punter tasted the stuff and found out his bar-girl was drinking thimbles-full of tea, he might get violent. One tart's tonic cost HK$5. As an insurance, he therefore adulterated it.

The system worked thus: a sailor would enter the bar and

order a drink, paying about HK$8 for a beer. A bar-girl would then approach him and start to engage his conversation and attention. This was usually done by asking his name and where he came from, placing a hand on his thigh or tucking fingers into the side of his waistband. The next move was invariably, 'You buy me one drink?'

At the affirmative, the bar-girl was automatically served a tart's tonic. The unit cost of one glass was about ten cents so the profit margin was enormous. From each tart's tonic, the girl received a percentage – usually 25 per cent. In this way, she was able to earn some money even if the encounter did not lead to sex. Her time, therefore, was not wasted. Furthermore, because the drink was essentially non-alcoholic, she could down vast numbers of them in an evening without the least effect. And did: the frequency of tart's tonic consumption increased as the punter got drunker and the hour later. It was not impossible for a sailor to spend more on tonic for the girls than on his own booze for, if he seemed a likely candidate, and business was momentarily slack, more than one girl would give him her attention, taking him into one of the cubicles, fondling and teasing him, kissing and caressing him and ordering even more glasses of doctored tea.

If a punter wanted to 'take a girl out' – in other words, have sex with her – he would tell the girl and she would inform George. The full payment was then made to George and the girl took her client off either to an accepted brothel (where she rented a room or bed-space – George, I am sure, maintained a cat-house nearby) or to a room she hired in a neighbouring tenement. If the client wished to extend his time of joy, he had to pay the girl extra and she then passed this on: if he did not pay, he would meet with a resounding beating. Heavies from the local Triad society ranged the streets as debt collectors for pimps and bar owners, most of whom were either members of the same brotherhood or paid protection money to it.

I went to the Liberty Bar at least once a week for about eighteen months in the early sixties and came to know George and some of the bar-girls well. The reason for my regular visitations was not what it might have seemed. I was primarily there as a beneficiary of another of George's artful alleged scams.

Whilst at school, I joined a rock band made up of fellow pupils: I was the bass guitar player and a background singer and it must be said I was diabolically bad in both roles. The band, originally known as the *Kay Gee Five* (we were pupils at King George V School, known as *KGV*), was called *The Kontinentals*. Despite my considerable shortcomings we did well and received a fair number of bookings to play at private parties and in a particularly rundown little dive in Tsim Sha Tsui called the Bayside Niteclub. We even graduated to playing tea dances in the Paramount Night Club in Central and, for one glorious week, found ourselves on stage in the City Hall with Chubby Checker, Bobby Vee and the Ventures. To keep ahead of the other local groups – and one in particular, a Filipino band called *The Fabulous Echoes* – we had to be sure of getting the latest material first. This was where George came in.

Every so often, and particularly just after the US Navy had been in port, I visited the Liberty Bar either alone or in the company of Gerald Laishley (rhythm guitar/vocals) or Anders Nelsson (singer, guitarist and subsequently bass player after my demise): Gerald, *aka* Gerry Layton, has been a professional musician in Vancouver most of his adult life and Anders is now the most successful rock promoter in south-east Asia. Our destination was George's jukebox.

A girlie bar needs three ingredients to be a success – good-looking girls, cold beer and hot music. George had all three and, where the music was concerned, he had the hottest. Records appeared in his jukebox within a week of their arrival in the Billboard top charts. To this day, I cannot hear Del Shannon's *Runaway* and the Everly Brothers' *Cathy's Clown* or *Walk Right Back* without being instantly transported back to the dark interior and cymophanous violet air of the Liberty Bar.

Going in always elicited the same remarks.

'Hi! How you?'

'You wanna beer?'

'You buy me drink?'

'You still cherry boy?'

This last comment had nothing to do with fruit. A cherry boy is a virgin.

We would sit with the girls a while, buy them glasses of tonic and ourselves beer then, before the first sailors began to arrive, we thumbed ten cent coins into the jukebox and scribbled down the words of the songs, listening at the same time to the melody. In this way, we had top ten hits in our repertoire before the records reached Moutries, the main Hong Kong record shop, or our competitors.

The wonder was how George acquired the discs. It was one of the girls who told us. Although she may have been lying, the scam was typical of the sort of thing bar owners did – a good example of the resourcefulness of the Chinese business mind.

All drinks in the Liberty Bar were paid for on order with no tab allowed. However, according to our bar-girl informer, a shakedown could occur . . .

Preferably early in the evening, an American sailor would enter the bar, alone or with just one comrade: assuming he looked a likely target, innocent of the ways of cat-houses and their owners, he was permitted a tab. Ideally, his companion would be given one, too. On this would be listed his drinks, his glasses of tart's tonic and anything else he might have: ultimately, if things worked well, there would also be a quick-time turn with one of the girls as a bottom line, so to speak. At the end of the evening, payment would be demanded. The sailor, having been encouraged to overspend (and perhaps having had his wallet lightened but *not* emptied whilst engaging in his rapid romp), would find himself short of funds. At this, George would go spare but, after threats to call the police, the US Navy Shore Patrol and the Triad heavies, he would relent and propose a deal: if the sailor returned to the bar with the top ten records from his ship-side mess jukebox, or obtained these from shipmates, he would overlook the debt. It was well-known throughout the bar-owning community that the US Navy welfare organisation air mailed top hit records to ships on foreign station. To ensure the sailor returned, his watch, graduation ring or – even better – his comrade would be kept in ransom until his return.

Apparently, this wheeze seldom failed and the Liberty Bar had the best music in the whole of Wanchai. Quite why other bars had not cottoned on to this trick was one of the enigmas of my teenage years over which I still puzzle.

When not scrawling down song lyrics, I often wandered Wanchai and, in 1967, the Vietnam War under way and the Americans committed militarily with vast numbers of sailors and soldiers visiting Hong Kong on R&R, I spent almost every night for three months in those streets. They had more life in them after nine o'clock than Coney Island on Labor Day. I watched pickpockets at work, pimps touting for business, sailors and soldiers fighting, whores walking along the pavement with their johns. This Americanism became current in Hong Kong at that time: the local slang for a prostitute was *loh siu seung*, which translates literally as rat box. The urban services department used to nail small boxes to lamp-posts in which local residents dropped trapped or poisoned rats for collection and incineration. As all Chinese whores were petite and their johns generally much taller, the sobriquet seemed particularly apt.

The fights were as spectacular as anything Hollywood could have arranged, but real. I saw a clumsy knifing once and observed more knock-out punches than I can count. All these fights were broken up by the Shore Patrol. This consisted of three or four heavily built stokers (or the modern equivalent) under the command of a junior officer. All were equipped with night-sticks and rode around in a open jeep. They wore pristine white uniforms which never seemed to get besmirched with dirt or blood and a black armband with the letters SP embroidered on it in yellow. And they were utterly ruthless, pole-axing any recalcitrant matelot who crossed them. To watch them was to see professionals at work: I am sure they enjoyed their occupation as much as George did his.

But that is all history now. Wanchai where all the bars existed has been tamed by glass-plated skyscrapers and the proximity of the ultra-modern Conrad and Island Shangri-La hotels. Even the old Luk Kwok Hotel, the setting for the Suzie Wong novel, is now an example of modern architectural imagination umpteen stories high: what is more, it is now over 500 yards from the sea shore. Reclamation has added a lot to the Wanchai waterfront and where the old Fenwick Street pier used to stand is now the lobby of the Hong Kong Arts Centre. There are only five girlie bars left in Wanchai where, in 1960, there were over 200 and one of these has English and Australian barmaids whilst another is little more than a tourist-infested topless bar. In short, the area has been gentrified.

A few girlie bars of the old sort remain but they are sorry reincarnations, mere intimations of their predecessors. One of these is the Red Lips Bar, tucked away behind a staircase in Lock Road, Tsim Sha Tsui, surrounded by camera and hi-fi shops, bespoke tailors, jewellers' emporia and restaurants not to mention a dozen or so top-class hotels including the world-famous Peninsula less than 200 yards away.

It exists in a time warp. Captain Kirk might beam in at any minute and, once his eyes adjusted to the gloom of bare, forty-watt red light-bulbs, he might think he was in a Klingon hell. There are no pretty Chinese girls here but older, street-wise and hardened Filipina whores with hands like talons and pock-marked faces. They smell of fake designer perfumes and wear miniskirts as taut as drums and little wider than fashion belts. They do not ask your name or where you are from and go straight to the buy-me-a-drink ploy.

At least that has not changed. The tart's tonic comes in whisky slugs and is not sherrified tea but Diet Coke or 7-Up. It costs HK$20 a glass whilst a beer costs $10. Behind the bar perches an old crone who might conceivably be someone's great-grandmother. She has none of the aplomb, guile or entrepreneurial skills of George. There are a few cubicles and ceiling fans but no jukebox, no wooden floor for dancing, no violet lamp and no paper bags of peanuts. The whole place smells of sweat and, faintly, of drains.

Sitting at the bar counter in 1993, buying a tart's tonic for an old Filipina biddy in a tank top and skin-tight slacks, and not far off my own age, was one of the most miserable destructions of nostalgia I think I've ever experienced.

Riding Fragrant Waters

Established by an enterprising Indian, the first ferry service to operate across Hong Kong harbour began in the 1840s, running at irregular intervals four times a day from Victoria to Kowloon Walled City. Apart from this, the only method of reaching the mainland, unless one was in the military, was to hire a sampan or small junk. Even though the British gained possession of Kowloon in 1860, there was no regular ferry service until 1880 when another Indian, Dorabjee Nowrojee, started a regular service between Victoria and Tsim Sha Tsui.

The lack of a service prior to this was not really surprising. Few island residents had need to visit Kowloon on a frequent basis and the place was still considered wild China in the European subconscious: in 1862, a battle raged at Tsim Sha Tsui between local Hakkas and Puntis which could be heard across the water and it was 1864 before the designation of building plots was decided upon.

The world-famous Star Ferry was formed in 1889, crossing the harbour between a pier by Statue Square and another at the very same site as the present Kowloon pier. The latter was a grand affair with a ten metre high, balustraded façade, two landing quays and a covered rickshaw rank extended into what is now the bus terminus: it was destroyed in the 1906 typhoon. The Island pier was similar but with a clock tower added: it has been a tradition ever since that a clock be mounted there.

The early ferries were steam driven but, in many other

respects, the modern craft follow the design of the earlier vessels. The slightly pitched roof in imitation of a tarpaulin remains constant as does a central funnel, a ring of life-buoys on the railings and a two-deck passenger accommodation with the upper deck being more expensive than the lower where coolies (or, today, those with heavy loads) travelled. Another feature of the ferry that has lasted is its push-me-pull-you construction. There is no dedicated bow or stern with each end having a lower deck wheel-house, rudders and propellers: each journey is a reverse of the previous, avoiding a waste of time in backing out from a berth. Early craft had both decks open but later the central section of the upper deck was an enclosed cabin unlike today where the ends are enclosed and the centre open. All the ferries have been named after stars – *Morning Star, Golden Star, Northern Star* – and all have had a white band with a star round the funnel.

With the exception of the war years, when the Japanese used them to travel to Canton, the Star Ferry has never operated outside the harbour and, until recent years when two new harbour routes were added, plied only between Central and Tsim Sha Tsui. When the war ended, there were no Star Ferries afloat: some had been sunk in 1941 and the Japanese had scuttled the rest in the harbour just before the surrender. However, in 1946, the wrecks were raised, repaired and rebuilt, service has continued unabated ever since except during typhoons.

There is a timelessness about the Ferry – no local calls it the Star Ferry. Despite a little winch assisting the gangway operator, the radio pay phone on the top-deck funnel housing and the illuminated advertisement boards in the cabins, much remains unaltered. The seats still have reversible backs so passengers can face the direction of travel, the decks are still wooden and the crew members still wear a uniform unaltered in decades (blue for winter, khaki for summer) and there are still notices on the top deck warning against pickpockets and prohibiting spitting. The MTR has not – as was feared by many – made the ferry redundant. It carries thirty-six million passengers a year and the fare across the harbour is HK$1 – the cheapest of its sort in the world.

Any journey through the harbour shows the astonishing range of other passenger vessels in use. The Hong Kong and Yaumati Ferry Company (*HYF* on the funnels) has run vehicular ferries between Central and Yaumati since 1932 (not made redundant by two harbour road tunnels) and operates passenger ferries on twenty-three routes to outlying islands carrying forty-one million passengers per annum. Not only traditional boat-type vessels are utilised. High-speed green and white ferries move towards Lantau with their bows raised; small hovercraft head for Tuen Mun, bouncing over the wakes of larger vessels; red and white hydrofoils, riding out of the water on wings and powered by Boeing jet engines, swerve majestically by *en route* for Macau; large vessels looking like mini-cruise ships and flying the Communist red flag steam slowly out to Guangzhou; fast catamarans zip over the water heading for the mouth of the Si Jiang, Wuzhou and Nanning. There are even still some wallah-wallah boats plying their trade like water-borne taxis to ships at anchor but their business was badly hit by the road tunnels: people no longer had to rely on them after the ferries stopped running at midnight.

Hong Kong's ferries have played their part in local history, too. In the 1920s, it was a HYF ferry *en route* to Central from Kowloon that was hijacked in the middle of the harbour by audacious pirates and steamed out towards Tuen Mun. The passengers were eventually released, unharmed. In the war, Star Ferry vessels were used to transport prisoners-of-war to and from forced labour projects, much to the chagrin of those who had ridden the same craft dressed in dinner suits, tropical whites or mess uniforms.

Over the years, Hong Kong has suffered brief periods of civil unrest: in the 1920s, anti-British sentiments in Canton led to strikes and boycotts, in 1931 there were anti-Japanese riots in Kowloon and, in 1956 and 1967, disorder flared up because of civil war in China and the Cultural Revolution respectively. All these were inspired by external forces: the only truly local rioting was inspired by the Star Ferry.

In March 1966, it was announced that top deck fares were

to be increased by five cents to twenty-five cents. Mrs Elsie Elliott, a local councillor and champion of the poor Chinese, opposed this and, on 4 April, ferry commuters faced a unique sight. At the Star Ferry pier, there was a lone demonstrator dressed in black and bearing a placard exhorting support for Mrs Elliott. His name was So Sau-chung. Within a day, he had attracted vast crowds and, that night, a group of ten demonstrators led by a European part-time teenage actor called Brian Raggensack, marched down Nathan Road with a banner. A huge following gathered behind them and the riot police arrived. Rioting ensued for two nights. A building was set alight, shops were looted, cars overturned. The police reported firing sixty-two live rounds in addition to sixty-two wooden bullets (the precursor of the infamous rubber bullet) and 772 tear gas shells. Hundreds were arrested and scores injured by flying wooden splinters, glass and baton charges. In due course, when the hubbub was over, the fares were raised.

Not only ferries operate in the harbour, the busiest in the world with the highest through-put of freight traffic: Hong Kong handles more cargo per annum than the whole of Britain and every other country save Japan and the USA. Massive cargo container vessels move inexorably through the western approaches on their way to the Kwai Chung cargo terminal, smaller freighters ride the tide moored to buoys. Tugs tow massive lighters between the ships and the shore. With the huge reclamation projects underway, Hong Kong waters currently contain over 25 per cent of the world fleet of dredgers which dig and dip for bottom muds, dumping their noxious cargo into barges. Floating Pimms palaces sail by sampans, the decks of one resplendent with well-dressed ladies, the other with an old man doing a bit of fishing or washing his dishes. Fishing junks chug through the choppy waters and grey police gunboats patrol beside pilot vessels, garbage scows, barges of sewage and domestic waste heading for the open sea or the landfill sites, customs and excise craft, sailing yachts out from the Royal Hong Kong Yacht Club at Causeway Bay and the occasional military inflatable speedboat. There is a speed limit in the harbour which varies from place to place for different types of vessel —

which is just as well for, on an average day, there can be as many as 280 *moving* craft in an area of approximately thirty-five square kilometres at any one moment.

Only one vessel blatantly ignores the speed code – the *dai fei*. This is a highly specialised vessel capable of speeds in excess of almost any other in Hong Kong: they are the latest additions to a fleet with a long Hong Kong tradition – piracy.

A *dai fei* is a very aerodynamic, ten-metre long, steel-hulled speed-boat, a spartan craft with no formal cabin, lavatory or other refinements whatsoever. To the stern is bolted a rank of five or six of the most powerful outboard motors money will buy working in tandem from a single throttle, fuel supply and steerage mechanism. Made in Hong Kong, it is no small wonder the craft is called a *dai fei* which means big wing – it flies. This vessel is capable of speeds up to sixty knots, outrunning even one of the Boeing-powered Macau hydrofoils. The wheel-house cockpit is surrounded by a sheet steel bulkhead and the windscreen is made of either pressure or bullet-proof glass. A hold behind the cockpit, lined and floored with steel, is made to carry cargo but has no covering other than a tarpaulin.

In the third quarter of 1992, car theft in Hong Kong rose by 924 per cent over the previous year. This dumbfounded the authorities for Hong Kong, being an enclave, was never bothered by car theft save the odd vehicle being 'borrowed' by British soldiers returning to barracks penniless and late at night. Commercial theft was virtually unknown for there was nowhere to take a vehicle for resale. What changed the situation was China's liberalisation. It was no longer frowned upon to be wealthy in China and the new rich entrepreneurs wanted the trappings of their Western counterparts. As foreign cars are hardly ever imported into China, the Hong Kong Triad gangs and mainland gangsters seized their opportunity.

Not any car disappears. What vanishes over the border are top range Mercedes Benz, BMW and luxury Japanese models, skilfully broken into in car parks and 'exported' sometimes before the owners miss them. Many are ordered and stolen specifically, to the tune of HK$139 million between 1 July and 30 September, 1992.

The means of extraterritorial transportation is the *dai fei* and the system is as simple as it is effective. An order comes down from China for, say, a black BMW 5-series. As the density of luxury cars in Hong Kong is the heaviest in the world, the thieves can find and mark one within hours. Armed with mobile telephones, they then call up a *dai fei* to a particular quay, diverting it (and the car) if there is any sign of police activity in the vicinity. If all is clear, the car is driven to the quay, quickly loaded and covered with a tarpaulin, the paintwork protected from rubbing or knocking against the hull by inflated lorry tyre inner tubes. The vessel then casts off and heads for China. The chances of being intercepted in the crowded waters of Hong Kong by either the marine police or the Royal Navy are low, despite both enforcement agencies being equipped with high speed pursuit craft. If they are confronted, the *dai fei* crew do not surrender easily. Many of them being disaffected or redundant People's Liberation Army soldiers, they are well armed with automatic rifles, sub-machine guns and even grenades.

Dai fei hunting is dangerous work. A chase has all the exhilaration of a Hollywood thriller but without the special effects. This is for real. Police and naval gunboats patrol the sea until they visually see or pick up on radar a fast-moving craft off the high-speed ferry routes. They intercept them by bisecting their path and lowering two fast pursuit craft which are little more than speedboats or inflatables with a very high power-to-weight ratio. Boarding parties set off after the *dai fei*. Everyone is armed but, unlike the pirates, do not have steel cladding to protect them.

If luck is on their side, the pursuit craft gradually overhaul the *dai fei*. The wind is strong enough to blow a man overboard and the shock of hitting the waves (or harbour flotsam) is bone-jarring: indeed, the risk of death by either falling overboard or sustaining terrible injuries as the pursuit craft bounces and tosses about, the action increasing considerably as the boat comes into the wake of the *dai fei*, is very great. Wrenched muscles and broken bones are a common hazard.

As most, though not all, smuggling takes place at night, the pirates use no running lights and their vessels are dark coloured, the danger of being rammed is ever-present. Most of the action has to be conducted by the light of an unstable spot-lamp or two.

Once alongside the *dai fei*, anything might happen. The pirate captain may swerve to swamp or ram the pursuers, or he might accelerate away. The pursuers hail the *dai fei* and tell it to heave to which it may, or may not do. Bluff and counter-bluff are brought into play. The chase continues. Other patrol vessels move in to block the pirates' course. Guns are drawn. Shots are not infrequently exchanged. In October 1992, a British naval rating, somehow managing to board a *dai fei* at speed in darkness, shot two of its crew members with his service 9mm Browning whilst endeavouring to fend off a thrusting knife and dodge a bludgeoning three-metre bamboo pole, and cut through the fuel lines.

At the end of the chase, assuming it to be successful, the *dai fei* is confiscated. All the pursuers are soaked to the marrow, ache in every cell of their bodies, are queasy from the motion and exhausted. Unlike the luxury craft Florida drug-runners utilise, it has little value save as scrap although the engines may be sold and, no doubt, frequently end up on another *dai fei*. The impounding of one has little impact on the business as another may easily be constructed.

The Chinese authorities have made some attempt to stem the piracy of cars. They will no longer initially register right-hand-drive cars (China drives on the right) and a minuscule proportion of those stolen are returned to Hong Kong but these measures are scant deterrent. Chinese officialdom being corrupt to the core, the registration wheeze is only nominal and the cars returned not so much of a disincentive to thieves as an assistance, for those brought back to Hong Kong increase demand in China.

What does upset the Chinese government is the *dai fei* operators' other line of tax-avoiding business. China has a multi-billion US dollar trade deficit but the new rich want luxuries – fridges, colour television sets, CD players, video recorders. And the pirates provide them with their *dai fei* fleet – or *cheung fei*, meaning medium-sized wing: these are not so large as the former but able to maintain comparable speeds.

Their cargo is not stolen. The operators legitimately buy a consignment of electrical goods in bulk from a wholesaler, load up their vessel and set sail for the biggest market-place on earth. No crime is committed in Hong Kong for, being an entrepôt port, it is not illegal to export anything from the territory save narcotics and firearms. This luxury trade, which extends to Japanese wrist-watches, designer clothes and, reminiscent of British pirates in the eighteenth century, French cognac which is much prized in China, is easier than car smuggling. Cars have to be on- and off-loaded at a dock and local officials given their tea money, a euphemism for bribes: other contraband can be run up on a deserted beach with no bribery to reduce the profit margin, just a few *yuan* for the coolies helping with the landing.

Yet, despite there being no crime committed, the Royal Navy and Royal Hong Kong Police are expected to risk life and limb countering this trade: anti-piracy control is part and parcel of a border agreement with China and has caused a great deal of suppressed animosity in police and combined forces messes. Lives are jeopardised (and lost) in these deadly chases which, unless a car is involved, are legal enterprises until the *dai fei* crosses the territorial waters boundary at which point, in any case, the British hunters have to turn back for lack of jurisdiction. And the Chinese authorities make less effort to stop this game in their waters than the Hong Kong government does. It is an unequal and unfair business.

As in much of Hong Kong, little has really changed in the harbour over the years. The cargo ships are bigger and more cumbersome, the ferries more plentiful and varied, the dredgers equipped with bigger scoops and the luxury launches sleeker but it is still a place of business, the vessels weaving and crossing, passing and turning with the alacrity of whirligig beetles. Amazingly, there is hardly ever a collision.

Walking down Paak Faan Gai

By the time this page is printed, Kowloon Walled City will no longer exist, having collapsed under the wrecker's ball-and-chain. All the residents, property owners and factory proprietors will have been compensated (for a total sum in excess of US$450 million) and will have departed for resettlement flats in Kowloon or condominiums in Vancouver, San Francisco or Toronto.

On the first day of demolition, the world's last real criminal barrio will disappear.

Before the British acquired Hong Kong, Kowloon was a sparsely populated promontory of low, scrub-covered hills with a few hamlets the occupants of which farmed the valleys and the land near the shore, fishing what is now the harbour. The best farming land lay where the airport is today. It was ideal because it was swampy and the main crop was rice grown in paddyfields: on the other hand, it was also malarious. Just behind this agricultural area of some one hundred or so acres, there rose a conical hill dotted with substantial rocks and crowned with a group of huge boulders whilst to the west there was another hillock upon which the exiled Sung boy emperor had set up his temporary court. It follows that where there was good farming there would also be a settlement: a small hamlet of some dozen or so houses and a temple was located at the foot of the conical hill.

What this hamlet was called is uncertain: it seems not to feature on any maps until the late seventeenth century although Kowloon appears on a coastal chart of 1425 and the village of

175

Tsim Sha Tsui, which stood on a sandy beach under what is now the Peninsula Hotel, was included on maps as long ago as the sixteenth century.

It is believed that the hamlet was provided with a stockade: however, no archaeological traces exist and no written records have yet come to light. However, in 1810, a small fort was constructed there as part of the imperial defences against piracy, acting as a subsidiary to Kowloon Fort which stood on a hillock next to Tsim Sha Tsui: that hillock survives to this day close to the Star Ferry and is the site of the Royal Hong Kong Marine Police headquarters. It was manned by men of the Tai Pang Brigade.

When Hong Kong island was ceded to the British in the January of 1841, the Chinese authorities, wary of British infiltration and influence, reduced the Tsim Sha Tsui garrison but increased that of the small fort which they set about strengthening along with the now expanding hamlet until, in 1847, it became a defended settlement of six and a half acres.

It was a substantial fortress with four main gateways, a number of cannon embrasures and six square watch-towers, all built of hewn stone and grey mudbricks. A spring rose from beneath the conical hill the southern slope of which was included within the walls to prevent a rearguard assault. The garrison numbered 150 men under the command of a *fu chiang*, or brigadier, and kept in close contact with other, lesser forts in the vicinity by way of land runners and patrol junks. Whilst certainly not impregnable in the face of a concerted attack by foreigners, the walled town was nevertheless secure by Chinese standards.

The settlement soon expanded further. Within stood the *yamen* (the mandarin's office and residence), a temple and about forty houses: outside sprang up houses, shops and assorted businesses including several brothels and opium dens, occupying the former paddyfields to the edge of the beach across which a wooden jetty was erected. It might be said here was the start of modern Hong Kong – traditional practices were being suborned by trade: indeed, the overseeing mandarin of Sun On County, which included Kowloon, reported 'the Kowloon people mingle.

with foreigners and their custom is that they value money and material matters and disparage poetry . . .'

In 1860, the Kowloon peninsula and Stonecutters Island came under British sovereignty in apparent perpetuity. An army camp was established, the British eager to gain control of the mainland facing the island as a military buffer zone: China was in turmoil with the Tai Ping Rebellion in full flood and there was a danger that this might spill over and affect the tea and opium trade. The Tsim Sha Tsui fort and guard stations were closed down and a boundary line demarcated across the foot of the Kowloon hills: at its eastern end, it reached the shore of Kowloon Bay a hundred metres or so from the walled town.

This became an important centre of official Chinese activity. A customs post was erected there, under the command of an English excise officer, to license opium trading: the Chinese customs service was almost entirely run by expatriate Englishmen. The garrison was increased to keep an eye on the British and more houses were erected to cater for the increase in trade. The border between Kowloon and China was not closed and Kowloon Walled City, as it was now named, was frequently visited by British soldiers and local residents. Kowloon itself acquired a dubious reputation for it was considered to be very much 'the other side of the track' or, in this instance, harbour. The Walled City became a little kasbah which added spice to colonial life. Foreigners went there either by sedan chair from Tsim Sha Tsui or by boat from the island (the wooden jetty was replaced by a stone one to accommodate this tourism) to smoke opium, dally with whores, purchase antiques or get a taste of the real China.

By 1898, the walled city garrison stood at 544 soldiers with 200 camp followers, mostly officers' families, whilst the surrounding town had a population exceeding 5000. All seemed stable: the colonial administration turned a blind eye to the trippers and the Chinese ignored the locals' mercenary materialism because the mandarin was able not only to tax the trade but also take a considerable sum in back-handers. Everyone benefited.

Then came the Convention of Peking on 9 June 1898. Anxious

to extend its territory and provide a greater buffer zone against land-borne attack, Britain obtained the New Territories under a ninety-nine-year lease. However, it was agreed Chinese officials could remain in the walled city except, as a clause put it, *so far as may be inconsistent with the military requirements of the defence of Hong Kong.* The British were not bothered by Chinese officials remaining and assumed they would soon leave whilst the Chinese authorities were pleased because it was said that if an emperor lost a city during his rule then he would be unable to enter the royal temple for shame would prevent him from facing his ancestors' spirits.

All went well until the next year when local peasants rebelled against the British and attacked surveyors and cartographers mapping the new region. The Governor of Hong Kong, Sir Henry Blake, asked the Viceroy of Canton for protection and requested the Chinese customs post in Kowloon Walled City be closed down. The Viceroy sent 600 troops, half of whom moved into the Walled City, Blake assuming this was to defend the customs post. British demands and deadlines for the removal of the troops were met with procrastination so British troops and the Hong Kong Volunteers occupied Kowloon Walled City and the Chinese officials exclusion clause was activated.

This military intervention set the stage for eighty years of political argument, infrequent diplomatic incidents and wrangling, claim and counterclaim over sovereignty and uncertain jurisdiction. In the meantime, Kowloon Walled City took on the role of a mini-state within a colony surrounded by a nation, all but ungoverned and outlawed. It became, in effect, the tiniest city state in the world ostensibly controlled by the British, just as ostensibly owned by China but actually governed by self-appointed rulers who were invariably gangsters.

Over the years, various confrontations have taken place. In 1947, the British suggested demolishing the city and building a park but the Chinese rejected this saying it should remain as an official residence for their representative. In January, 1948, 2,000 squatters were evicted and their huts demolished. Localised rioting ensued, the Chinese government tried to intervene and the Hong Kong Government considered handing the whole place over to the United Nations whilst taking the Chinese to the international court to sort out jurisdiction. Other mini-riots and disagreements ensued until, in 1966, during the Cultural Revolution, the Communist flag was raised in the city. Officials tore it down and bloody rioting followed. Even the occupying Japanese had not escaped censure although little was done about their activities when, in 1943, they set about pulling down the walls and many of the buildings, using Allied prisoners-of-war working as slave labour. The masonry was used as hard core to extend the airport less than 400 metres away.

British policy towards this tiny enclave, now without a wall, was conducted on softly-softly lines. The police patrolled it and on occasion made arrests, but generally it was left well alone, regarded as a hornets' nest not to be kicked unless absolutely necessary – as in 1975 when security forces moved in to dismantle two buildings which posed an obstruction to the airport flight path.

Urban planning laws, rigorously applied throughout Hong Kong, tended to be ignored in the walled city, the residents in the immediate post-war years inhabiting squatters' huts which, over the years, gave way to buildings up to twelve storeys high. The thoroughfares in the 'new' city metamorphosed along the line of the *hutongs*, alleys and lanes of the original city, the buildings constructed cheek by jowl and crammed into the tiny acreage so close together as to shut out sunlight from ground level even at high noon.

This is how Kowloon Walled City remained, a confusing warren of almost subterranean passageways and wynds from which no sky could be glimpsed nor fresh breeze felt.

To enter it, even as recently as 1980, was to invite trouble. Or worse. The domain of Triad society gangsters, drugs dealers and hardened criminals, a lone European venturing into its midst would most probably never be seen again. No Chinese went in unless he was a resident, a Triad official, a felon or someone with specific business therein. The police patrolled in units of four or more. The health authorities kept away as did the factories and schools inspectorates, the telephone and utilities companies, the immigration and customs organisations.

Kowloon Walled City was a no-go area.

After Margaret Thatcher signed away Hong Kong's sovereignty without so much as a by-your-leave from the population, things changed. Kowloon Walled City became an anachronistic anomaly. The future landlords, the Communist Chinese, requested it be emptied of people and eradicated. Accordingly, from 1988 to 1992, it was systematically vacated to become a shell of dangerously semi-derelict buildings populated by enormous rats, cockroaches and, no doubt, ghosts. Plans were set afoot to demolish the lot, save the *yamen*: the mandarin's building was mooted to become a museum and the rest a public park. The 1947 plan, it seems, might come to fruition after all.

On several occasions, I have been into the walled city with the Royal Hong Kong Police. The first time, just before the depopulation commenced, was to accompany a vice squad patrol to check up on the last of the city brothels. In the company of a European inspector, a sergeant and half a dozen constables, I climbed out of a police minibus in Tung Tau Tsuen Road which borders the north of the walled city and stepped into what seemed from the pavement to be nothing more than a doorway without a door. The alleyway into which we passed was not much more than a metre wide with sloping stone steps worn by decades of passing feet. Although it was early afternoon, the sun high in the sky with a temperature in the mid-eighties, the alley was in semi-darkness and the air chilly. After the bustle of the road, it was surprisingly quiet. Stumbling onwards in indian file for about ten metres, we turned a corner by a blackened wall upon which was stuck a poster warning in English and Cantonese that rat bait was laid nearby. I realised with some alarm I was already lost: it was impossible to tell in which direction I was facing. The inspector called a halt.

'Let me give you a few words of advice,' he began, checking the flap on his revolver holster was closed.

I expected to be cautioned about Triad knifemen, drug dealers

and dope fiends: in the circumstances, a warning about white slav-
ers and Fu Manchu himself might not have been inappropriate.

'Don't touch the walls if you can avoid it,' he continued,
'and watch where you step. If it's vertical, it's probably covered
in shit and if it's horizontal, it'll be slippery with it. Puddles are
not all they seem and the drains are worse than any nullah you've
ever encountered. Don't look up if you can avoid it. Any liquid
dripping from above is not a shower of summer rain.'

At this point, two of the constables produced what I thought
were short night-sticks but which proved to be folding umbrellas.
They smiled politely at me as they unfurled the ribs.

'And stick together,' the inspector finished. 'You'll not come
to any harm: we've cleaned out most of the heroin dealers. But
you'll easily get lost and it can take an hour to find your way out
and longer if we have to search for you. Now,' he stopped fingering
his holster, 'we're not going straight to the knocking-shop. They
know we're here already so there's no surprise to be gained. Word
travels fast hereabouts. Instead, we'll give you a guided tour.' He
smiled at the sergeant. 'The A Tour.'

We moved off, turning round corners and rising up and
down undulations in the flags or concrete underfoot. Here and
there, we climbed or descended stone steps illuminated by low
wattage neon bulbs. Down the centre of some of the *hutongs*
flowed little open sewers rimed with grey sludge. The air was
fetid and stank of sewage mingled from time to time with
different contrasting scents – dried herbs, dead fish, carbolic,
industrial cleaning fluid and boiling sugar. Here and there we
passed closed doors of steel shutters behind which an assortment
of human and mechanical activity emanated, all echoes killed by
the close confines of the alleys.

Halting once more by a doorway, one of the constables spoke
to an unseen occupant. From above came what I assumed to be the
incongruous sound of a cicada, a sort of broken hizzing noise. As
there appeared not to be any liquid dripping down from on high
and the constables' umbrellas were closed, I risked glancing up.
The sight was staggering. I had expected to see at least a distant

crack of light but there was not the merest hint of sky or day. Instead, about two metres over my head was a dense cross-hatchery of galvanised steel pipes and metal brackets, wires and poles. From these was festooned a copious debris of paper, scraps of cloth, plastic bags and indescribable tresses of filth. It was like being in the intestines of some infernal machine. The insect noise was an electric spark dancing gaily across a gap between a wire and one of the pipes.

'Ingenious, isn't it?' the inspector commented, moving to my side. 'It's all legally supplied these days but it didn't used to be. The water pipes were tapped into the mains in the outside world, by-passing the meters. The electricity was likewise siphoned off from the grid. And town gas, when it reached here. The telephone wires were illegally routed to the exchange network. God knows how *that* was achieved, but it was. When the whole lot was legalised, however, the actual supply system could not be altered, the original means of delivery being utilised all the same. That's what's hanging over our heads. Reach up there and – zip! – you're fried. And, apart from providing utilities, the whole mish-mash stops the rubbish falling to the ground.'

He turned to one side and pointed to an oblong hole the size of a narrow coffin under a wall, shining a bright policeman's torch into it. The beam flickered upon a torrent of fast moving water.

'That's water coming from the springs which used to supply the city in the last century. Not that you'd drink from it now. I would reckon a good many people have vanished down that gap, whole or butchered.'

We started off once more, the inspector not speaking again until we arrived at a T-junction.

'Here, we are in Tai Ching Street,' he said, nodding in the direction of the dark alley behind us, 'and this salubrious boulevard before us is called West City Road. Just beyond here is the edge of the walled city, where the wall was. Come.' He led the way down the alley, negotiated a dog-leg bend and suddenly, to our right, a shaft of sunlight burned in. 'This is where the west gate stood,' he explained. 'More or less.'

I peered into the glare and was able to make out an expanse of bare earth with a vast orange bulldozer parked upon it.

'That was an area of shanties,' the inspector observed, 'until a few months ago. It was cleared,' he added bluntly.

With that, he made off again and we all traipsed behind, round two more dog-leg bends into another dingy *hutong*.

'This is Sz Kung Street,' the sergeant informed me, pointing to a black and white sign nailed to the wall. 'Each house has got a number.' He tapped on a tin mail box nailed to a wall. 'The post is delivered here every day.'

I was by now completely disorientated. It was like being in some chthonian labyrinth. This, I thought, was how tame rats felt in experimental mazes. At that moment, I caught sight of my first Kowloon Walled City wild rat. It was sitting level with my head next to a hole in a rusty iron down-pipe. It was, I guessed, about the size of a small cat. One of the constables jerked my arm and grimaced. The rat departed quicker than the eye could see.

'Big brutes,' the inspector remarked. 'If you come in here on a night patrol, when most of the people are asleep, it's as if you've found the Pied Piper's stables. They scatter everywhere. When I was younger, we used to boot them into the piping. They were more brazen then.'

A doorway loomed and we entered it to discover a much-battered lift door. The inspector pressed a button.

'It'll only take a few of us at a time,' he remarked as the door opened on a tiny Otis lift, the aluminium step polished smooth and the floor badly dented: four of us squeezed in and the doors shut. 'It's the only lift in the city. Never serviced, of course,' the inspector went on. 'I often wonder about the state of the cables . . .'

We rose at infinitesimal speed, floor numbers flicking on and off in a cracked lighted panel. At last, the lift juddered and the doors creaked open, depositing us on the roof of the walled city where the sudden direct sunlight blinded us. All around was a tangled forest of television aerials, washing lines draped with laundry, corrugated iron cocklofts and shelters, cages of bars, railings and rolls of barbed wire demarcating one person's roof-space from the next. I followed the inspector, climbing over low walls containing small neat gardens of potted chrysanthemums, kumquat and azalea bushes and even, here and there, boxes of lettuces. Hens scrabbled and clucked in coups, pigeons cooing and murmuring in lofts made of packing cases.

'A good number of the pigeons you eat in the classy restaurants come from here,' the inspector informed me in passing. 'They're one of the walled city's main exports.'

A whine began to build inside my head. I do not suffer from vertigo and wondered vaguely what it might be, praying it was not the onset of a migraine. The inspector nodded behind me.

'Duck!' he said.

I turned to come face to face with the sharp end of a brand new Bae Airbus. It was leaning to one side at an altitude of about a hundred metres and was not more than 300 metres off. I could see, in fine detail, the line of panels on the fuselage. It flew nearer still, banking more steeply, its huge wheels lowered, the landing lights brilliant on its wing bases. It was not as noisy as might be expected: there are strict sound parameters in Hong Kong. Then it was gone down through the aerial jungle, disappearing over the far side of the city. After a pause, there was a deep distant thunder as the engines reversed their thrust.

'Some years ago,' the inspector recollected, 'one of the landlords decided to stick another three storeys on his building. Many of them have been added on to in a vertical direction over the years. We came in and said he couldn't do that. He more or less told us to bugger off – what he did with his property was up to him. This was the walled city. We shrugged and said, "OK, but you'll lose the floors with the first wide approach." He took the hint.'

Jumping from flat roof to roof was an exhilarating experience. Although the distance was never more than a metre or so, it was unnerving to think that if one missed a footing the next stop was the grid of pipes and wires. Glancing down between the buildings, where window overlooked window at a distance of centimetres, I could see why no light reached the ground: the gaps were filled with strata of garbage.

Finding a staircase, we started to descend, going past heavy steel doors on apartments and flatlets. One or two doors were open and I glanced through them: the confined living quarters were incredibly neat, spick and span. Caged birds sang in the windows and one flat had a huge fish tank filled with neons and zebra-striped angel-fish. Beds were mostly of the bunk variety and the walls were covered in shelves with books, pictures and televisions upon them. All the floors were carpeted or covered in rush matting and, by almost every door, there was a square of cardboard or newspaper upon which an entrant could deposit his outdoor shoes.

'How many people live in the city?' I asked the sergeant.

'I don't know,' he admitted. 'Not exactly. But there are about 10,000 registered families. Maybe 30,000 total.'

'And *un*registered?' I said.

He shrugged and smiled.

Back into the labyrinth we plunged, setting off along more all-but subterranean alleys. At intervals, we met residents of the walled city. Contrary to my expectation, they warmly greeted the policemen and paused to pass the time of day. Some smiled at me. Children walked by on their way to school, dressed in pristine blue and white starched uniforms, old men sat on chairs by doorways and smoked whilst younger men moved by carrying loads in tough plastic sacks or suspended from poles over their shoulders. Housewives stood aside to let us through, their hands holding bags of groceries, live hens or crabs, their wings or legs or pincers pinioned with twine. At one point, a man approached us carrying a squealing piglet under his arm, trussed in a cylindrical woven bamboo cage.

'This street,' the inspector said, halting by an open doorway from which came the suck and thump of a vacuum plastic forming machine, 'is known colloquially as Paak Faan Gai. *Paak faan*, as you know, is white rice. But in here it is slang for No 4 heroin.

Until six months ago, you could walk along here and buy it by the kilo.'

'Where are the peddlers now?' I asked.

'Moved out. Moved on. A number have decamped to the Wong Tai Sin resettlement estate. We keep tabs on them. The addicts are still here but you don't see them much. Not now. You need to come in the evening to catch a sight of them. Poor bastards. Many of them are looked after by Jackie Pullinger.'

Jackie Pullinger is a charismatic Christian missionary who arrived in Hong Kong on the back-packing hippy trail in 1966, received her mission from Christ and has, ever since, worked to rehabilitate addicts in the Walled City. Without methadone. Her system of cure is simple: she and her helpers pray with them, see them through the agonies of withdrawal with just the strength of the word of God. Miraculously – and no cliché is intended – it works and she has saved hundreds from the snare of heroin, curing and rehabilitating them.

'Drugs,' the inspector continued, nodding a greeting to a passer-by laden down with bundles of cotton waste, 'and the walled city have been synonymous for decades: one of the other alleys is Guang Ming Street – Bright Light Street. Needless to say, the sun doesn't shine in. It got its name from being the place where all the opium dens used to be.'

Turning left, we were suddenly in daylight again. At the centre of the walled city is a large courtyard containing the remains of the *yamen*, a clinic and a school. It was incongruous to say the least to discover traditional Chinese village houses in a canyon of semi-derelict high-rises with stained concrete walls, narrow, barred verandas and poles of laundry hanging out from the windows. There was even a tree or two growing there, bizarrely garlanded with garbage. Passing through the archway into the *yamen* yard, I could not prevent a minatory shudder from icing my spine: it was on this very spot the mandarin had summarily (and frequently) beheaded petty criminals as recently as the turn of the century. On a wooden bench nearby sat three old crones, knitting children's sweaters in bright yellow wool.

Leaving the old ladies to their work – they waved me farewell – we re-entered the alleys and came upon two heavy cannons lying alongside the pathway. Water was gushing from above and the sergeant opened an umbrella and held it over me.

'All that's left of the Imperial Chinese Army,' the inspector commented, putting his boot on one of the guns: I noticed the leather was filthy and looking at my own shoes saw they were just as soiled. 'There were more but the others have gone. Probably made into counterfeit fifty-cent coins. Who knows? Originally, they stood on stone mountings near the *yamen*.'

Our next stop was the Tin Hau temple in Tin Hau Temple Street, yet another alley. Like the *yamen*, the temple was an ancient building but without the expanse of sky overhead: indeed, to protect it from falling rubbish it was entirely covered by a thick wire mesh covered in litter. A grim and snarling chow-dog chained in a box by the door forbade entry. His warning seemed to be echoed by the carving of a snarling dragon over the lintel: gore, or it might have been some effluent from overhead, dripped from its maw. Beneath it were carved two characters.

'*Jung lung*. Dribbling dragon,' the sergeant translated. 'He is dribbling for blood, for victims.'

I assessed the length of the dog's chain and thought I could just get by the creature to enter the temple but I reckoned without an old woman who glowered and shook her finger at me. One of the constables spoke harshly to her but piloted me away. The temple caretaker was the only unfriendly face we had seen.

The walled city is more than a residential area. It is riddled with shops, bustling factories, thriving businesses and 'other establishments' of which the brothel was but one. Some of the shops cater for the local residents, selling groceries, fruit and all the other necessities of modern life. Others offer a far more bizarre trade, as the inspector pointed out when we arrived in a wider-than-usual alley called Kwong Ming Street.

'Having a problem with your gnashers?' he enquired pausing before a glass counter in a little shop. 'He'll fix you up.'

The shop sold second-hand sets of dentures. Rows of the

things were lined up on the shelves, pink plastic set with rows of teeth, some bleached white and others yellowed from age, nicotine or just ill-use.

'Where do they get them from?' I asked.

'People come here and trade their loose set in for some new ones. Sometimes relatives bring them in after the owner's passed on. Sometimes they come from funeral directors. Dentists' assistants or nurses sell them: it's a perk of the job.'

Just down the street from the spare teeth shop, close to another selling second-hand artificial limbs and a wide range of second-hand, chromium-plated surgical instruments of the most gruesome appearance, was a grimy factory making fish balls. Rather like round fish fingers, these are a delicacy of Cantonese cuisine. Trays of them stood under a filthy lamp, the ceiling hung with stalactites of grease, the tiled walls smeared where attempts had been made to clean them down. A man with a smut-stained apron, stripped bare to the waist, was scooping them with his hands into a large vat. By the door, an old woman seated at a wooden trestle was hand-wrapping bright green boiled sweets in cellophane, her gnarled fingers deftly twisting the wrappers. Onto a corner of her folding table water dripped incessantly from the dimness above.

'They *say*,' the inspector remarked, stressing his words carefully, 'the fish balls served in the Mandarin come from the walled city. I'd not swear to it. Couldn't afford the libel award. But these are the best in the colony. I can vouch for that. Certainly, 90 per cent of all the meat- and fish-balls eaten in Hong Kong come from here.'

'What happens if there is a fire?' I queried.

'The fire brigade treat it immediately as a grade 1 occurrence regardless of information. Frankly, it astounds me the whole place hasn't been razed to the ground. There was a blaze here last week, in a pork fat rendering works. Nobody injured. Not even smoke inhalation.'

We moved on, passing workshops in which men were welding cycle frames, repairing televisions and car gearboxes, pressing out plastic bottle caps, forging washers, winding wool or spinning yarn onto spindles and turning wood screws: at the height of industrial activity in 1987, there were over 900 commercial businesses in the Walled City. All the machinery looked on the point of mechanical collapse. At first glance, I took one workshop to be a Chinese sausage manufactory for the ceiling was hung, I thought, with red, salami-type sausages: they were in fact latex rubber penises fresh from the mould.

The sergeant touched my elbow.

'Come this way, sir,' he suggested. 'This may interest you.'

We went down some steps and entered what at first looked like a sort of warehouse. Chairs and tables were piled on a tiled floor and the place seemed to be partitioned into areas by steel grids. At the far end was an altar beside which a ragged man was sleeping on bare planks inside a steel bunk, half covered by a moth-eaten quilt.

The altar was nothing like as elaborate as that to be found in most temples, being little more than a long table with two red pillars on either side of a single small idol behind which were draped red and gold curtains. On the altar was arrayed a number of exceedingly brutal-looking weapons. One was a spiked ball, another a chain with a blade attached to it and a third a throwing star: against the wall leaned a number of sharp iron pikestaffs.

'A Triad temple, to the god Kwan Tai,' the sergeant said quietly then, taking my elbow, he led me away not, I sensed, out of deference to the sleeping down-and-out.

At last, we reached the brothel. It was not what I had expected. Too many hours spent either at the movies or in the girlie bars of Wanchai had conditioned me. The place was little more than a small and uncomfortable apartment entered by way of a polished wooden door with a spy-hole in it. Inside, the cramped area was divided into three or four wooden boxes vaguely reminiscent of confessionals. They had carved posts and, inside, raised board floors strewn with bedding. A red light in each was the only concession to it being a whorehouse. There was no one present – no pretty young concubines, no fat and worldly mama, no long-haired or long-legged oriental beauties. There was, however, a vague hint of exceedingly cheap perfume, or it might have been expensive disinfectant, and the acerbic whiff of incense from a little shrine above one of the bed-boxes.

'They'll be outside,' the inspector predicted. 'The place is illegal but we don't really bother with it too much. We just keep it on its toes. After all, it's been here for decades, serves a purpose and, besides, the whole of this pile is coming down in a year or two. It's due to be cleared of residents in three phases starting in just a few months.'

'Who uses it?' I inquired.

'Coolies, mostly. Drug addicts. Street sleepers. That sort of thing.'

'And the girls?' I went on, naively.

'The girls, as you put it, have a combined age of well over 200. There are four or five of them. Work it out for yourself.'

Close to the brothel was an illegal dentist's surgery. The proprietor was a smiling, chubby man of about fifty in his shirtsleeves. His dentist's chair was ancient, the drill belt-driven. Over it hung a cluster of four lamps of the sort one sees in pre-war gangster films, the glass orbs dropping to an almost-feminine nipple. The walls were lined with mirrors, little medicine cupboards and a pink domestic sink beside which rested a glazed stone water purifier. Above the mirror I noticed a cross with a tiny crucified Christ upon it.

'There are eighty-six illegal dentists and sixty-eight illegal doctors here,' the inspector remarked after exchanging greetings with the dentist. 'By illegal, we mean unlicensed. They may be qualified – indeed, most of them are – but in Communist China in the Fifties. They learnt their trade all right, but in Russian. Many of them could probably pass the licensing exams if they sat them, but they can't manage as they don't have the command of English.'

Down a short passageway by the dentist's shop, we hit daylight once more. Traffic buzzed past some cooked food stalls and the air was suddenly fresher, warmer, cleaner. At the curb stood the police minibus.

'Fancy a beer? Come to our station mess,' the inspector invited me. 'Or perhaps you'd rather be hosed down.'

As we got into the vehicle, I spied a very old crone watching us through eyes disguised as pinholes. The inspector followed my glance.

'That's the youngest one,' he said and slammed the door across.

Later, in the police mess at Kowloon City police station, I was presented with a tie awarded to officers who serve in the Kowloon Walled City precinct. It is a tasteful dark blue and made of silk. Embroidered upon it is the grimacing dragon's head above two characters – *jung lung*.

Laap Saap

I forget exactly in which year it happened but it must have been 1961 or '62. There was a bad squatter area fire, with thousands of shanty-dwellers made homeless, and the pupils of King George V School, Kowloon held a fund-raising drive to help with the relief. It was organised, I seem to recall, by a very pretty American girl in my year called Roxy Drysdale. The deputy headmaster was a delightful man called Alec Reeve who, in retrospect, must have been a flawed judge of character for he declared that if the pupils raised a certain (and to him improbable) sum, he would jump in the harbour. The inevitable, of course, happened. The ceiling of donations was exceeded and he and another master had to bite the bullet. Or, in this case, swallow the water.

With the whole school massed and cheering, the two masters leapt into the sea and swam from the Star Ferry to the Kowloon Public Pier. This, to my mind, was an act of bravery. The currents could be vicious, the harbour contained scavenging sharks and not far from the pier was a sewage outfall. Both masters, however, survived and honour was gained.

They would not do it now.

Depending on who one listens to, the population of Hong Kong ranges from between six to eight million: official figures hover around the former but large numbers commute from China daily to swell this assessment. So many people crowded into a land area of around 1100 square kilometres, much of which is mountain, means just one thing – pollution. Hong Kong is not in the same league as Calcutta or Mexico City and the air is not as foul as that of Los Angeles but it has a serious pollution problem which seems to have no effective remedy in sight.

In many respects Hong Kong, like much of the Orient, has always seemed dirty to foreigners. Hawking (that is, spitting) in the streets was commonplace until a decade or so ago and is not unknown now. Laundry hung out to dry on poles from tenements drips on passers-by as do air conditioners. A child peeing in the gutter is not frowned upon and nullahs are a part of the urban plan. It is the Chinese way to dump rubbish into the street, sometimes tossing it out of a window: walk in any town in China and you will see food discarded on the roadway where it is consumed by animals. This attitude, which I do not condemn for it is as much a cultural deviation as it is an anti-social one, is not pleasant: I have on more than one occasion over the years been showered with the remains of a rice bowl and was once narrowly missed by an entire fish carcass. Yet one should accept this: it is a part of the scene and, I would argue, considerably less disgusting than the splatters of drunks' vomit one finds on the pavements of London. The trouble is that Hong Kong streets do not have free-ranging dogs, hens and pigs as Chinese ones do and the nature of the pollutants has changed. In other words, old-fashioned garbage disappeared in natural ways but modern trash does not, as language now has it, bio–degrade.

There was a time in my childhood in the fifties when Tsuen Wan was a small industrial town through the centre of which ran a river fed by the slopes of Hong Kong's highest mountain, Tai Mo Shan. Most of the factories in those days were involved in textiles, established by mill-owners or weavers and dyers who had fled from Communism with their machinery: in fact, Tsuen Wan was an industrial centre (of a sort) long before that. There had been rope- and sail-making shacks on the shore at the turn of the century alongside a small boatyard making sampans and small junks and, above the village near the hamlet of Chuen Lung, eight water-wheels well over a hundred years old pounded sandalwood chippings to dust with heavy hammers for use in the making of joss sticks.

Driving through Tsuen Wan, I used to hold my breath at a certain spot for the air held a strange and choking taint caused by a dyeing works. I have not encountered that smell anywhere else in the world. Yet the worst thing was the little river for, according to what the dyeing works was processing that day, it changed colour. Sometimes it was bright red or canary yellow. If one passed when the colours were being changed, the discharge gave the river a curiously marbled quality.

Today, Tsuen Wan is an industrial metropolis of high-rise factories, breakers' yards, container terminals, oil depots, shopping centres, workers' apartment towers and the main terminal yards for the Mass Transit Railway. It is no surprise therefore that, although the river no longer gruesomely rainbows into the sea, is it just as lifeless, slick with oil streaks, covered with a detritus of litter and grey with sewage. Nothing lives in it at all save bacteria.

Take a ferry ride anywhere in Hong Kong waters and you will see the most astonishingly comprehensive range of *laap saap*, the Cantonese for garbage. It comes from a wide variety of sources despite there being official action and legislation with high-falluting names – the Water Pollution Control Ordinance (WPCO) which sets up Water Control Zones (WCZs), the Dumping at Sea Act 1974 (Overseas Territories) Order 1975, the Waste Disposal (Chemical Waste) (General) Regulations and the Marine Disposal of Sludges Scheme.

Hong Kong harbour is so full of flotsam there have been special little craft invented to hoover it clean. These are the most bizzare-looking boats which seem to defy all principles of buoyancy and appear to be in a permanent state of near capsize. They are about the size of a small lorry, painted bright orange with a high cab like that of a crane and a sort of scoop affair on the front: one cannot refer to bow or stern for it is hard to tell which is which. They chug slowly through the harbour with ferries, hydrofoils, merchant ships, pilot boats, hovercraft, fishing junks and luxury powerboats sweeping past them, rocking them precariously with their wakes. Only sampans pose them no threat.

Examples of what they collect may be found at the tide-line on any beach. Early in 1993, I walked along a measured fifty paces of beach at Nim Shue Wan on Lantau Island, flotsam-spotting. It is not, I would hasten to add, a hobby of mine nor of anyone I know. My tally of objects observed is as follows: plastic and glass bottles, soft drink tins, bicycle tyres and wheels (separate), sun-dried turds (human and bovine), pellets of plastic or nylon and sections of expanded polystyrene packing, plastic off-cuts from shoe soles, rice straw, lengths of driftwood, a Kodak film box, gobs of oil and diesel fuel, dead fish, seaweed, a number of small anonymous bottles of injection material (the kind with little rubber stoppers for the hypodermic needle to go through), still sealed and unused but without their labels, flaccid condoms, light bulbs, an empty, bright yellow, chemical drum with no indication whatsoever of the erstwhile contents save for an ominous stencilled skull and crossbones, plastic bags, a split bamboo scaffolding pole, paper (news and toilet), bottle-tops and other picnic refuse (not flotsam, admittedly), lumps of cork, waxed paper cups, a denim stevedore's peaked hat, and a decomposing cormorant being desultorily picked at by a small crab which was the only living thing on the strand. At least I did not find what I once had seen floating in the harbour, by the Kowloon Star Ferry in 1954: that was my first dead human being, a man face down wearing a coolie's baggy blue trousers and a white vest, his skull cracked open like an egg and surrounded by a halo of tiny silver fish.

Despite the heaviest road traffic concentration in the world, not to mention the dense industrialisation, air pollution in Hong Kong is not as bad as might be expected. Most days, the sky is hazed, as it very rarely was prior to 1975, but the air does not catch at the throat as it does in Rome or Tokyo. What makes the air pollution most uncomfortable is the high humidity which comes with the summer months. Once again, there are more acronyms to protect the sky — the atmospheric equivalents of

WCZs (ACZs) and APCO (Air Pollution Control Ordinance) not to mention AQOs and the Air Pollution Control (Furnaces, Ovens and Chimneys) (Installation and Alteration) Regulations. Needless to say, these may carry the clout of the law but much of Hong Kong's air pollution blows in from the industrial Chinese hinterland where APCOs and ACZs are ungazetted and would be either ignored or become a good source of tea money or squeeze if they were.

Six million people also create a lot of domestic trash: to be exact, some 24,000 tonnes a day. This is dealt with in landfill sites, three vast rubbish dumps into which the garbage is dropped once it has been collected by trucks in the street, delivered to refuse transfer stations, compacted into containers and transported on to its final destination. As with all major cities the world over, these landfill sites are inevitably and inexorably filling up. Hong Kong's answer to this problem does lie in part in recycling: in 1991, the latest year for which figures have been published, Hong Kong exported 1.3 million tonnes of waste paper, metals and plastic, to a value of HK£2.3 billion whilst local reprocessing saw to half a million tonnes of paper, metal, plastic, used lubricating oil and glass. Some rubbish is incinerated. Yet despite this, more landfill sites are being created. One of these is called the West New Territories Landfill. It is a massive artificial valley, dammed with an earth wall, just a mile or two up the coast from Mr Cheng's fortified house. The new road which cuts across the mountain above his valley gives access to it. If he were not being evicted because of the deepwater quay, industrial complex and power station, I have a feeling he would be living next to a garbage dump meant to cope with the next twenty years' worth of Hong Kong's trash.

With so much industry, chemical waste is a pollution problem, too − all 120,000 tonnes a year of it − not to mention dust from factories, building sites and land reclamation projects, noise from almost incessant traffic and the ubiquitous construction site pile-drivers, the euphemistically-named 'livestock waste', landfill gas and car fumes.

Hong Kong does better than many cities in combating these hazards: it has the highest number of cars per capita running on unleaded petrol (must have an acronym here – ULP), the strictest smoke regulations in Asia bar Japan and the pollution laws have teeth. Fines are crippling, unavoidable noise is restricted to certain times of the day (but not halting the twenty-four-hour construction of skyscrapers – heavy irons beams and the like are moved through the streets only in the early hours) but this still means that unfortunate residents next to a building site can be woken by an hydraulic hammer at seven in the morning.

Of course, the main problem is sewage.

Vast treatment works deal with all they can but they are insufficient to cope with the capacity. Furthermore, a lot of places have either no sanitation at all – like the tens of thousands of squatter shacks – or are connected to a system which has either not been upgraded or is itself insufficient for the volume passing through it. Add to this the amount of filth that goes into rainwater gullies and storm-water drains and the result is an appalling mess.

When I was a child, the waters of Hong Kong were rich with marine life. Sharks cruised the harbour alongside multi-coloured Portuguese man-of-war jellyfish which could kill a child or a man with a weak heart, coral reefs – the most northerly in the world – existed off Lamma Island, fishing junks trawled between merchant vessels and warships at anchor, the sea was aquamarine in the sunlight and little boys caught crabs from the jetties in the typhoon shelters. Now, the sharks keep clear and the jellyfish are hit by pollution which dissolves them, the coral reefs are all but extinct due to pollution and heavy propeller disturbance, the fishing junks are reduced to half a dozen optimists and there are few crabs to be caught. The sea, even in the depth of winter with clear blue skies and a high sun, is at best dark blue and usually greyed.

How much sewage is produced every day is not published: the Hong Kong government is shy of promulgating any pollution sensitive figures for they are aware they are containing the problem, not eradicating it. What is more, the government is prone not only to inadequacies but also to downright stupidities on an almost monthly basis. One of the latest, most dramatic and certainly avoidable was caused by a newly completed area of reclaimed land which may be a boon to industrialists, exporters and property developers but has had dire environmental consequences.

Stonecutters Island, in Hong Kong's western harbour, has been a closed military base for over a century. As such, it has avoided urbanisation and disturbance, the waters around it famous for their blueness in the middle of the otherwise leaden harbour. Despite the proximity of Kowloon less than a mile away, the island is home to kingfishers, egrets and herons and houses the biggest black-eared kite community in the world. All these birds depend upon the island's peace for breeding and the surrounding waters for food.

On 11 August 1992, Stonecutters was joined to the mainland by the North West Kowloon reclamation: eleven days later, the north shore of the island was inches deep in dead marine life. Mullet, bass, grouper, trigger-fish and bottom-dwelling crabs had all shared the same indiscriminate fate: the sea floor was also littered with countless dead fish, crustaceans and shellfish. None of the creatures showed any signs of physical damage and it was established the water was almost completely anoxic. Sewage, trapped by the new landlock and abetted by neap tides, had emptied the water of oxygen.

Despite warnings from Hong Kong's Environmental Protection Department (EPD – another acronym), a predicted catastrophe had occurred. Once Stonecutters was de-islanded, the tides could no longer flush its waters clean. Flush is an appropriate verb for this section of the harbour is especially polluted by sewage, not to mention industrial effluent: every day, 288,000 *tonnes* of raw sewage were being pumped out close to the island. Until the reclamation closed the channel, this was swept out to sea and diluted.

The disaster was totally avoidable: to coincide with the reclamation was the construction of a sewage treatment works to deal with 70 per cent of the daily filth but this was still five weeks away from coming on line when the reclamation was finished. The Secretary of Works was aware of the mis-timing but the infill was completed before the treatment plant 'because of tight schedules'. The reclamation is to be a new container terminal and could not be delayed. In Hong Kong, money talks louder than mullet.

The EPD, which is an advisory body with no legal teeth, issues Environmental Impact Assessments (EIAs) for all major developments but these are regarded by the government as ignorable formalities, regardless of the high profile 'green' credentials of the Governor, Chris Patten, who has declared a war on pollution. Public environmental concerns are blatantly disregarded if they are deemed to be too expensive or reduce the operational effectiveness or time schedules of a project.

Hong Kong's name means Incense (or Fragrant) Harbour. In actual fact, it probably never referred to the quality of the sea in the modern harbour but to the area around Aberdeen, named after Lord Aberdeen who was the British Foreign Secretary in 1844 and has the name Heung Kong in Cantonese. Around this one-time fishing village, now a major industrial and residential city on the southern shore of Hong Kong island, the slopes of the island of Ap Lei Chau and the valleys between Aberdeen and Shouson Hill were covered in perfumed *kuan heung* or sandalwood trees. These were dried, pounded into powder and made into joss sticks. Indeed, before Hong Kong island gained its present name, it was known as Hung Heung Lo Shan – or Red Incense Burner Mountain. These days Aberdeen and Hong Kong harbours have a less than fragrant perfume.

Some good may come of the Stonecutters Island calamity. The military are due to leave the island and pressure is being put on the Hong Kong government to ratify a five-year-old demand that Stonecutters be gazetted a bird sanctuary and declared an area of specific scientific interest – it is rumoured to have a unique snake population – but this begs two questions. How many kingfishers will want to have Container Terminal No. 8 as their nearest neighbour? And who will give a damn after 1997?

Pirate's Cave, Shark's Mouth

'No need for you to take a ferry to find a pirate,' a Chinese friend told me: he pronounced it *py-wrat*. 'Maybe once, if you take a ferry to the islands, a pirate would find you. But today – why go to Cheung Chau? Plenty of pirates here in Central.' He gazed upwards at the forty-eight storey silvered glass oblong of 1 Exchange Square. 'You want to see pirates, go to the Stock Exchange.'

He chortled quietly at his own joke but I detected an inkling of personal chagrin in his humour, appreciating as I did the irony of his comment: he had, I knew, lost over HK$25,000 on the market – and over $40,000 at the races – all within the space of three days.

'The pirate I'm going after is dead. Long ago. More than one hundred years.'

'Best for a pirate. Dead. Good pirates are dead pirates.'

He glanced briefly, and with a hint of longing, past the Henry Moore bronze statue and into the mirrored doors of the main lobby to the skyscraper.

'But good day for you. Sea calm, sun not too hot. If you want to eat on the island, go to the food stalls near the fire station. Best noodles in all Hong Kong. Very good seafood.'

I walked against the current of early morning office workers, smartly dressed shop assistants and secretaries in tight skirts teetering on high heels which increased their average height to just below that of my shoulders, office managers and clerks in grey lightweight tropical suits with a briefcase and a mobile phone both held by the same hand, messenger boys in shirts and jeans, building labourers in dusty shorts and stained vests with hats of folded newspaper on their heads, shaped like origami boats. They were all coming from the Outlying Islands ferry pier. I was hurrying towards it.

The pier is a concrete and iron jigsaw, the floors stained with rust and the green paint of the iron meshing which contains all the queuing lines. I paid HK$6 at the window for a one-way ticket to Cheung Chau and passed through the ancient turnstile, the steel prongs polished by decades of thighs and children's hands.

There were hardly three dozen passengers waiting for the ferry. Five were old crones in black, traditional smocks and baggy trousers, their grey hair cut short and severely scraped back as if greased. They clucked together like broody hens, nodding at each other and cackling. A couple in their twenties held hands over a red, white and blue plastic shopping bag of gargantuan proportions. They did not smile or coo at each other like lovers but sat forlornly staring at their bag. The man, shock-headed and with a prominent Adam's apple which bobbed up and down as he swallowed, wore a black mourning arm band.

Just as the metal gate clanged open to allow boarding, a party of six-year-old school-children arrived followed by two coolies carrying funeral goods on poles slung over their shoulders.

Every child wore a school uniform of tartan trousers or skirt, a white shirt, a tartan bow, white socks and brown shoes. Each carried a miniature haversack several of which had working electric clocks the size of dinner plates sewn into them. The children chattered and giggled but stayed in a row, controlled by two schoolmistresses: no matter where you are in the world, a school-teacher is unmistakable. These were both in their late twenties. One wore jeans and a blouse, the other a pair of slacks, a shirt and a gaudy pink anorak. They also wore harassed looks and did not speak to each other but fussed around their charges, reminding me of a rural Chinese duck farmer guiding his flock.

I let the other passengers embark ahead of me. The ferry was built for 600 passengers and we were not sixty.

The coolies with the funeral goods went on last. Their loads were bulky but light. I surreptitiously slipped my automatic camera from my pocket and took a frame of them from waist level, aiming by instinct. It would not be polite to be discovered photographing such items and the coolies would be suspicious. I wondered if they were on the way to the same funeral as the young couple.

When a Chinese dies, or on the anniversary of his death, offerings are burnt to send to the spirit in the after-world, to ease his life there and see he is all right. Whoever was to receive these goods would be a fortunate ghost. Made of coloured tissue paper stretched over a bamboo frame and doped to make it tight, much as model aircraft are constructed, there swung ahead of me down the gangway a substantial three-storey house about four feet tall, a brace of pagodas, a bicycle, a table and chairs and what was recognisably a Rolls-Royce. The predominant colour was red. The Roller was golden. Someone in heaven was going to achieve all the riches they had sought in life.

I settled into a seat on the air-conditioned top deck, put my camera bag on the formica table and, purchasing a polystyrene cup of dark jasmine tea, watched the waterfront of Western District slide by through the windows. The dumb-bell shaped island of Cheung Chau is ninety minutes' ferry ride from Central, via the island of Peng Chau.

Chau means island in Cantonese, *Cheung* means long. Originally, it was two islands but ancient currents 3,000 years ago joined them by a thin spit of mud and sand 200 metres wide. This isthmus, now covered by the main village on the island, has been settled for longer than Hong Kong itself, most of the time by fishermen or pirates, according to the season and the variety of catches to be landed or hijacked from the South China Sea.

Today, the island is a time capsule, three kilometres long and a kilometre across at its widest point. The pirates have gone for there is more to be made from fishing and in the workplaces and offices of Hong Kong. Yet Cheung Chau retains an air of the past. There are no motor vehicles on the island, save a red Land-Rover equipped as a fire tender, for there are no roads, only village streets and pathways up the two hills. There is electricity and telephones, TV aerials and bicycles, Coca Cola and Pepsi, yet there are also wooden hand-carts, rattan fish and chicken baskets, cane hats and wooden junks which might have been pirate vessels for some of them are over a hundred years old. Had they still been pirate vessels they would have been invincible – not one uses sail now but powerful Volvo and Honda diesel engines.

The ferry turned in a slowing arc of frothed wake and flotsam through the entrance in the protective breakwater to the typhoon shelter of Cheung Chau Wan. The fishing fleet was in, a wedged mass of several hundred wooden junks packed against the *praya*, or quay. Sampans with sputtering motors scuttled like water beetles between vessels at anchor and the shore, their hulls protected by old car tyres, their ribbed bat's-wing awnings made of tarred canvas or multi-coloured plastic sheeting. Every one was piloted by a woman in smock and trousers, every face sea-tanned and salt-roughened. A grey police gunboat lay alongside the ferry pier, its deck cannon covered by a tarpaulin sheath.

I was the only European on the *praya*. Tourists do not often come to Cheung Chau: it is too far from the luxury hotels, the camera stores and jewellers' shops, the tailors and the restaurants. It exists in few of the guide books except as a mention. And the Westerners who live on the island and commute daily by ferry (or private company launch) to Hong Kong were far away in their air-conditioned offices.

It being mid-week, there were no picnic parties of laughing Chinese youths laden down with food hampers, cameras and transistor radios, no expatriates visiting resident friends, no luxury cruisers wallowing at anchor off the shore, no water-skiers ripping the sea apart. This was a working day.

The night's catch was unloaded and on offer along the *praya*. At the stern of every junk, neatly reversed against the quayside like a car into a parking lot, was a lean-to stall with the fish for sale swimming in seething masses in trays and buckets, fed with running sea-water from hoses snaking onto the vessels. Red mullet hung in some of the trays, their fins winging slowly like a punkah-wallah's fan. They were like fish already butchered, their colouring so scarlet and raw. Wrasse, dressed in their bizarre pyjama colours of canary yellow and jade stripes, were thrashing in a wooden bucket. In shallow trays, semi-translucent shrimps scuttled and scrabbled over each other, their feelers waving and the organ-stops of their eyes curiously pathetic. Emerald and azure crabs, their claws bound tightly by bamboo twine, snapped and blew complaining bubbles in a blue plastic crate.

On the quayside was also landed a shark. It was about five feet long and was the only creature not still alive. It was torpedo grey with a stiff fin and slits in its sides like the jet outlet cowlings on a fighter aircraft. Its eyes were sunken into the sockets, not by death but by design. Out of curiosity, I touched the fin: it was as hard as tyre rubber.

The owner, protective of his prize and assuming me to be a tourist for I was slung about by a camera bag, muttered, 'No touch! No touch.'

'*Nee doh ah. Gay do cheen?*' I asked.

The fisherman gave me a surprised stare and held up his hand, five fingers spread.

'*Ng baht mun!*'

Five hundred dollars: it was a fair price, I guessed, for the shark's fin. I asked him if I could have one or two of the creature's teeth. He laughed and said I could if I bothered to get them for myself.

I knelt on the flagstones, warm from the sun, put my camera bag down, rolled my short sleeve into my armpit and pushed my hand under the beast's snout, sliding my palm along between the cool, rough flesh of the snout and the damp stones of the quay. I had to burrow the length of my forearm before my fingers met the mouth. Inevitably, a small knot of spectators gathered to see the unusual sight of a *gweilo* on his hands and knees fumbling in the maw of what I was by now hoping was a very dead shark.

Sharks have renewable teeth. The snatch-grab-and-twist manner of their feeding causes teeth to break off, so behind the front row of undifferentiated teeth are ranks of others which move forward as those on the leading edge are lost. Quite often, one or two of the teeth in use are ready to snap free and it was a few of these I wanted.

The top jaw usually carries the bigger teeth, and as the shark is a streamlined animal, the lower jaw is aft of the other. Once I had my arm inserted under the head, I had to twist it to reach upwards. To achieve this manoeuvre, I had to lie down. The now quite substantial crowd moved back to give me room and fell silent, assuming the moment had come for me to either do a Jonah and disappear into the beast or for it to come to life and consume my forearm.

My face was level with the shark's. Its eye was like a steel ballbearing, glazed by contact with the air, a primitive invention of a time before gods created love, hate and merriment. My fingers pressed through the slit of cold lips and I felt the first needle-sharp teeth.

The owner of the shark was finding all this activity a boon to his business. The crowd were not only watching the spectacle but also eyeing his other, less deceased catch. From ground level, I saw him selling half a catty of prawns to a woman in a white blouse with a baby strapped upon her back in an embroidered cotton sling. The infant was gazing at me with eyes as expressive as those of the shark.

I found a loose tooth, pressed my finger against it and pushed. It budged. The shark gave a spasm. Its snout lifted an inch off the pavement and fell back again. A few of the crowd, standing close by, stepped smartly backwards. I let out a reflex grunt – in retrospect, it might have been a strangled scream – and immediately broke into a cold sweat. The crowd, however, roared with laughter.

The fisherman, in order to enliven what he now saw as a brilliantly conceived sales pitch, had stood upon the shark's tail and kicked down on it, lifting the head. I glanced along the lead-grey flank of the creature to see his foot, in a pink and mauve plastic sandal, ready to kick again. The sweat on my neck heated up and I gave him what I hoped was a viciously reproving stare. He grinned widely and kicked once more to prove it was he who was alive and not the shark. The head raised and flopped back down. Three of the teeth jabbed painfully into the palm of my hand.

Animated conversation erupted. There was much speculation as to how long a shark could survive out of water, how strong their jaws were, what had happened to a certain Mr Fong who had fallen overboard from the ferry several months previously and why I was lying with my arm up the sharp end of a shark.

For a few minutes, I tugged and wrenched my way along the jaw then, satisfied, I stood up. Several of the crowd applauded but the rest were silent and bemused. Until now, they had had no idea what I was up to: perhaps the shark had attacked me whilst swimming and swallowed my watch was one explanation I overheard whilst lying prone in a sweat.

I held my finds out. My hand was oozing blood from the punctures, the teeth lying in a swelling maroon puddle in my palm.

'*Chi sin aah!*' I said loudly, and tapped my head with my free hand. The crowd, once more, broke into peals of laughter. Indeed, in their minds I was as mad as a hatter.

The fisherman rinsed my arm down with sea-water from a hose, the salt stinging the lacerations. I wondered if it was not better to stink of shark than to be cleansed by water from Cheung Chau harbour. He thanked me quite profusely for drawing the crowd so expertly. He had sold out of prawns and had only three crabs left. In turn, I thanked him for the teeth. He put his hand in his pocket and I thought he was going to offer me a part of his take – his money-pouch was bulging with coins. What he produced, however, was not a roll of dollar bills but a fistful of shark's teeth.

'Good for touris'!' he declared in pidgin English. 'You take some. No money.'

In one of the narrow streets, I found a traditional medicine-cum-pharmacy and purchased a roll of bandage. The shopkeeper obligingly strapped up my hand, first sprinkling a greenish powder over the wounds. To make the blood hard quick, he told me. The bandage was HK$2.50 and the few pinches of powder HK$27.80.

I had my trophies, though, and studied the teeth as I sat at a table outside a small tea-shop, sipping my second cup of the day. In all, I had retrieved four. Each was about an inch long, ivory white and shaped like the spear-head of a Chinese war-lord's ceremonial lance. They were very sharp at the point with the bladed sides serrated like a blunt saw. I could understand why they were once used as arrow-heads by pirates.

The coast of southern China has been ideal pirate waters for over a thousand years and well into the present century. Coastal traffic was massive even before the Europeans started to trade in the Orient. Fishing villages and the *yamen* of the local mandarins were ripe for raiding. The millions of islands, coves and little river estuaries gave safe hiding, fresh water, women and recruits.

The China Coast pirates were notorious ruthless killers. They not only sacked ships for their cargoes and wealth but set them to the torch, the crews battened below decks. These would have been lucky ones. Others would have been torn on the rack, trailed live behind the pirate craft as bait for sharks, marooned on waterless islands, cast adrift, mutilated and maimed and then set free as a warning to others not to resist. They were a scourge not only of the traders, but also the Imperial forces which were no match for them. China, despite its long coastline, has never been a maritime nation and has always lacked an effective navy. In short, the pirates were virtually invincible, the more efficient or merciless of the chiefs becoming in time important warlords in their own right.

Cheung Po-tsai was one of the most infamous. He frequently harboured his fleet in Sai Wan, the next bay south from Cheung Chau Wan on the western leeward facing side of the island which hooks around at its southernmost end. The stories of Cheung Po-tsai are legion and mostly legendary but that he existed is historically – if tenuously – recorded fact. His reigning years were, it is thought, the last decades of the eighteenth and beginning of the nineteenth centuries. He was so successful in his piracy the Emperor's forces could not outwit him. Instead, diplomatic discretion being deemed the better part of military valour, he was eventually offered an admiral's rank in the Imperial Navy and put in charge of the anti-piracy fleet which he commanded with equal efficacy against his former brethren-in-crime. In short, the buccaneer became the bailiff.

Like all larger-than-life men whose legends are confused, Cheung Po-tsai's are woven with what are probably the skeins of narrative about other pirate leaders. It was said he had a fleet of over one thousand war-junks equipped with cannon, his men numbering 10,000. It is claimed he could raise a sea-fog in which to waylay ships or through which to make his escape and could command dragons to fly over enemy vessels, setting them on fire.

The truth is he probably had a fleet of about a hundred sea-going vessels but could draw upon local minor pirates to join him in any big conquest. His followers probably never numbered over 2,000 at the very most. He apparently invented the art of laying a smoke-screen and firing buckets of fir cones soaked in burning pitch from a deck-mounted ballister. Rumour has it that he also had an English concubine with whom he lived in a sumptuously furnished cavern on Cheung Chau.

The story goes as follows: he raided and captured a British clipper bound for Yokohama, putting half of the crew to the sword but capturing the rest whom he intended to hold ransom in case of British reprisals. Amongst the clipper's complement was a young woman in passage to Japan where she was to be wed to a British official at the Japanese court. Being a gentleman, and not wanting to harm a woman, Cheung Po-tsai did not throw her into his dungeon with the crew but took her to his cave where she fell in love with him, bore him several children, befriended his Number One Wife and lived out her days on Cheung Chau. The crew were kept imprisoned for a year or two then set free aboard another British vessel. However, a number of the British tars decided piracy with Cheung Po-tsai was preferable to serving before the John Company mast so they too remained out east and became, in due course, wealthy taipans.

So much for mythology: and yet there is a lone grave on one of the uninhabited Soko Islands to the south-west of Cheung Chau which might give credence to this tale. It is overgrown and extremely difficult to find now – if, indeed, it has survived the ravages of time – but it is the final resting place of a European woman dating from the turn of the eighteenth century. On the other hand, Cheung Po-tsai's cave does exist. It is marked upon the Ordnance Survey map of Hong Kong.

I finished my tea, paid the waiter (who asked to see my shark's teeth: word had travelled fast) and set off through the village, heading south, passing little workshops making the metal frames of hand trolleys, repairing bicycles, assembling plastic flowers and manufacturing genuine American Indian bead jewellery for export to the souvenir shops of Arizona and New Mexico.

Cheung Chau, in recent years, has become a fashionable middle-class residential ghetto. I walked by building sites of compact luxury condos in the making, the fresh concrete facing as white as an alpine piste in the sunlight slamming down from directly overhead. Taking a stony path up a tree-covered hill, I passed a primary school from within which came the high-pitched chant of maths tables in Cantonese mingled with the discordant clang of a piano suffering from an existence in the humid tropics and incongruously playing *Tipperary*.

The path levelled out beyond a foul-stinking public lavatory decorated with the insignia of the Urban District Council, a stylised red chrysanthemum flower on an orange background. Walking was easier now. My camera bag seemed to weigh less, my wounded hand, which had throbbed as I climbed the hill, settled into a mild ache. I imagined this was caused by a billion bacteria, ecstatic at their release from the polluted waters of the harbour, replicating by the milli-second in my palm.

The path, now concreted, twisted through groves of thick

bamboo and fir trees of the variety often seen in classical Chinese paintings. Huge brown butterflies with yellow markings flitted ahead of me: birds called sorrowfully from the warm shadows or darted across the pathway. In the dry bamboo leaves, skinks rustled as they ran. These beautiful lizards grow to about thirty centimetres in length. They are sleek and polished, their backs dark khaki, their bellies pale yellow whilst down each side of their bodies is drawn a delicate golden line. They feed on cockroaches and flies, moths and butterflies, ants and grasshoppers, tasting the air for the proximity of prey with a thick black tongue like a cord of wet licorice.

At a narrow valley called Shui Hang, I came face to face with a chow dog sleeping on the steps leading down to an ancient gateway with a curled roof. It was badly in need of repainting, the plaster flaking away from the granite beneath and the writing – THE SHUI HANG ICE BLOCK FACTORY: estbl. 1922 – was faded almost to invisibility. In the lush trees behind huddled a filthy black godown of corrugated iron from which projected a steaming funnel. Into the centre of the gate arch had been mounted a circular concave mirror to reflect away evil spirits.

As I approached, the dog awoke, stood up and growled ominously. The ruff on its neck stood out like a lion's mane: it is arguable that the chow is the Lion Dog of ancient Chinese mythology. It is also infamous for its bloody-minded temperament. I pretended to ignore the animal and drew nearer. It increased its growling, lifting its upper lips in a grimace of anger.

There is a Chinese saying which, roughly translated, goes *He who hollers is a coward: he who whispers is wily and brave and would have your guts for garters.*

I stopped. The dog came forward, its curved tail erect and its ears flat as an irate leopard's. Its teeth were distinctly reminiscent of the shark's but not quite so clean. I stood my ground. To back up was unconscionable. I was damned if I was going to lose face to a Chinese dog. Besides, there was no other path to Cheung Po-tsai's cave. Perhaps, it occurred to me, this dog was a descendant of one of the pirate's hounds. He must have kept them if only for food in the winter months when braised or stewed dog is considered a delicacy.

The chow strutted a few steps further, growling even more ferociously: but I heard the music of a steel chain on stone. The dog was tethered to an iron ring set into the gateway. With courage borne of certainty, I set off again. The dog lunged at me but fell short, snapping at the air with foam-flecked lips. Still it did not bark.

At a junction with another path was an old cast-iron signpost. It had been painted cream with red lettering in both English and Chinese characters but it was now scabrous with rust. It read: *CAVE OF CHEUNG PO-TSAI ◊ 1 klm.* Below it was a newer sign of the sort used to direct traffic – *CHEUNG PO-TSAI ROAD.*

The round bay of Sai Wan contained a small fleet of sampans and the decrepit remains of a luxury launch. The houses on the edge of the beach were certainly over a century old and might well have been built by the pirates. A new jetty and breakwater stuck out into the bay but, that apart, the scene might have been untouched by modernity. Until, that is, the path reached the thin beach. On the sand was a derelict sampan, two definitely unseaworthy fibreglass ski-boats lying hull up and an agglomeration of filth including a drowned kitten, a very large decomposing eel of some sort, and some obviously human detritus. In the shallows was a submarine forest of plastic bags. Once more, my hand throbbed.

I hurried by, climbed the last hillock before the southern shore of the island and stopped at a brand-new pavilion. The roof was made of pristine green glazed tiles. The stone seats were clean and the trees hissed in a gentle breeze zephyring off the ocean. Beside a litter bin and two as yet unused public barbecue grills stood another signpost – *Cheung Po-Tsai Picnic Area. No littering.* Just as there are legends about famous men so are there those who would make currency from them. As there is a Benjamin Franklin Restaurant in Boston and a Bonnie Prince Charlie petrol station at the Kyle of Lochalsh, I see no reason why Cheung Po-tsai should be ignored.

I passed this place by and took to a narrow track through boulders on the crest of the hill. Soon, there were steps edged with bricks and mortar and, finally, a jumble of large rocks at the head of a steep stony slope into the sea which was utterly calm, just sucking at beds of kelp on the water's edge.

Under a red and white Hongkong Bank golfing umbrella squatted an old hag. She was wizened and her feet clearly bound, making her at least seventy years old, a veritable age for a Chinese. She was eating rice and boiled fish out of a lunch pail with a plastic Chinese spoon. Upon spying me, she rapidly abandoned her repast and struggled to her feet. She muttered something I did not understand and pointed to some calligraphy crudely painted upon the rocks. (Whilst I can speak some Cantonese, reading it is quite beyond me: I can recognise Ladies, Gents and Exit, and the numbers up to ten but other than that, I am at a loss.)

I smiled and went to pass her by. At this point, an unspoken international language took over. She held her hand out and said, quite clearly, 'Sa'am mun...'

Not wanting to appear churlish and assuming her to be a well-heeled beggar – the lunch pail was a new one with insulated sides – I gave her the three dollars she demanded. At this, she beckoned me towards a slit in the rocks and, from a bag on the ground beside it, handed me a battered silver aluminium torch, considerately switching it on in case I was ignorant of the technicalities of such a modern marvel.

I left her with my camera bag and eased myself in through the slot, dropping into a hollow under the boulders. Underfoot was sand littered with a broken bottle, two Coke cans and a nondescript piece of plastic. I followed a sort of passageway through the boulders. Most of the time, the torch was redundant for daylight seeped in through the many cracks between the stones overhead.

I found no cave, just a series of small sandy openings similarly littered. In the farthest, half buried in the sand, was a pair of knickers. I clambered up a slippery chimney, arriving just behind the old woman who had returned to her luncheon.

My cameras were safe. I returned the torch, switching it off. The old dear took it and grinned at me, almost mischievously. It occurred to me then that she had never been into the cave. I wondered if she considered herself as the guardian of a palatial subterranean boudoir decked out in fine silks, hung with tapestries and provisioned by sweetmeats beyond the dreams of a starving man.

Such – again – is the stuff of legend.

Walking back to the ferry pier, I thought of the fate of the British seamen who were probably the only long-term occupants of those crannies in the rocks. And of the lovers who used it now, unaware of the anxiety and long months of boredom the prisoners must have suffered.

Back at the *praya*, the fisherman welcomed me with a broad grin. The shark was gone: I was informed it had been sold off to a restaurateur from Hong Kong. For HK$780, including the fin. The fisherman now had a bucket of octopuses. Would I like to see one? I said I would. He plunged his hand into the bucket and brought out a drab sandy brown octopus with a leg-span of about thirty centimetres. He held it out to me and its tentacles snagged on my flesh, suckering its globular head in to my arm. Water dripped down to soak the bandage. Once anchored, the octopus did not move. Several of my previous audience gathered round in the hope of a repeat show but the ferry was in and due to leave. I purchased the octopus for HK$12 and the fisherman jerked it from my arm, the suckers leaving marks on my skin like ordered ringworm. He placed the creature in a polythene bag half-filled with water from the hose and tied a knot in the plastic. The thumbs-up sign which followed indicated that he hoped I would enjoy my seafood supper: it is possible on Cheung Chau to buy fresh fish and take them to a restaurant to have them cooked.

Halfway back to Hong Kong, I tore the bag open and let the octopus go over the side of the ferry. It hit the water and was gone. I put the plastic bag in the litter bin on the open deck but, just before entering Hong Kong harbour, I saw it blow out and whisk away towards the waves.

'You find a pirate?' my friend asked me as he joined me for lunch the next day.

'I found the cave.'

'What did you do to your hand?'

'A shark bit it.'

He made no comment for a moment.

'But it's all right. I saw Dr Vio. No infection. A herbalist put something on the cuts in Cheung Chau and that did the trick, it seems.'

'Good!' he exclaimed then, after calling the *dim sum* girl over to our table, added, 'Next time you want see shark, no need go to Cheung Chau. Better go to Sai Kung. Good shark fishermen there.'

At the next table, a mobile phone chirruped. A young Chinese executive put it to his ear and there was a brief conversation involving a series of high denomination numbers.

'Or maybe,' he said thoughtfully as the girl put two steaming wicker baskets on our table, 'you just stay in Central. Plenty of shark in Central. You want see shark, go to the Stock Exchange.'

Hing Loon

'Hello, my ol' frien'! How are you?'

This is the exact greeting I always receive on entering Joseph's shop. It is invariably followed up by, 'You wan' a beer? Orange? Coke?'

'I'll have a Coke,' is my usual response as I sit on one of the low, red stools in front of a glass case, the heavy safe on my right and the rest of the shop to my left.

'How your wife? Your son? He mus' be a big boy now. How your daughter?' He thinks for a minute. 'Alexander an' Emma. You wife Helen.'

'They are well. And send their regards.'

'Good! Good!' He pours the Coke into a glass. 'How long you come to Hong Kong this time? Maybe you should stay for a long time now. Come home for a long time. And you mus' buy something for your wife. Present for her. You cannot go back to her without a present. She will be very angry.'

At this, I laugh and Joseph grins. It might be his usual sales pitch but he knows it does not work on me. I do not enter his shop just to buy a gift – although I always purchase something from him. I come in here to be with an old, old friend and wallow, just for half an hour, in an atmosphere of sentimentality, nostalgia and, frankly, love.

There are three places which linger in my mind from childhood, the memory razor sharp and exceptionally detailed. The first is the mess in the NAAFI officers' club on Chatham Road. Situated in a row of arched Nissen huts, it was squeezed into a narrow strip of land between the road and the marshalling sidings of the Kowloon–Canton Railway. The tables were made of woven cane with glass tops, the chairs of a similar construction but with thin cushions upon them contained in flowered print material which matched the curtains and with comfortable curved back and arms. The mess-boys were young Chinese in white *sam*s and black *fu*s who always wore felt slippers in which they glided silently over the polished linoleum tiles of the floor. It was there I was first introduced to a pleasant addiction I have had ever since – the taste of Coca Cola. Served in a green glass bottle with fluted sides, a waxed paper straw protruding from the top, it was both sweet and tart, the ideal cooler for a child in the tropics. Sipping on the straw to make it last, the steam engines trundling by on the other side of a small but sparse military flower-bed of marigolds and salvias, is a memory I have never lost.

The second place is a cake-shop-cum-tea house called Tchenko's – although I may have the spelling wrong. Long since vanished, it was to be found on Middle Road, between Ashley Road and Hankow Road, and was owned by a White Russian family which had, I presume, fled the Bolshevik uprising and arrived in Hong Kong by way of Harbin, Wei Hai Wei and Shanghai, moved on over the decades by successive wars or civil rebellions. The interior of the cake-shop was like a cross between a Viennese café and a Chinese tea-house. There were a few tables set up with a counter to one side filled with the most exquisite confectioneries imaginable: cakes in chocolate the shape of butterflies, banana buns and profiteroles, éclairs which oozed cream and coffee gateaux. How these remained in such condition in those days before the invention of air conditioners is a marvel. The counter, I suppose, must have been chilled but the sun still shone through the tall, narrow doors and in summer the temperature was seldom below 30°C in the shade. Wooden ceiling fans like the propellers of First World War aircraft, with gleaming brass bosses and varnished blades, stirred the hot air and shimmied a potted palm in one corner. The chairs were upright in the style of traditional Chinese furniture, just as formally uncomfortable and made of dark-stained rosewood with rattan seats. Coca Cola was not served here, only a variety of teas served in thin, bone china cups. The cakes were baked sins, so rich and wicked were they – or so my mother claimed; yet she never spurned one.

The third place was just around the corner and up Hankow Road, on the right. That was the premises of Hing Loon Curio and Jewellery Company. The proprietor was Mr Chan, Joseph's father.

When I first entered the shop in the summer of 1952, it was a substantial establishment with two wide shop windows crammed to bursting with curios of the sort for which the Orient was famous. My mother had entered the shop with me in her wake. It was, I recall, summer for the weather was baking and I was wearing my Kowloon Junior School uniform, my shirt sticking to my back with sweat and the backs of my knees itching with prickly heat. Whilst my mother inspected brooches or bracelets, I was placed upon a stool and told to wait. After some time, I became increasingly agitated, partly from boredom and partly because of the itching which was exacerbated by the stool. Suddenly, I found myself being addressed by Mr Chan.

I do not recall his exact words but he offered me a drink, enquired after the year and month in which I was born and gave me an ivory carving of a monkey and an ivory crucifix on a chain of beads carved into little balls of flowers. The monkey, he stated, was my birth animal. As I didn't understand, he explained how each year in the Chinese calendar is dedicated to an animal on a cycle of twelve. Mine was a monkey. I treasured the monkey for years, but lost it in the many moves of house a colonial family was obliged to make: the cross and beads I have to this day, a reminder of Mr Chan's generosity.

Mr Chan died two days after Christmas 1990 at the age of eighty-three – or eighty-four, as he would have had it, for the Chinese consider themselves to be one year old when born.

He had opened the shop on 1 February 1935 at 30 Hankow Road in Tsim Sha Tsui. The building was not new, the front arcaded with the pavement running along behind colonnades: most of the shopping areas of Hong Kong were so constructed for the arcading allowed relief from the sun, gave cover from the tropical rains of summer and provided a roof for street traders. With the shop came living accommodation into which Mr Chan and his wife moved and it was here that she gave birth to their two sons. The first, Henry was born in October 1939, the second Joseph in November 1940.

From the start, the shop was a curio, furniture and jewellery emporium. It was skilfully sited only a few hundred metres from Kowloon Docks, two hundred from the southern boundary of Whitfield Barracks, the main army base in Kowloon and only a few minutes' walk from the Peninsula Hotel, opened just six years earlier and already a mecca for film stars, tycoons and a new breed of human – the tourist – which slightly increased in numbers in 1936 with the opening of an air route to London. It was also a time when Tsim Sha Tsui began to turn its trading attention towards the tourist rather than the resident, a state of affairs that exists to the present day.

The business was only six years old when the Japanese invaded Hong Kong. Tsim Sha Tsui, being on the tip of the Kowloon peninsula, saw a good deal of gunfire but much of this was directed towards the British holding out on the island and there was comparatively little damage done to Kowloon. Tsim Sha Tsui also avoided the street fighting that took place in Kowloon Tong, Mong Kok and Kowloon City.

Many Hong Kong Chinese were killed in the battle: no statistics were ever compiled of the numbers but a conservative estimate would put it at around 32,000 on the mainland with double that on the island. Many tens of thousands fled the colony in the twelve months after the Japanese takeover but Mr Chan decided to take his chances and remain. There was nothing for him to return to in China, no family who could support his own and, as many other local Chinese believed, he thought the Japanese could not last forever and that, eventually, the British would return and normality proceed.

Realising there would be little call for curios and camphorwood chests amongst the Japanese occupiers, Mr Chan hid all the prize items of his stock and the shop metamorphosed into a general store selling groceries, meat, tinned goods and confectionery.

Times were hard indeed: he had a wife and children to support whilst food was frequently very scarce and rationed. By 1943, a catty of *wong tong* (raw sugar) cost HK$30 (against a pre-war price of about ninety-five cents), rice became very scarce and, by the winter of 1944/45, meat was so scarce that the remaining population of Hong Kong was reduced to cooking and eating rats and, in parts of Kowloon, cannibalism of the dead was not unknown.

How Mr Chan maintained sufficient stock to keep in business is a matter for conjecture but he was almost certainly forced to buy it on the black market. With the currency devalued, a black market was unavoidable and operated by local pro-Japanese Triads and the Japanese themselves. Large stocks of Red Cross food were stockpiled by the occupying forces and gradually released onto the market, keeping prices high. Bartering was also widespread and it is likely Mr Chan used some of his stashed jewellery and jade to purchase provisions from fishermen, New Territories farmers and the Japanese. As soon as Hong Kong was liberated, Hing Loon emerged from the ashes of war and groceries to become a curio, furniture and jewellery company once more.

To enter Hing Loon was like stepping back in time. The shop was piled to the ceiling with goods. Furniture made up the largest items, camphorwood chests carved with junks and mountains and dragons stood one on top of the other protected by squares of card, coffee and occasional tables balanced over chairs with the glass insets (protecting carved pictures) wrapped in corrugated paper and square rosewood chairs tottered on the top, their seats padded with square cushions covered in brocade.

Around the walls stood heavy, ancient glass-fronted cabinets. These were of Chinese design and came from the era when Chinese art copied Western and vice versa. The sides of the cabinets were carved (naturally with dragons and so on) whilst the shelves were jammed with all sorts of items – jade and porcelain opium lamps,

Ming and Tang bowls and vases, carved ivory animals and boats (and, out of sight at the back, in deference to propriety, copulating figures) with entire tusks carved into classical Chinese tableaux, cloisonné vases and paper-knives, soapstone and jade statues, rotund rosewood Buddhas and coolies with poles over their shoulders, filigree pictures cut out of cork and pottery statuettes of Kwan Yin. Along the top of the cupboards were arrayed lines of white porcelain lamp bases fashioned like cages with lights inside them, large wooden models of junks in full sail (with every detail faithfully copied – how I long today for one of those old models: they were superb!) and miniature camphorwood boxes, replicas of the huge ones, which were jewellery cases.

Where the walls were not covered by furniture or display cabinets, they were hung with hand-painted silk scrolls of sinuous ladies in flowing gowns, finches perched on bamboo fronds and boughs of plum or peach blossom, thick stencil-cut Chinese characters in brass (wall hangings or tea-pot stands) and wide brass trays.

The jewellery was kept in glass counters lining either side of the shop. Row upon row of rings, bracelets and pendants glittered in the bright light beaming down from cantilevered spotlamps or neon strips high above, beside the ceiling fans. Unmounted stones – topazes and aquamarines, rubies and garnets, zircons and diamonds, glistened like coloured eyes. Gold chains hung like molten larva from black velvet boards. Silver charms lay in ranks – fish that were hinged and wriggled in a life-like fashion when shaken, rickshaws and sampans, dragons and the character *sow*, meaning long life, minuscule Buddhas and all the animals of the Chinese calendar.

By the mid-fifties, Mr Chan was joined in the shop by his two sons who served behind the counter, learned the trade and, when the old man retired, stepped into his shoes. Yet Mr Chan never really left the business. Right up until his death, he sat in a little chair at the back entrance, squinting at a newspaper or dozing, dreaming of the old, hard, good times with, in the gloom behind him, a tiny red spark of light burning over the shrine in the back room. When he died, it was discovered he had retained a hoard of superb curios and jewellery which are now, bit by bit, appearing in the shop stock.

In 1963, Hing Loon moved for eight years to Lock Road, the next street over towards the main Kowloon thoroughfare of Nathan Road but, in 1971, it moved back again, this time to 44A Hankow Road, at the north end next to an alleyway notorious with locals for its junk curio stalls, silk tie vendors and kelter traffickers.

For over forty years and right up to her death, my mother stayed in touch with Joseph (Henry died tragically young in the eighties) and the shop has provided me with all my cufflinks and gold chains, brooches and pendants and rings for a succession of teenage girlfriends and, later on, my wife. But we are not the oldest client: he is Mr Ivan Hall of Salt Lake City, Utah. Once a purser on President Lines ships, he still purchases items by post.

Today, the shop is no longer on the street: Joseph lets the ground floor premises and has moved to the third floor. Although the shop is smaller, it is virtually unchanged from how it was in his father's day save that the company no longer deals in furniture (but can get it if required). The cabinets remain packed with goodies, the glass counters remain with their intrinsic strip light and, tucked into the hinges and joins, a history of the shop, of sorts . . .

Years ago, shop keepers used to collect tourists' or business-men's visiting cards and wedge them under the counter. Few continue to do this – but Joseph does. For all to see is a long line of past customers going back over a quarter of a century and coming from practically every country that has ever exported a tourist.

One can no longer saunter into the shop: it is protected, as many such businesses are now, with a strong steel door and a toughened glass window. Robbery is on the increase with so many Vietnamese refugees in Hong Kong and the border open with China.

'So what you going to buy this time?' Joseph asks as I sip my Coke.

'What have you got?' I ask, which is a moderately stupid question yet he knows what I am referring to – what he has that is either new stock of modern design, or antique or recently discovered in and released from Mr Chan's cache.

'Lots of things . . .'

He begins to produce packages wrapped in triangles of newspaper. These are the special items not displayed under the glass. We talk them over.

'Any of these copies of an order?' I enquire.

Joseph pretends to look hurt then grins broadly. 'Oh! You got a good memory!' he exclaims. 'You don't want to let me forget!'

This refers to a pendant I had Hing Loon make for a girlfriend called Judy in 1963. It consisted of a peardrop-shaped cage of gold bars containing a single loose pearl. When I visited the shop in 1985, after an absence of eighteen years – and, it must be said, was instantly recognised by both Joseph and Henry despite being accompanied by my nine-year-old son – I spotted an identical pendant at the back of a tray next to a pair of matching earrings. I bought them for my wife.

'That was my design,' I remonstrate. 'You should give me a cut of the profits. How many more you make over the years?'

I would not really want a royalty: I'm certain I've earned it over and over again across the years, in discounts on other purchases.

Deciding what to buy, I set it aside and we talk of the old days. I might be a Chinese shopkeeper from down the street save that I'm English and there are few other such long-standing companies left now.

'What will you do in 1997?' I enquire. 'Let your son take over?'

'My son will not take on the shop. I shall retire before 1997. In that year, the shop will close and I am going to emigrate with my wife to California. I shall try my best effort to carry on the shop as long as possible . . .'

And so, by 1997, Hing Loon will be no more. It will become

one of the many old-established firms Margaret Thatcher's government has sold down the river, displacing its proprietor and his family who saw through the war and the bad times afterwards, who have been staunchly and loyally pro-British for three generations and who helped, in their way, to rebuild Hong Kong into the power-house it is today. When Hing Loon (and all the other Hing Loons) are shut down, then that will be the end of the real Hong Kong.

Of Double Quinellas
and Multiple Tierces

The Chinese are a race of inveterate gamblers. Why this is so is the subject of much conjecture but the preoccupation may have its roots in the early discovery of mathematics, the understanding of statistics or probabilities and the arithmetic of chance. Games of chance are legion and any activity which may be governed by probability is regarded as a potential source of gambling for everyone from the menial coolie to the multi-millionaire.

Every day in the parks of Hong Kong groups of elderly folk can be found playing Chinese chess, *tien kow*, 'money cards' (the tenth century forerunner of royal playing cards), *kap tai shap*, *tiu yu*, *sap tim pun* ('half past ten') or *wei ch'i* (known in English as Go). No money is seen to change hands as gambling in a public place is illegal but be assured no game is solely for fun. Every street has a mah-jong game in progress somewhere in a tenement or mah-jong school. Children toss coins or play scissors–paper–stone and coolies play *fan tan* with a bag of pebbles. Chinese blood sports range from cricket-fighting through cock-, dog- and cat- to horse-fighting. Yet for the Hong Kong Chinese, horses are not for fighting. They are for racing.

On the first Sunday of November 1637, Peter Mundy reported that he attended the races held on an artificially levelled square before the church of Sao Domingos in Macau. The races were attended by the Portuguese *cavalleros*, each having their personal 'Negroes or Caphirs, Cladd in Dammaske' by their side: the

224

site is today marked by the Rua dos Cavaleiros. It was the most incongruous of race meetings. The horses were bred in Mongolia and none was bigger than twelve and a half hands. No Chinese attended. It was the first horse race to be recorded in the Orient.

The history of horse racing in China is a history of the foreign presence and the opening up to the world of the Orient. Wherever Europeans held trading franchises, wherever there was a trading post or legation, customs station or treaty port, there was a racecourse. From Canton in the south to Chungking in Szechuan province to the west and Newchwang north of Korea, horses raced. Fierce rivalries grew between the trading houses (the *hongs* or 'noble houses'), expatriates, nations and racecourses, the rivalries based not upon trade, jingoistic pride and profit but upon the value, efficacy and standard of the ponies.

Inevitably, racing threw up its characters – men and women of fortitude, determination and skulduggery. Dr William and Sir Robert Jardine, Sir Victor Sassoon, Raymond Toeg, Frans August Larson, the 'Duke of Mongolia', Sir Hormusjee Mody and Sir Ellis Kadoorie – these were names of the China Races. They established rival cups and trophies, went to extraordinary lengths and risk to buy horses from Mongolia, transported mounts across China by special train, ship or river steamer. They braved the Taiping Rebellion, the Boxer Rising and the civil wars of the early twentieth century to get their horses to the next race. The first anti-foreign action of the Boxer Rising was the burning of the grandstand at Peking racecourse: the foreigners incarcerated in the Foreign Legation in Peking during the famous siege were obliged (finally) to eat some of their racehorses but only after the supply of pet dogs and cats had been expended: a race meeting in Shanghai took place whilst, at the very gates to the course in Bubbling Well Road, public executions of socialists and Communists were being carried out with swords and axes.

The racecourses were as unusual as their founders, the strangest in the world. Shanghai was reclaimed from marshland and paddy; the Happy Valley racecourse in Hong Kong was built upon a malarial swamp with the express permission of the Colonial Office (who were misled about the plans); Tientsin was dirt tracked because, in northern China, it was next to impossible to grow grass – races there were held up by sand- and dust-storms; Chungking racecourse was built on a boulder and mud island in the centre of the Yangtse which disappeared every rainy season and was rebuilt for each meeting. Villages were re-settled, clan graveyards flattened, sacred hills levelled and diplomatic incidents caused by the siting of courses. Yet they went ahead.

As much as the races threw up remarkable humans and venues, so did they ponies, some of the most fleet, superb animals that ever raced – Tetoy, Teen Kwong, Black Satin, Blackberry and Bengal. In the annals of horse racing, these animals must be unique for they raced supremely well and were champions of international stamina and standard yet they were never bred from, never turned to stud. All were flat racing mounts: steeple-chasing was never popular in China because the Chinese did not take to it. They found it highly amusing when the jockeys fell off, much to the consternation and annoyance of the foreigners who did not like to lose face. In addition, they disliked the betting odds of steeple-chasing.

Needless to say, the introduction of horse racing brought about a new market in China – the horse fair. In Mongolia, horses were being bred for the Europeans, traded in Mongolia itself or in horse fairs in China, just over the Great Wall. Where horse markets were established, so was 'horse trading'. The currency of horse dealing was the Mexican silver dollar.

The China Races had, at one time, the richest stakes in the world – for the Shanghai St Leger. By 1926, the Shanghai race clubs (one European, one Chinese owned) were taking US$40,000,000 *per annum* in ticket sales alone. Horses changed hands for large sums of money. Entire fortunes were gambled – and lost – at single meetings. The Chinese took to the new sport with gusto for, by the mid-nineteenth century, racing was not the exclusive domain of foreigners. At first, towards the end of the eighteenth century, Chinese attended the races to watch the Europeans eating – with knives and forks. This, it seems, was as much of a spectacle as the racing. Yet the meetings were also attended by mandarins and their retinues. Mandarins even presented cups. As time passed, more and more Chinese attended, were invited, became members of the jockey and race clubs, owned horses, raced them and trained them and provided their own jockeys. It is historically accurate to say that the Chinese first integrated into foreign society – or vice versa – through the auspices of horse racing.

Horse racing has been extinct in China, prohibited under Communism, for decades but under the 'new liberalisation' movement has recently begun again. In theory, betting is still prohibited which begs the question why the horses race at all: to race horses without odds is akin to knitting with noodles. Utterly pointless.

In Hong Kong, the sport has never ceased, save for the war, and continues through a nine month season with meetings twice weekly, usually one at Happy Valley and the other at Shatin, the most advanced racecourse in the world reclaimed from the sea in 1977. All racing is controlled by the Royal Hong Kong Jockey Club, abbreviated to RHKJC but referred to as the Jockey Club by all and sundry. It was inaugurated in 1884 and given a royal charter in 1960. It owns and operates both racecourses and over a hundred official off-course betting centres – bookmakers and freelance betting shops are illegal – in addition to maintaining 850 horses, new mounts imported at a rate of about 175 a year: all their grass and hay fodder is flown in daily from Australia and the USA. Trainers and jockeys are licensed and housed by the RHKJC, being paid a retainer plus prize money percentages. As well as racing, the RHKJC also operates a twice-weekly lottery on behalf of the Lotteries Board called the Mark Six where six numbers out of forty-five are selected by computer, all proceeds going to social welfare programmes: the annual turnover of the Mark Six exceeds HK$1,600 million whilst the betting turnover per annum on horses is well in excess of HK$45,000 million (or about £4,050 million). From this, the RHKJC takes about 7 per cent commission, the government between 9 and 16 per cent in tax: the remainder forms the dividend.

Although it is a limited company with no shareholders, the RHKJC does not hoard its profits. In the ten years from 1977, it spent HK$11,050 million on arts and cultural activities, handicapped and blind persons centres and training units, community facilities, schools and a university of science and technology (Hong Kong's third university), hospitals and youth programmes. Over the years it has also constructed Asia's largest seaquarium, built Victoria Park out of a swamp (a sweet irony considering the origins of the first racecourse), extensively funded cancer and heart disease research, founded hundreds of educational scholarships, paid for floating clinics for island communities and bankrolled the Hong Kong Academy for Performing Arts.

To go to the races in Hong Kong is unforgettable. I am not even an amateur punter and would never dream of going to Ascot or Aintree, never back the Grand National favourite with a flutter: yet I never refuse an opportunity to race in Hong Kong. It is one of life's most pleasant, self-indulgent, luxurious but simultaneously generous pastimes. Invariably, my hosts are Jane and Peter Binstead. Jane was at school with me, Peter a Hong Kong businessman and a Voting Member of the RHKJC. This affords him (and, by proxy, me) a perk I would amputate one of my minor limbs to own: a place in the Voting Members' box.

Happy Valley is synonymous with Hong Kong horse racing and it is here most of the history of the sport in the colony occurred: and most of the tragedy which is not restricted to heavy losses of dollars and reputations. The racecourse was the scene of the worst civil disaster to happen in the entire British Empire. In the early years, most punters watched the races not from the grandstand by the finish line but from a series of three-storey terraced matshed stands built of bamboo poles lashed together with rattan strips and covered in woven panels with wooden board floors erected at the north-western end of the track by the main gates. At the rear of these was an area where Chinese vendors set up sweetmeat and *dai pai dong* stalls whilst, under the stands or on the terraces, many Chinese played gambling games between the races.

On the sunny afternoon of 20 February 1918, the racecourse was crowded. Chinese New Year was close by and the multitudes included punters, their families and the entire staff of some of the smaller commercial companies who had given their employees a day at the races: the main race of the day was to be the hotly contested China Stakes. At 2:30, just as the bell rang to signal the start of Race 5, one the matshed stands began to collapse, dominoing into its neighbours. At least 5,000 people were sitting in them and the screams echoed across the course. Then the inevitable happened. One of the stands must have knocked over a *dai pai dong* stall and caught fire. Within twenty seconds, flames appeared. The fire raged for twenty-three minutes. Elegant Edwardian ladies pulled up their skirts and shredded their petticoats for bandages. Gentlemen stripped off their shirts and Chinese merchants and coolies alike joined together to rescue the trapped, many of whom were women and children of all races but predominantly Chinese. The trapped panicked and there was a stampede. Lt Col John Ward, present with members of his regiment, ordered a bugler to sound fall in, mustering his officers to assist. Every motor vehicle in Hong Kong was requisitioned to form a fleet of ambulances and arc lights were erected so rescue or recovery of the victims could continue into the night. In all, 604 were known to have perished with over 400 injured: the actual death toll was probably higher.

Today, huge banks of halogen lamps hang over the racecourse but not for such a macabre reason. Happy Valley is the spectacular setting for fortnightly evening racing, the horses running on a grass course surrounded by the tiered ranks of the windows of high-rise luxury apartment blocks, skyscrapers and colourful illuminated advertising hoardings. Atlas and moon moths, like languid nocturnal birds, flutter around the brilliant lamps, beetles circle like fast-flying miniature missiles and a myriad smaller insects glisten like stars in the sky.

Yet, for me, I prefer Shatin and an afternoon there with Jane and Peter is a wondrous interlude in life. We always meet at the Hong Kong Star Ferry where I get into their Volvo for the ride to the racecourse.

'Ready to lose some money?' is Jane's usual greeting, accompanied by a mischievous grin.

Peter is marginally more circumspect and terse for he has to chauffeur us through Wanchai, along the eastern corridor motorway, under the Eastern Harbour Crossing tunnel beneath Lei Yue Mun, through Yau Tong, Kwun Tong and the tunnel beneath Tate's Cairn then navigate round Shatin to the racecourse entrance negotiating along the way traffic lights which invisibly change, suicidal taxi drivers, traffic jams, *pak pai*s bent on self-destruction, articulated container lorries, air freight cargo vans, youths on high-powered motorcycles, speeding sports cars and sedate limos. Jazz or Sixties hits play on the stereo, to aid his concentration or encourage a what-the-hell bravado: the Volvo is ancient.

We arrive at the racecourse an hour before the first race. Crowds of punters are streaming in from the racecourse railway station. Uniformed guards watch over them, checking tickets and eagle-eyed for mobile telephones. The racecourse is the only place in Hong Kong free of their cheeping tones: a man with a mobile could report to any number of illegal bookies. Other hi-tech gadgets are permitted so some carry miniature pocket televisions or radios to listen to the coverage and others may have small, recondite racing odds computers like calculators.

The Volvo is left in the Voting Member's multi-storey car park beside red Ferraris and gold Rolls Royces (with gold-plated fittings), Aston Martin Lagondas and Lambourghinis, Mercedes Benz 500s and 8-series BMWs. The wealthy of Hong Kong are serious car owners. Entry to the private boxes, which are some twenty metres above the terraced stands, is by way of a modernistic covered footbridge, steel and mahogany panelled elevators and corridors of thick-piled carpets. Guards check passes by the footbridge. Even these have a certain style to them. Members' badges are not plastic cards as they might be in Britain but engraved, embossed and enamelled brass, a different design for each season, curiously manufactured by a company in Bombay: this, I was once told, obviates the risk of temptation by local factories from making extra runs of badges as they might designer dresses. The meeting badge for that day is a thick cardboard emblem printed and numbered on forgery-proof paper. Each must be prominently displayed in a button-hole.

At the door to the box, Jane sighs. Passing inside, the cares and worries of the playgroup she owns dissipate like joss stick smoke: for Peter, the world of commerce disappears and he steps suddenly just a little more lightly. These are reflexes of which I am certain they are unaware.

'Did you bring a pen?' Jane asks in a pedantic fashion, taking a slim Parker from her bag with two official programmes, handing me one.

I nod. That lesson was well learned years ago.

'And the racing pages of the *South China Morning Post*?'

I nod again and remove them from my pocket. She approvingly smiles her puckish smile once more.

Peter finds our table – for this is no ordinary box. It is more like a *very* expensive restaurant. Beautifully prepared tables for about 200 people line a room three deep. The rear wall is made of wood panelling hung with racing prints whilst the other wall is an expanse of sloping, grey-tinted, plate-glass windows giving onto the track. A few friends may join us to make a party of six. Drinks are served by waitresses in smart uniforms controlled by a *maître d'* and a few more senior waitresses. For a while we talk about the general affairs of life but, gradually, the conversation veers towards the day's mounts. A trainer friend of Peter's, David Oughton, drops by and has a quick drink followed by a personable young Australian with a deceptively quiet voice: less than a quarter of an hour later he is stridently announcing odds, riders and form over the public address system.

Then we eat. The meal is a buffet but with a difference. The Savoy could be shamed by what appears: platters of *sushi*, spiced baby octopuses, dish upon dish of ice ridden by New Zealand oysters flown in that day, patés and cold collations, a tub of Sevruga caviar, a square metre of smoked salmon, salads and vegetarian options. Decorative vegetables are intricately carved into dragons, fish, flowers and leaves but, surprisingly, never horses. There might even be an ice statue. To partake of this repast requires experience: on her first visit to the races, my wife piled up her plate not realising this table was just the *hors d'oeuvres.*

The other punters with whom we share this luxury are divided equally between Europeans and Chinese. Everyone is smartly dressed (except, perhaps, for a foreign visitor used to watching horses race with a plastic beer mug in his mitt) and discreet in the way of the very wealthy.

By the time the entrée is over (roast beef, duck, prawn curry, more vegetarian courses) and the dessert consumed (trifles laced with sherry, fresh tropical fruit salad with liqueur, mousses and other, less recognisable decadences), glasses refilled for the umpteenth time and coffee served, the first race is not far off.

Betting in Hong Kong is a complex affair, not just a matter of prophesying first past the post or place. It involves quinellas and trebles, tierces and double trios. The quinella names the first two horses in any order in a race of three or more and a double the winner in two nominated races; the treble predicts the winner in three nominated races whilst the tierce guesses at the first, second and third placed horses in their correct order in a race; the double quinella goes for the first and second past the post in either order in both of two nominated races. There is also the six-up and the double trio, the bonus and the consolation. The across-board minimum wager is just HK$10 (about £1).

'Well,' Jane remarks as she licks her chocolate mousse spoon for the last time, 'now for some serious business.'

She reaches across the table to a communal stack of betting tickets and begins to complete them for the first race. The win, progressive win and quinella odds, with the place investment and win dividend prediction appear on closed circuit television sets suspended from the ceiling. The whole odds and betting system is computerised and one marks the reverse of one's card by blocking in little boxes. This done, we go to a row of private desks to the rear of the box. Here, tellers in smart uniforms take our wagers and slip the tickets into a code reader: the computer registers our blocking and prints our details on the reverse of the ticket in English and computer bar-code.

The race is only a few minutes off so we go out to the tiered balcony before the box windows: the warm humidity of a sub-tropical afternoon strikes us as the door opens. The view is staggeringly spectacular. In the distance across the half-kilometre wide oval course rise the green wooded mountains of the Kowloon range with the hump-back peak of Ma On Shan off to the left. The foreground is a serrated wall of white skyscraper apartment blocks, the centre of the course containing an ornate park of walkways, lakes, fountains and tropical plants. In fact there are two concentric courses, the outer one lush with emerald turf like a priceless Tientsin rug and the inner a sand-coloured Equitrack. Directly in front of the grandstand complex, across the tracks, are two computerised tote indicator boards and a huge colour television screen, the largest in the world. Below on the terraces are the ordinary punters – twenty or thirty thousand of them. The noise is astounding: it is like standing over an infernal beehive.

The horses are already out on the course, milling around and being led into the starting gate by the *mafoos*, the Cantonese word for a syce or groom. Over the public address system comes a fanfare and they are off. The apine buzz of the crowd below increases. A running commentary in English comes out of the speakers and, on the TV screen, a picture of the race is broadcast with the numbers of the leading horses highlighted in coloured squares, updated by computer as the order changes. As the horses round the last bend before the home straight, the crowd begins to roar. The order numbers vanish from the screen.

It is at this moment, in the first race, I always steal a glance at my fellow Voting Member punters. Ranged along the balcony are millionaire Chinese businessmen accompanied by demure wives, expatriate bankers or stockbrokers with glamorous spouses, exquisite young women with handsome beaux and a smattering of the general glitterati of Hong Kong society. This is a moment of real humanity. The strictures of that society are fleetingly abandoned. The taipan in an Armani tailored suit is seen to be no more than the taxi-driver in a T-shirt. Just like the masses below, they shout and call, bellow encouragements (or threats) at their horses or stand in silent disbelief at the ineptitude of beast and jockey.

As the jockeys pass the finish post, rise in their saddles and allow their steeds to slow, the crowd drops its noise and the others on the balcony turn to go back to the air-conditioned box. This is the time to briefly study the tote board which illuminates the accumulated stake money on the race: a commonplace example of what might be seen is what I noted on my programme for the eighth race on 7 March 1993. The event was the Newbury Handicap: 1,200 metres with a total prize purse of HK$500,000, the winner taking HK$285,000. The field was of fourteen horses and the total sum bet on them was HK$179,688,270 – or about £17.4 million.

For the remainder of the afternoon, conversation at our table is muted. Drinks glasses are refilled almost without notice as we study form, keep our wagers secret and visit the tellers where winnings are assessed by computer and paid in cash or, in the case of very large sums, by cheque drawn on a Hong Kong bank. I am a modest backer of horses and have never won more than $1,000 on a race but I have seen an elderly Chinese gentleman with a gold pocket watch leave the desk with well over a $100,000 to his credit.

By the time the last race ends, the sun is lowering over the racecourse, the crowds in shade and the horses streaking for the post with their shadows winning half a length ahead of them. As soon as the results are ratified, hoards of people set off leaving the racecourse by the public gate: we leave by the member's entrance and join the queue of very pricey automobiles. Free of the racecourse we do not join the stream of Kowloon-bound traffic but drive north up the Tolo Highway, the motorway towards

China. Our destination is Beas River, the RHKJC country club near Fanling.

Situated next to the Fanling golf course, Beas River was one of the first places to be overrun by the invading Japanese on 8 December 1941. Across the valley now taken up with quiet rural rides and a taxing, fast cross-country course, bullets whizzed and mortars crumped. The nearby slopes of Fuk Tsuen Shan, or Fir Hill, contained slit trenches and an observation post manned by C Company of the 2/14 Punjabis but they were soon out-numbered: rusty bomb fins and shrapnel may still be found in the trees.

We drive in through an austere, grand gate arch almost as old as Hong Kong. In 1841, when the first land auction was held, the noble house of Jardine, Matheson & Co. built their Number One House on East Point, in what is today Causeway Bay. This was its gate, donated by Jardines to RHKJC and rebuilt, numbered piece by piece, here.

The clubhouse is cool and very uncolonial with horse-racing prints hanging on the panelled walls, cups and shields in glass cases and comfortable leather armchairs scattered about: only on looking out the window is one made aware that this is south China not Sussex. A Hakka woman in a broad-brimmed hat surrounded by black curtaining drapes tends the flower-beds and, by a pathway, there stands a huge fifteen-metre high tree frequently found as a pot plant in English doctors' surgeries or London office lobbies. Nearby are tennis courts, a dressage arena, a large swimming pool complex, ponds of fish and walks through trim gardens. Yet this is not just a luxurious country club for humans. It is also one for horses.

All RHKJC mounts are extremely pampered. When in the racing stables they have an indoor exercise swimming pool of their own, temperature-controlled loose-boxes and, it is said, the best veterinary equine hospital in the world. Yet when their racing days are over, they are not necessarily exported to stud, shipped off to France for the racks in butchers' shops or shot and given to the local foxhound kennels as they might be in Britain. Instead, they are pensioned off to Beas River where they become mounts for leisurely hacking, cross-country riding, dressage and riding instruction.

Their accommodation is the equine equivalent of Claridge's or the Waldorf Astoria. The two-storey stables are airy, light and air-conditioned or heated according to the weather. Fly-zapping ray lamps line the walls. The loose boxes are kept clean and the horses frequently groomed by trainee *mafoos*, club members or their children who are responsible for some of the liveried animals. Every loose box bears the occupant's name and lineage and, if necessary, a warning. The label on Club Whisper's box had a notice advising that he bites: he is a bay once operated by a syndicate including Peter amongst its owners and has lost me hundreds of dollars over his track career. Close by are octagonal rolling boxes, pens with six foot concrete walls filled with sand into which the horses go in turn to snort, charge round in a circle, whinny, neigh or roll and an indoor riding school with slowly gyrating ceiling fans and floodlights.

Before dinner, Peter occupied with club business, Jane and I walk through the grounds and down to the cross-country course. It is cool now, the sun setting and the paper-bark trees casting long lines across the grass. We always talk over our schooldays together, dredge up names half remembered and faces long forgotten. She speaks of her business and what they might do in retirement, asks after my family, my work, my latest book. Eventually, we turn by the dressage ring, walk past the stables and head back for the clubhouse, the last of the sunlight full in our eyes.

At length, Jane enquires, 'Had a good day?'

There is no need to answer this question: she knows I have.

'And how much have you won?' she goes on.

'How much have you won?' I demur.

'That would be telling!' she retorts, her puckish smile back again.

'I have lost $520,' I admit.

'Never mind,' she answers, touching my arm with mock sympathy. 'It'll pay for a hospital bed.'

By MTR to Poverty

The Mass Transit Railway is Hong Kong's Underground or Metro. Opened in 1979 as a fairly simple network, it has expanded so that, today, it operates on forty-three kilometres of track which reach virtually every urban sector of Kowloon and Hong Kong Island, additionally reaching out to Tsuen Wan in the New Territories. It runs trains every four minutes out of rush hour, every two minutes during it and carries well over two million passengers a day.

Riding the MTR must be the only reasonably pleasurable metro journey in the world. In rush hour, the trains are jam packed but not to the extent that one is crudely man-handled aboard as in Tokyo, jostled dangerously as in Paris or hustled as in New York. One may be elbowed but this is a commonplace in Hong Kong where, if British law and order has impinged itself, the art of queuing has not: it is best, in the circumstances, to elbow back. No one will mind. This is China.

What is so impressive about the MTR is its efficiency, cleanliness and space. Discreet signs warn of hefty penalties for eating, smoking, littering and flicking one's ticket with a fingernail. The stations are exceedingly spacious with all walls tiled and colour-coded so one can tell, as the train pulls in, which is which: not that this is necessarily essential for the train driver announces the next station as he leaves the last. This, however, requires a tuned-in ear for all the drivers seem to have attended the same school of pidgin pronunciation so that, after giving the information in Cantonese, he goes on to say something like, *'Nexstashnjawdung'* with a most un-oriental nasal twang. To the uninitiated tourist, this is gobbledegook. (It actually states 'Next station Jordan'.)

The ticketing system is entirely computerised. All tickets, be they for a single journey or stored value, are made of thin flexible plastic rather like a starved credit card. When received, the amount paid is recorded on the ferrous oxide reverse of the card. Once purchased, it is taken to the barrier and sucked through a slot, popping up for the passenger's retention. At journey's end, the ticket is placed into another barrier slot and either returned with the journey value deducted from the stored value, or retained by the machine for re-issue. This explains the curious fine for flicking tickets, a rule frequently heard pondered upon by tourists: a flicked ticket not only annoys but also risks being bent and therefore unrecyclable.

The trains are eight cars long and built in Britain: quite why a similar design has not been introduced on the London Underground beggars belief. Each train unit looks from the inside like one long, articulated carriage. There are no interconnecting doors so one can stand at one end and see right down to the other, over a hundred metres away: as the train moves along, rising or descending, turning tunnel corners, one can see the whole structure flexing. The minimal seating runs along the walls and is made of continuous stainless steel benches. The floors, walls and ceiling are made of the same metal or polished aluminium. Straps, bars and thin tubular pillars afford a hand-hold for at least 80 per cent of all passengers stand during their journey. Every train runs on schedule, its timing controlled by a central computer system and the fares are, for a subway system which is not state subsidised, the lowest in the world.

The MTR does have its faults, however. One is that, although the network has expanded considerably since its inception, the volume of passengers at rush hour has reached saturation point, a fact not publicly admitted but evident. And there are platform marshalls in natty day-glo yellow jackets but they are still not the strong-arm passenger loaders of Tokyo. Another worse error of judgement is that the designers, for some inconceivable stupidity, did not put a station at or even near the airport although they did link the system in to the Kowloon–Canton conventional railway network.

These criticisms apart, it is fair to say the MTR is as modern a means of urban travel as a Boeing 747-400 is of international travel. What are not so up-to-date or pristine are some of the destinations outside the stations.

Diamond Hill is the MTR stop a kilometre due north of the airport at the foot of the Kowloon hills. Twenty years ago, it was a barren series of foothills in the centre of which was a quarry from which, once a day, the dull thump of high explosives could be heard echoing off the rock faces. Since then, it has developed somewhat but not in the fashion of the rest of Hong Kong. Whilst roads and factories, high-rise apartment blocks and skyscraper banks have evolved, Diamond Hill has remained like a monument to the past for it is still a squatter area.

Coming out of the MTR exit to the north of the station is to experience what tourists refer to as culture shock. Not three metres from the colour-coded walls, swept steps and steel handrail is Tai Hom village.

Squatters, along with the utterly homeless, are an integral part of Hong Kong and its history. There has not been sufficient permanent housing for the entire population since the thirties. When the Sino–Japanese War started to impinge itself upon Kwangtung province, thousands fled their farms and villages and made for Hong Kong to escape the same fate as the populations of Nanking and Shanghai – the carpet bombing of residential areas, the bayoneting of civilians and the worse threats of disease and starvation. By the end of 1938, the population of Hong Kong had increased by almost a million over what it had been a decade before and, of these, half a million were estimated to be street-sleepers.

I have vivid memories of this sub-class of the truly unlucky. As a child living between Mong Kok and Ho Man Tin in Kowloon in the early fifties, I came upon them every day. They nestled in alleyways, under staircases, close to the railway embankment. Every nook and cranny was a potential home, every box a possible shelter. Nothing was ignored which could be pressed into service.

One family – for the street-sleepers were not necessarily single folk – had staked their claim to a section of space off a narrow *hutong* which ran between Soares Avenue and Victory Avenue. It was a fetid passageway about a metre wide down one side of which ran an open drain slick with fat deposits and excrement. On the coldest of days, it reeked: in summer heat, it was unbearable. Cockroaches scuttled across the walls in broad daylight, rats slipped noiselessly in and out of holes and cracks, oblivious to cat or man. Halfway down this alley, where the buildings in the former street backed onto those in the latter, there was a gap of about two metres. Overhead, the sky was criss-crossed with washing poles, intertwined drain and sewage pipes, cables and metal spikes around the lower pipes to deter burglars. The concrete ground was black with ingrained filth.

The family home comprised three tea chests, a part of a larger crate and a section of canvas with an arrow stencilled upon it: it must have once been the side of a military tent, perhaps left over from the war. In this collection of débris lived a man, his wife and three children, the oldest a girl of about eight – my own age. The man worked as a general coolie. For some months, I saw him frequently on my way to school where a hillside was being cut back. He had a bamboo pole thicker than my leg with which he humped wicker baskets of stone from the hillside to waiting lorries and he seemed to work all day long for he was there when I passed by at eight thirty and was still there at three thirty in the afternoon. He wore a small coolie hat with red characters stencilled upon it, the property of his employers, and was bare to the waist. His chestbone was sunken and he went barefoot over the sharpest gravel on his way to the lorries.

His wife did not work full-time, for she was often to be found tending her children with the help of the eldest of them, but she was not always at home. Perhaps she begged, using her children as a tool of her trade, but I doubt it. Although there were beggars in Hong Kong, they were not plentiful. The Chinese do not resort to beggary as, say, the Indians do, except as a very last resort. It is not so much a matter of pride as a belief that one should help oneself: poverty is not a state of resignation but a spur to get to something better.

At night, the family remained in their hovel. They cooked over a little clay brazier of charcoal and ate mainly plain boiled rice with a bit of fish and some vegetables. The husband smoked thin cigarettes, his wife sewing or rocking one of the children to sleep. When the family slept, it was in a foetal position in one of the boxes. Where they washed themselves, relieved themselves, did their laundry and hung it out to dry I never discovered but, one day as I was walking to school, I met the oldest child. She was on her way to her school, too. Her white uniform skirt was stiff with starch, her blouse pressed as if it had been steam ironed with the navy blue edging to the collar sharp. Her sandals were polished and her black hair shone. I stared at her and she smiled coyly back at me. We walked side by side in silence down Argyle Street. I might have been falling in love. At Gullane Road, we had to part for my school was to the right and she was heading on towards Kowloon City.

A fortnight later, the family was gone. All that remained were the tea chests and crate and these soon vanished, no doubt to be utilised at a different site. I am quite sure the family had gone up in the world, graduated from a *hutong* to a squatter shack.

Walking through a squatter area prompts mixed emotions. For friends unused to the Orient, it produces a deep and abiding sorrow. They feel they must do something to alleviate the lot of the residents. Chinese friends are somewhat more stoical: that is the squatter's fate just as it is the millionaire's to ride in a Rolls-Royce. My first reaction is one of humble admiration for the survivor, for the tenacity of the human spirit to ride the odds and break them.

In official Hong Kong government jargon, Tai Hom is not

a squatter area but a cottage area. The difference is a fine one of definition only. A squatter area or habitation is constructed either upon government-owned or private agricultural land whilst a cottage area has a degree of official blessing and, therefore, semi-permanence. Squatters are controlled by regular patrols which move them on but cottage area dwellers are somewhat safer in their tenure. They can count on their home being demolished sooner or later but not at the drop of a hat and, before they are displaced, they can be more or less certain of being re-housed in a resettlement estate. Squatters wind up in a THA – a Temporary Housing Area.

From beside the MTR exit begins a warren of alleys, passage-ways and wider thoroughfares. Unplanned, these have evolved almost organically, like the tendrils of a fungus working its way through a matrix of dead wood. The shacks and occasional ancient stone building through which they wend teem with life. Little shops sell every conceivable product from blocks of Cadbury's chocolate and Hershey bars to National Panasonic television sets. *Dai pai dongs* sell cooked chicken's feet and boiled fish-heads, crisp dumplings of batter stuffed with meat or noodles all prepared over open ring gas burners which hiss and roar as the flames are charged. Small workshops turn out wood screws, washers and ball-bearing races or repair motorbikes.

As with all squatter areas, there is little organised sanitation and one side of Tai Hom is bounded by a noxious nullah into which seeps a large quantity of effluent gathered from sewers under the shacks. Electricity and telephones are laid on, water coming from a series of standpipes and dubious connections which snake across the ground. It is government policy to bring amenities to such places but this is not always as efficient as it might be.

Most of the buildings are made on frames of wood with either timber walls or sides made of beaten metal sheeting. Doors are wooden or metal and most are faced with sliding grilles such as used to be found on lift doors. Windows are usually small and barred whilst dogs lie chained in corners ready to pounce on any intruder, animal or human. A good number of the buildings are two storeys high with narrow balconies on which laundry dries in the sun or children play. Not far from the MTR exit is a small playground with gaily painted climbing frames and a swing with a crash mat beneath it. Wherever there is room, flowers are growing in the barren earth or glazed brown pots decorated with rich golden dragons.

From the outside, a squatter hut can look pretty much like any hovel anywhere but the interior can be very homely and comfortable, in the oriental fashion. Each property is divided into a number of rooms: the living/dining room is the central hub of family life and will contain chairs, a table, a television and have pictures on the walls with carpets on the floor; a small kitchen is usually equipped with a miniature refrigerator and a cooker with rings and grill but no oven, washing up being done in a sink; a bedroom or two containing beds, a cupboard and shelves for clothes. Floors are frequently tiled for ease of cleaning. All the walls are painted in bright colours and everything is invariably tidy. It is the Chinese way to be house-proud and a squatter is just as meticulous about his shack as a millionaire is of his mansion.

Every construction looks flimsy but is surprisingly solid. They withstand typhoons, torrential rain and, for a surprising length of time, bulldozers that might be sent to clear them. What they cannot contest is fire.

A squatter blaze is a terrible sight. They were commonplace in the fifties, always occurring in the winter months when rainfall and humidity were low and the winds brisk and cool, leading to tens of thousands being made homeless in the space of less than an hour. Once the flames took a grip they spread with the voracious avarice of a pine forest conflagration, the fire leaping not just narrow *hutongs* but even twin carriageway roads. A family's home could be razed in minutes and because the squatter areas were usually in the foothills of Kowloon and supplied with neither access roads nor water, fighting a blaze tested the ingenuity and efficiency of the fire brigade to the limit.

Squatter fires usually began in one of three ways: they flared up because of an accident in one of the numerous little factories set up in their midst, because of a domestic accident or, on occasion, on purpose. The latter was organised by the local Triad society, partly as a service to the local inhabitants and partly as a means of generating income. The system was ingenious: word would go around that a section of shacks was to be torched. Local residents prepared for this by removing their valuables, translocating their old folk and animals and getting ready to run when the shout went up. One hut would then be ignited and the fire began. Hoards would flee ahead of it and gather on the perimeter of the area to watch the holocaust. The fire brigade would soon arrive but the fire, being set as far as possible from the nearest road or hydrant, would do maximum damage before being brought under control.

The benefits were legion: the homeless received charity and, if available, were re-housed in resettlement tenement blocks; the health authorities were temporarily rid of a source of disease (especially cholera and typhoid) and the Triads had a new area in which they could do business by re-building new shacks for new squatters, charging for concrete bases and the provision of illegal utilities.

At the age of nine, I saw a squatter fire at close hand. A large part of the hilly area of Ho Man Tin was covered by squatters' hovels through which I used to wander in search of puerile adventure. Late one afternoon, I was walking up a track from Waterloo Road when a tidal wave of people came rushing down it towards me. They were waving their arms and shrieking. I was terrified. There was nowhere to hide. Yet they ignored me and rushed by, shoving me aside and jostling each other. Behind them, against the blue of the sky, a thin wisp of smoke was rising in a column before bending under a breeze. Other people were running towards me now, shouting and screaming. Children were being dragged along. Dogs yapped hysterically. An old man, I remember, hobbled past me at speed, pulling an old pram behind him laden with cooking utensils.

The smoke quickly thickened and I could hear the distant clamour of fire engines. The crowd which had hurtled past me was returning now, standing around me. The people were horrifyingly quiet. No one spoke and even the dogs fell silent. From the squatter area came the terrible click and crack of flames. Every now and then, there was a miniature explosion. The fire engines turned up the track and stopped. The crowd parted to allow firemen to rush by unravelling hoses or swinging long-handled axes. In the meantime, the fire was raging. Dirty flames leapt metres into the air and the sounds of the inferno were punctuated by the crash of roofs, accompanied by showers of sparks. Dense, acrid black smoke drifted towards the crowd. I did as everyone else, covering my mouth by pulling the neck of my vest up over my nose.

Suddenly, the conflagration reached a hut at the head of the track. Fingers of smoke seeped through cracks in the walls then, without any warning, the whole building erupted into flame: one moment it was there, the next it was a ball of flame. The firemen turned a hose on it but to no seeming effect.

When it was all over, an area of some two or three hectares was flattened. The ground was covered in damp ash and charcoal with metal frames poking up here and there, of a chair or a bicycle.

The fire, which was reportedly started by a man spilling a tub of the hair oil he was making on an open stove, could not have lasted more than thirty minutes. Four thousand people had been rendered destitute. No one had been killed: the death toll from most squatters fires was very low indeed, but the toll in human spirit and hope must have been enormous.

Today, in Tai Hom, hope flourishes. The squatters here are not down-and-outs by a long chalk. I have watched a man exit from a squatter hut wearing a smart suit and carrying a briefcase, bid farewell to his children and then, not twenty paces off, answer his mobile phone. No one here is ill, dirty or necessarily poor. They are all doing the best they can in the circumstances and display the very qualities that have made Hong Kong what it is today

– resourceful, hard-working, diligent, determined and ambitious. Without the likes of these folk, Hong Kong would be an abysmal failure.

Living in the General's Shadow

On the afternoon of Tuesday 22 January 1907, the Governor, F.H. May, and Mrs May attended the opening of Mr A.H. Rennie's new flour mill in Junk Bay. Along with other dignitaries, including Sir Paul Chater and H.N. Mody, doyens of the business community, they were shown around the ultra-modern factory. However, an incident occurred which, in the light of future events, was somewhat unfortunate and would have been considered downright inauspicious by any Chinese. Riding to the top floor of the building on a sack lift, Mr Mody was too slow in jumping off and was thrown to the floor, knocked semi-conscious and required the ministrations of Dr Thornicroft, another guest.

Alfred Herbert Rennie was a Canadian businessman. Born in 1857, he had held a series of junior but important civil servant posts in Manitoba before moving to Hong Kong in the late 1880s where he joined the colonial civil service to become acting assistant harbour-master, acting superintendent of the Water Police and acting sanitary superintendent: indeed, all his posts seem to have been in a *pro tempore* capacity. After ten years, he resigned and went into business as the China representative of the Puget Sound Milling Co. and later the Portland Flour Mills Co., gaining a considerable knowledge of the cereals trade. It was, therefore, seemingly appropriate he should found the Junk Bay mill, both Chinese and expatriate businessmen financially backing the enterprise.

The mill was constructed at the foot of a steep hill in a little cove on the western shore of Tseung Kwan O (known in English as Junk Bay although the literal translation is The General's Haven, O being a harbour or safe anchorage) around a headland to the east of Hong Kong harbour. A 200 metre-long concrete quay was reclaimed with the mill standing on it: imported wheat was delivered directly from cargo vessels into the mill, processed and shipped out again for Hong Kong. The very latest machinery was used with Swiss-built diesel engines powering the whole plant which was managed by Rennie with a head miller, Mr Gaddie, working for him.

For a year, all seemed to go well. The mill did a brisk trade in the face of fierce overseas competition and the characteristic conservatism of Chinese traders whose native caution made them reluctant to change brand allegiance. The first annual general board meeting reported HK$77,000 of the development debt had been settled and there was credit of HK$83,000 carried forward. It was then things started to go badly. First, Rennie bought several speculative shipments of wheat on the rising American market which promptly collapsed; second, trans-Pacific freight declined so it became as cheap to ship milled flour to Hong Kong as it did grain; third, wheat was now being grown in Manchuria more cheaply than North American grain; finally, and perhaps more significantly for it indicates a weakness in Rennie's business acumen, there was no local market for *offal*, the milling term for bran, shorts and mill feed which in America had a market value as animal fodder and which made up a quarter by weight of grain stocks.

At four thirty on the afternoon of 14 April 1908, *en route* for the mill in his steam launch across Lei Yue Mun, Rennie jumped overboard. Around his neck he had tied a six-foot length of rope on the end of which was a steel despatch box such as companies used in those days to keep documents free from the jaws of cockroaches and the ravages of the sub-tropical climate. Despite the launch steaming at top speed through a choppy sea, the helmsman managed to bring her around. The boatswain, To Yau, risked his life by jumping into the sea with a lifebuoy but Rennie refused to grasp it. The Chinese kept his master afloat, despite the weight of the box, until the boat drew alongside but Rennie lost consciousness and attempts to revive him on deck were in vain.

Two days after the suicide, it was noted in the *China Mail* that all the assets of the mill had been seized by the bank. Rennie's investors cut their losses, withdrew from the business and the mill was, in time, abandoned.

I suppose Rennie's mill was always doomed and its owner fated to kill himself: Mody's accident as well as Rennie's suicide would have been expected by any necromancer had one been called in to advise on the siting of the factory. At the time Rennie built his flour mill, the place was known as Diu Kang Leng or Hanging Neck Hilltop. How this name came about is uncertain but legend says it was a spot favoured by suicides. After the collapse of the mill, the place was renamed Tiu Keng Leng, which means Mixed Scenery Hilltop: the name sounds the same (more or less) but the bad luck has been exorcised by the change.

After the mill collapse, Tiu Keng Leng was all but deserted. Apart from a few subsistence fishermen who set up shacks beside their dip-nets in the little bay, no one lived there. At least, not until June 1950 when Rennie's Mill took on a new lease of life.

Apart from a privately owned ferry which visits it hourly, linking it to Hong Kong, the only access to Rennie's Mill is Po Lam Road which winds around the side of a hill called Mau Wu Shan. Just wide enough for two cars to pass, overhung with trees on one side and with a steep drop to Junk Bay on the other, it leads nowhere else, coming to a dead end not far past the little cove on which the mill was built. Below the road, the entire head of Junk Bay as far as the village of Tseung Kwan O has been reclaimed and is a flat expanse of dusty land apportioned into building sites bisected by embryonic streets or avenues: by 1995, this will be a town of 200,000 souls.

'Look at this!' Stephen exclaimed, glancing out of the car window as the driver changed into second gear and slowed to allow a *pak pai* to edge by. 'The last time I visited Junk Bay there were – well, there were just junks here.'

Stephen is a senior publicity officer with the Hong Kong Tourist Association and an old friend. He had taken the day off to visit Rennie's Mill with me out of curiosity: certainly, he could not have argued that such a visit was part of his job's remit. No tourist would ever want to come here and not one of them would have been welcome. Rennie's Mill is not, by a long stretch of the imagination, a resort.

On my last visit to Tseung Kwan O, it was just a hamlet of traditional houses without so much as the smallest temple beside a creek, a few acres of paddyfields and a muddy beach with several sampans drawn up on it: the only way to reach the place was on foot from the nearest road at Tseng Lan Shue where I lived out the last of my teenage years.

'Have you visited Rennie's Mill before?' I enquired.

'Never!' Stephen answered abruptly. 'They're not fond of strangers. Especially nowadays. To wear a suit here is to ask for it.'

He looked down at his shirt and jeans to ensure he did not appear like an official. Betty checked her dress, too.

The post-war renaissance of Rennie's Mill began when Mao Tse-tung's People's Liberation Army won China from the Kuomintang (KMT) or Nationalist Army of General Chiang Kai-shek. Large numbers of KMT soldiers, accompanied by their families, fled China for Taiwan and Hong Kong.

The first to reach Hong Kong, a party of 148, arrived in November 1949. They were destitute. By the end of March, the numbers had swollen to 7,800, living as squatters on the site of the old Jubilee gun battery on Mount Davis with scant government and charity aid. Many were women and children: 500 were disabled or blind. Something had to be done with them. A refugee camp was planned for Mui Wo on Lantau but the would-be inmates were against it: in those days, Lantau was the back of beyond and they would be unable to find work there. Eventually, on 6 May 1950, funding was given by the government to build a refugee camp at Tiu Keng Leng. The cost was HK$103,000.

On 26 June, a mass transportation began. In truth, Rennie's Mill was as remote as Mui Wo. It could only be reached by boat or a footpath (and a three hour mountain hike) from Kowloon City. The government built huts on the site of the old mill but in insufficient numbers and many of the refugees took their squatter shacks with them in sections. For all intents and purposes, the move was a cosmetic one. The ex-KMT soldier problem was being swept under the colonial carpet or, in this case, behind the colonial mountains.

The people, however, were quick to adapt to the situation and, in retrospect, it was advantageous for it allowed them to retain the fierce pride and independence with which they had fought the PLA. Very soon, huts and small houses started to be erected outside the mill area, round the cove and up the hillside behind it. A self-government office was built, provincial associations formed and a market, library and school established, much of it with the help of local Chinese charities and sympathetic supporters: in later years, right to the present, the government of Taiwan also made regular contributions. Missionaries moved in with more schools and medical facilities. Shops opened and a ferry service started to Shau Kei Wan.

A military engineer, Hsieh Yu-chun, built a wide path through the settlement and made the track over the mountains an all-weather route. Five years later, Po Lam Road was built by the refugees themselves with Christian World Service Association funding. The Hong Kong Government, it seems, was reluctant to be seen to play a major role in Rennie's Mill, anti-government feeling fuelled when the authorities tried to cancel ration tickets: later, moves to turn the area into a resettlement zone rather than leave it alone were forcibly resisted.

The car stopped by a small tea-house and we got out. It was here we were to wait for Miss Cheng, the music teacher from one of the Rennie's Mills schools. She was to be our official guide.

No sooner had we settled at a table by the shop than an old man approached us. He was dressed traditionally but for an incongruous Western-style flat cap and a padded jacket for the

February wind was chilly and the sky overcast. Jerking his chin in my direction, he asked bluntly what we were up to. Stephen told him: we were waiting for Miss Cheng. The name-drop placated the old man but he was still curious about the *gweilo*. It was explained I was a writer, an old Hong Kong hand, who was visiting to pay my respects to the good folk of Tiu Keng Leng. This produced a wide smile showing blackened gums and three yellowed teeth. We shook hands, the old man's grip as firm as warm steel.

Sitting with us, he volunteered his history. He was a KMT soldier who had fought the Reds, been driven back right across Kwangtung province: for certain, he had killed Communists and he was proud of the fact. From his pocket, he produced a much-thumbed KMT identity card with his photograph. It showed a young, proud and handsome idealist in a military cap, his eyes serious but his lips just hinting at the smile of victory that would never be his. Folding the card away, he embarked upon a bitter tirade against the Hong Kong government whom he likened to a number of lower invertebrates and several words I did not understand but of which I caught the gist. After the initial expletives, Betty translated for me.

'I fought for freedom. For liberty,' she related. 'Tiu Keng Leng is the Lighthouse of Freedom. Now they want to move us again. Why? To fill in the bay, build factories, houses. Why? There are houses here now. And where will we live? Over there!'

He swung his hand in the direction of the reclamation and spat on the ground narrowly missing a cat curled up beside a blue plastic butt of water.

'We have to go and live in a flat. Higher than the mountains. I am not in favour of that. And do you know what compensation we are offered? Do you? I will tell you. $320 a square foot. What is that? Nothing! And if you have a two-storey house here, you only get what it covers on the ground. Not floor area at $320 but plot area. And those flats we have to move to? $600 a month rent. How can we pay that?' His next few sentences were not translated and Betty blushed slightly. 'We deserve better treatment. I am an old man. I am a freedom fighter. But what freedom? I am not free to die in my own place. Once again, we must move. All my life, I have been moving. Why can't we stay until I go to join the General?'

It was for this reason I wanted to visit Tiu Keng Leng: like Kowloon Walled City, it is doomed to the breaker's hammer, targeted for reclamation and rebuilding. The residents have been presented with an official *fait accompli*.

Miss Cheng arrived, a pretty woman in her early thirties with a serious air about her. A spokesperson for the Rennie's Mill residents, she shook our hands then led us along a concrete path beside the shop, the old man waving us off in a cheery fashion.

There is no vehicular access to Rennie's Mill. All the streets and roads are nothing more than paths rising and falling at various angles, keeping to the contours of the land and dropping in a series of corners to the mill site. At intervals along the path placards had been wired to the railings, painted in red characters. I asked Betty what one of them said and she replied with her voice lowered.

'It says, "Whoever destroys my home I will chop to death."'

The site of the mill contains a school, some administrative buildings and a small attempt at a museum containing some notice boards with photographs of the history of the refugee settlement. Everything was dusty and sad, as if the spirit of the people was beginning to succumb: the photos were fading fast and would soon show only the blankness of time.

On the dock, huge iron bollards showed where the wheat ships had berthed. Two small boys were flying a kite and shouted a cheery greeting to their teacher. Further along the quay, under a few trees, some very ancient men were sitting on a bench, chatting and gazing out to sea.

'These are our veterans,' said Miss Cheng, who spoke fluent English. 'They were not just ordinary soldiers but officers – majors, captains. The man at the end was in the battle of Nanjing. More than 1,500 of our citizens are over sixty years old.'

One of the old soldiers caught my eye. He grinned and raised his hand in a salute. I might have been an allied general inspecting their parade. His fingers were bent with arthritis and his chin covered in a grey stubble but there was something indomitable about him. He was a survivor. I wondered if he was the man, reputed to live here, who kept a dead Communist colonel's finger pickled in a vial so that the deceased enemy might never go to heaven: no Chinese may enter the hereafter unless his body is complete.

Everywhere we looked, Nationalist Chinese flags were flying – from poles rammed into cracks on the rocky shore, from bamboo sticks, television aerial masts, trees, railings. The red oblong with blue quadrant and white spiky sun added a hint of mobile colour under the grey sky. On the hillside above the bay were huge Chinese characters painted white: they spelt out Long Live President Chiang.

The Nationalist fervour of the ex-KMT veterans was one of the main causes for the 1950 Rennie's Mill plan. Close to the squatter site they occupied in Hong Kong, some Communist sympathisers were making a rowdy noise as they celebrated the Dragon Boat Festival; the KMT soldiers caught them and beat them to death. It was hoped Rennie's Mill might be remote enough to avoid further political reprisals.

'What will happen in 1997?' I enquired as we made our way out of the mill area towards the rest of the settlement.

'We do not know. Some people will go to live in Taiwan, especially the old men. Some may go to other countries and many will have to stay.'

'Will it not be dangerous for the veterans?' I asked. 'Will the Communists take reprisals even on such old men?' I had in mind the occasional body-snatching at Sha Tau Kok, not to mention the Tienanmen Square blood-bath. For a government capable of killing hundreds in front of the world's news crews, a few dozen old men would be as nothing.

'We cannot say,' she answered, noncommittally.

The bulk of Tiu Keng Leng exists around the cove, rising a hundred metres up a horseshoe-shaped valley on the far side of which is a large scrap-metal foundry. The cove itself is a fetid stinking stretch of water into which the effluent of 15,000 people, the present Rennie's Mill population, flows. The buildings are mostly low, single or double-storey structures made of wood, tin sheeting and corrugated iron, crowded cheek by jowl in ragged rows through which run alleys, *hutongs*, wider pathways and narrow stepped creeps. The main path is called Hsieh Kung Road, in honour of the engineer.

The whole place is a hive of activity. People come and go, exchanging greetings and arguing over prices, dogs and cats sleep or studiously ignore each other, filthy water rattles in drains and rats slip secretively in and out of culverts: in two hours, I saw more than thirty rats, a number far in excess of a year's viewing in Hong Kong proper. At one point, a gaggle of children went merrily by with a rat in a live animal trap, on its way to a drowning in the bay. Mah-jong tiles clattered in the recesses of shops and eating-houses.

Stephen halted by one of these. A woman in a tri-coloured Benetton sweatshirt was presiding over a large bowl of boiled eggs the like of which I had not seen before. The shells were as polished as dark walnuts. Being a gourmet of considerable knowledge, Stephen bought one.

'I have not seen these on sale for a long time,' he remarked, eating the egg. 'It is boiled in tea and special herbs.' He smacked his lips. 'You don't often find this traditional food.'

From somewhere up the hill came the strains of a pi'pa and a ch'in, two of the main instruments of classical Chinese music. The strains of their sad melody seemed to prophesy the future. They were not the only relics of old China. On the corner of one alley was a traditional bone-setter's shop next door to a barber's in which two men sat balancing side by side on stools reading newspapers as their heads were close cropped with a pair of ancient electric clippers. Just along the way was a dentist's on a shelf of which stood a massive model of a molar, cut away to show the ravages of rot.

An old lady, not four feet high, came hobbling towards me. I instinctively looked down to see if her feet were bound but they were not, just shrunk with age and use. Her spine was hunched, her dark grey hair combed back and cut short in a straight line at the nape, held in place by a tortoiseshell hair band. She was puffing on a long, thin-stemmed bamboo pipe from the silver bowl of which wafted a hint of smoke. As she drew level with me, she looked up and muttered something.

'*Cho san*,' I replied politely: but this is a morning greeting and it was now afternoon.

'You are wrong,' she retorted quickly in English, her voice squeaky and high-pitched, rich with humour. 'You must say *ng'on*.' She laughed, a little joyous cackle.

I was taken aback by her fluent English and my surprise amused her all the more. She reached out and put her hand on my arm, her fingers frail and twig-like.

'You don't speak Cantonese so well. You must take some lessons.'

She sucked on the pipe, smoke leaking out of her mouth as if her lips needed repairing where they did not meet. The burning tobacco smelled sweet and pleasant, unlike the sharp reek of Virginia tobacco.

'I'm sorry,' I apologised.

'No matter. No matter. Do not say sowry. You are still a young man. Plenty of time to learn for you.'

She squeezed my arm gently then, turning, set off on her way up a flight of steps. I sensed the pain of arthritic age in her every move.

Miss Cheng said, 'She was once a house servant for Europeans but now she is retired. All old people and orphans are looked after by us. It is our duty.'

From behind us swelled the stuttering din of a two-stroke motor: for a moment, I wondered what use a lawn motor was at Rennie's Mill. Around a corner appeared a strange contraption. It was like a hybrid between a market barrow and one of those mechanised ploughs seen in rural Europe, controlled and steered by a man walking behind holding onto a set of handle-bars. Yet this was no agricultural implement. In place of a plough was a reclining chair like that of an invalid carriage in which huddled an ancient man covered to his neck with blankets. The contrivance was being driven by a man in a white coat, another similarly attired attendant walking by the side holding a drip bottle connected to the man's arm. We stood aside to let the machine pass.

Miss Cheng explained, 'No vehicle can come here so anyone who is ill has to be taken up to the shop where we met. Then an ambulance can take them to hospital.'

We strolled on past a small, empty market. A prim roof stood on pillars over custom-built concrete and stone counters.

'The government built this market,' Miss Cheng remarked, 'but the people do not use it.'

'Why not?'

'They built their own,' she answered enigmatically.

Close to the old mill, she bade us farewell. It was time for her to go to her pupils. We left and began the climb up to Po Lam Road. Halfway up, we paused for breath and, looking back, I saw the proliferation of defiant flags shifting in a rising on-shore breeze. In the bay, the ferry boat from Hong Kong was docking. Some way out, a junk – perhaps the last to use Junk Bay as its mooring – was sailing slowly by under the power of diesel engines, the puttering of the water-line exhaust competing with the clang and rumble of the foundry. On its foredeck, a man was readying to drop anchor. I thought of the veterans sitting by the dockside far below, gazing out on the same scene, dreaming of conquests and going to join the General.

Shek O

Early in the twenties, a number of Peak residents got together to do something about their lifestyles. They were tired of existing for seven months of the year either in the mountain mists or above them, with nothing to look down upon except clouds and the distant summits of the Kowloon hills bleakly jutting above them like barren islands. There seemed little alternative to their predicament save moving lower down the mountain to Mid-Levels which whilst geographically acceptable was socially exceedingly undesirable indeed. If one resided on the Peak one had achieved a certain position, to be preserved at all costs: Mid-Levels was for lesser mortals, senior managers and compradores, those who had not yet made it up the social ladder – or, to be precise, the social mountain. It was all very well going down the Peak to the office, to the Hong Kong Club overlooking Statue Square or the Ladies' Recreation Club above Garden Road, referred to by excluded men as the Ladies' Recrimination Club, by which name it is still known to this day, although males are now allowed to be associate members. Yet it was altogether another matter to *live* on the lower slopes.

Then an idea was struck upon. Instead of living on the Peak, why not live in the country? Why not create a totally new, socially respectable residential environment? It was not long before it was realised this might become, with care, even more selective and élitist than the Peak itself.

When the round island road had been completed, a spur road

was built turning off at Tai Tam Gap to the east of Hong Kong island: running along the side of Tai Tam Bay, it led eventually to a quarry but there were plans to extend it further out along the D' Aguilar Peninsula then round the southern end of a mountain ridge called the Dragon's Back and, twisting through a windy pass between the ridge and D'Aguilar Peak, down to a small fishing village called Shek O.

Like many of the coastal villages, Shek O (Stony Haven) had a history of piracy. For most settlements, buccaneering was an opportunistic crime to which they turned as a supplement to subsistence farming and fishing but in Shek O, piracy seems to have been a major source of income in historical if not modern times. No pirates are recorded as coming from it during British colonial times but a mid-sixteenth-century map of the region specifically warns navigators against the *Pirates and fishermen of Nantou mooring* – the earlier name for Shek O.

The village was not unknown to the adventurous wealthy. Those who took to vigorous mountain walking or cross-country horse-riding knew the place, famous for its two sandy beaches and spectacular views over the South China Sea. The Royal Navy knew of it as a safe landing place as, no doubt, had the pirates and everyone arriving in Hong Kong by sea spied the beaches to port as their liner steamed into the beginnings of the strait of Lei Yue Mun.

From the point of view of would-be residents, Shek O had everything for the makings of a little paradise. A small rocky headland jutted into the sea between two uninhabited islets about 300 metres long and sixty wide, creating and sheltering two bays. The fishing village was small and ancient with a little temple and a population of about 200. To the north of the headland, for about a kilometre, the ground was made of rolling hillocks covered in low scrub, any flat land between being cultivated by the villages for vegetables and ginger. A number of streams trickled down from the Dragon's Back which provided a spectacular backdrop 250 metres high. The golden sand beaches, Shek O beach and Rocky Bay on the other side of the headland offered excellent swimming, the former having none of the undertow that make some of the island beaches notorious.

Despite the fact one could only approach Shek O by sedan chair over the mountain from the end of the road by the quarry, this seemed not to detract from the project and a leading local architect, Lennox Godfrey Bird, established the Shek-O Development Corporation in 1925. Shipping building materials round by junk and carting stone over the hills from the quarry, they built the first bungalows of the new estate on the hillocky area and, in true colonial fashion, inaugurated the Shek-O Club by erecting a clubhouse and, later, laying out an excellent golf course. The low scrub around the bungalows was cleared, formal gardens were laid out and trees planted.

Life in Shek O became idyllic although for a while some commuted to their paradise only for the weekends. Until the road was built down to the village around 1930, the journey from Central took over two and a half hours. The Club was the centre of the community with provisions being available and all mail delivered there. The bungalows bore no numbers and were known only by their owner's names. Bird believed Chinese buildings were especially typhoon-resistant so he designed a number of the residences with low-pitched Chinese-style roofs made of local tiles. Whether he was correct or not cannot be ascertained but those old properties which remain, having survived a good many typhoons, hold a certain charming quaintness, fitting in well to the area which is blighted nowadays by modern designs and sixties boxes.

Only the very fortunate lived at Shek O. Its exclusivity saw to that. The bungalows and later residences were amongst the most expensive in Hong Kong and remain so to the present: Jardine, Matheson have one of their taipan's homes here and it was said in the sixties Shek O had the highest population density of multi-millionaires in the world. The type who became a Shek O resident may be gauged from the fact that Bird's daughter had a windsock erected in the garden so her boyfriends in the RAF could drop love letters to her from their seaplanes and another had a pet leopard imported from China. The Shek O Country Club still has an exclusivity second to none in Hong Kong, a strictly limited number of members, a lengthy waiting list and a joining fee not for the faint-hearted or miserly.

Shek O reached its zenith in the sixties. At weekends, it became a thriving hub of swimmers and holiday-makers. The beach bore three lines of striped canvas beach tents with deck chairs and a folding table, roving attendants providing old kerosene tins of fresh water to clean off the salt of the ocean. Sweetmeat merchants wandered by competing with Dairy Farm ice cream sellers, newspaper vendors plied their trade whilst children or old ladies tried to hawk beach balls, cigarettes and plastic lighters, swimming rings and freshly caught fish or crabs. The sea was dotted with bobbing heads, splashing children and little rubber boats. Even the car park was taken over with sheds hiring out kiddies' bicycles, selling soft drinks and San Mig. beer, blocks of ice, flip- flop beach sandals, salted plums and near-inedible sandwiches of rubberoid cheese and (for some inscrutable reason) Marmite. At the headland end of the beach, under a roof of overhanging branches and broad leaves, was a little restaurant offering the simple fare of noodles, fish and rice.

In the daytime, a dip in the sea attracted little fish which nibbled fingers and tickled legs but Shek O was best visited at night when the crowds had departed, the restaurant was shut and the only sounds to be heard were the bark of a village dog and the soughing of wind in the Chinese pine trees bordering the beach. To walk the sand in the moonlight was a delight. Small crabs fled helter-skelter for their burrows and wavelets breaking on the sand sparked like distant heat lightning with phosphorescence: a jumping fish in the bay created glorious explosions of ghostly green light.

Nowadays, Shek O is returned somewhat to its former backwater status. Although served by regular bus and *pak pai* services, the beach is seldom as crowded or as busy as it was twenty years ago. The sea is occasionally polluted which puts swimmers off. Children still ride cycles round the car park, scratching the paintwork of Nissan and BMW alike, and the sheds still sell sweets and drinks, bowls of noodles and beach paraphernalia – even the restaurant under the tangle of boughs remains in business – but their trade caters more for the day-tripper than the swimmer, for those who like to walk in the hills. The paths once used by the sedan chairs are now busy with hikers, picnickers and ramblers and the Dragon's Back and surroundings summits of Pottinger Peak, Mount Collinson and Shek O Peak are designated a country park of desolate mountain-side and rocky outcrops, covered in scrub and wind-bent grass, only the narrow valleys sylvan and filled with muted bird song and fleet shadows.

Yet to go to Shek O is still to find peace, the same sort of escapist tranquillity the investors in the development corporation had sought. True, the headland is built up with houses (occupied by the modern equivalent of senior clerks, middle managers and compradores, which would not please the original expatriate community whose ghosts must be spluttering in their gins-and-tonic at this influx of common riff-raff), the village has expanded to cater for the increase of residents and the beach is cleaned daily on the weekends or at public holidays by a machine which sifts through the top layer of sand and extracts almost all the rubbish – flotsam left by tides and trippers – save the smallest cigarette filter tip, matchstick or viciously sharp drinks can ring-pull. What is more, the houses have been numbered but at least in a Shekoian fashion in keeping with the eccentric, exclusive past: the numbers relate not to position in a row or street but to the order in which the structures were built.

Despite all this, however, Shek O remains comparatively unspoilt by Hong Kong standards. There is now a white concrete lifeguard shelter on a pillar and red litter bins dotted about, but there are also on occasion one or two sampans riding at anchor in Heung To Wan, the bay in front of the main beach, although they are seldom engaged in fishing. Most often, they are used by locals to ferry out beach merchandise to weekend sailors on their luxury motor launches calling in on their circumnavigation of Hong Kong island. The only road into Shek O, passing the golf course, still skirts a few vegetable and banana plots beside little shacks and bamboo groves.

To walk through the village is to get the feel of times past. Even if many of the houses are modern cubes with iron-framed windows and air conditioners, they still have about them an air of attractive peasant shoddiness typical of any Chinese settlement. The alleys and single street twist and turn along the lines of the original *hutongs*. Bicycles and handcarts lean against walls next to galvanised tubs. Dogs lie dozing in narrow strips of shade in small forecourts, patios and minuscule gardens. Cats lounge in the sun, too hot to stroke, and hens cluck and scatter at one's feet. Women squat to their laundry at standpipes to gossip or loiter in twos and threes under broad-brimmed Hakka hats, hung with black fringes of stiffened cotton. Men lounge in the little shops or under trees, smoking, chatting or playing Chinese draughts. Young boys kick a shuttlecock of chicken feathers about with their heels.

In the centre of the village is a tiny, unprepossessing temple built not to attract tourists but merely to serve the religious needs of fisherfolk. Even they are not quite extinct and, most days, an old lady in a black silk jacket or a man dressed only in shorts can be found somewhere in the passageways sorting live prawns in a bucket, scaling fish or expertly cracking open sea urchins with a thin, pointed blade. Crime is low, as it must always have been, the main responsibilities of the few policemen stationed at the police post being traffic control, checking on hawkers' licences and preventing newly arrived expatriate ladies from bathing topless, which is illegal in Hong Kong.

Standing on the beach in the middle of the week in late summer, half a dozen people swimming in the sea or striking out for one of the swimming rafts, the rest of the world might have ceased to exist. The sea is blue, the sky cloudless. Beyond the rocky islet of Ng Fan Chau 500 metres offshore, the hump of Sung Kong island squats on the horizon with the white lighthouse of Waglan Island further out to sea on its left.

Neither island is inhabited. Until 1989, the latter was occupied by nine staff who tended the lighthouse and reported on the weather in the approaches but they are now defunct, made redundant by advances in navigational and meteorological technology. The former, Sung Kong, has an area of about three-quarters of a square kilometre and is composed of little more than a bleak, 140 metre-high hill projecting from the sea, covered in stunted bushes, surrounded by rocks and without even an unsafe landing point. It is said to have been used by the Japanese between 1943 and '45 to exile Chinese Kuomintang and Communist partisans, dumping them there to die of starvation, sunstroke or thirst, there being no fresh water or significant cover on the island. Word has it the castaways resorted eventually to cannibalism; human remains are still said to be found in crevices on the north side of the hill above a little inlet.

I cannot look at this panorama without a certain, deep sadness. Waglan was the first landfall in Hong Kong one passed close by when arriving on an ocean liner in the slower years of my childhood, before 747s and A-300s. My memory is quite clear of my first view of it from the boat deck of the P&O ship SS *Corfu,* early on a misty morning well over forty years ago. The lighthouse was still switched on, the sea running with a low swell unscarred by breaking waves. Someone standing by me – it might have been my father – handed me a pair of binoculars. I trained them on Waglan. Beside the lighthouse was a flagpole from which fluttered a dark blue flag with a Union Jack in one corner and a white circle in the centre. Near to the lighthouse tower were several buildings with red roofs which looked almost English. They were surrounded by low, green bushes but below them the island was just bare rock. To the right was a longer island with hardly any greenery on it at all. I was, I recall, somewhat disappointed. I had somehow built up the puerile expectation that all Chinese buildings were pagodas and that I should live in one.

A ship's officer walked by and I addressed him.

'What is the name of that island?' I demanded with all the officiousness of an adult passenger.

'Wag Lan,' he replied.

I laughed. It was absurd yet, at the same time, peculiarly and mystically oriental and, it seemed to me, utterly appropriate for the name of the gateway to China.

Box City

Between Jardine House and Swire House in Central, there runs a wide pedestrian bridge over Connaught Road, its floor expensively carpeted with hard rubber tiles and its walls lined with polished steel. In rush hour, more than a thousand people cross it every five minutes and, were it not for the street trading laws and a paucity of escape routes, I am sure it would long ago have been sequestered by any number of enterprising hawkers and peddlers. Instead, it has been expropriated by one man – a beggar.

It shocks to think what is conceivably the wealthiest city on earth has a beggar class. Social services and universal medical health care exist, low-cost or (if necessary) free housing is available and there are a large number of philanthropic charities and organisations ranging from world-class hospitals to soup kitchens run by religious foundations from Catholics to Buddhists. There is no need for any beggary at all and yet it exists.

This one beggar is perhaps the best known. Surrounded by hi-tech skyscrapers and with a pitch not fifty metres from a row of shops which include Gucci, Dunhill and Chanel, he squats right in the middle of the Swire House end of the footbridge with a plastic mug.

Dressed in fairly clean rags, he is hideously deformed. His hands are claws and what there are of his legs are twisted sticks of flesh with grotesque mockeries of feet contorted under him. His spine is hunched and his face has not gone unattended by his disfigurement. He has the look of a hellish creature from Norse mythology. When he moves, he does so in the manner of a baby yet to walk, shuffling along on his bottom and raising himself on his hands and bent arms.

At no time does he pester passers-by. He merely sits on the floor and awaits their benefice. Many ignore him but a fair number drop a coin or two into his cup. When alms are made, he raises one arm in thanks and mutters his gratitude. He does not smile (perhaps he cannot) and although I am sure he has long since learnt to stoically accept his miserable station, I sense he does not have the arrogance of so many beggars the world over of expecting a donation. There is something about him that tells me he is genuinely grateful for every dollar coin.

Whenever I pass him by, I drop a $10 bill into his cup. Ten dollars is less than I shall pay for a mid-morning cup of coffee and is no sacrifice on my part. He raises his arm and looks up and I catch in his eyes the strange depth one sees in a man who thinks a lot and I always wonder if, inside that grotesque form, there is a wise man considering the strange world spinning around him.

About a hundred metres off, on a flight of side steps going from the Mandarin Hotel down to the Star Ferry pedestrian underpass an old bent woman is usually to be found. She wears traditional Chinese clothes and holds a polystyrene foam cup to collect her contributions in. Her face is wizened with age and her hands shake but she is otherwise without apparent illness or affliction.

When I first saw her, I wondered if she was an old *sor hei* amah fallen on bad times. Believed to derive from the Middle Latin *amma* by way of the Portuguese *ama*, meaning a nurse, the word *amah* was an Anglo–Indian coinage of 1839 for a servant that was a child's nurse, more especially a wet nurse and particularly of Chinese extraction. However, in that mystical inter-relational way languages have, it might also have educed from the Chinese *nai ma* (literally translated as milk-mother): furthermore, Chinese children called their mothers *ma* (as did British children until recently) so a servant who took the place of a mother would be termed *Ah Ma*, the *ah* prefix being the usual way of addressing a servant. The *sor hei* amahs were a special group unto themselves. Admired, adored, respected or feared by generations of European children, they came from peasant stock in Kwangtung province. Many were illiterate and all were poor. Additionally, almost all had undergone the ceremony of *sor hei*, which was the taking of a vow of celibacy and, after this, had entered the sisterhoods of girls' houses (or spinster clubs) in their native villages. As spinsterhood was an alien concept to the Chinese and, in Chinese traditional society, single women were either whores, concubines or (exceptionally) nuns of either Christianity or Buddhism, the only other alternative open to many was to enter into service. This they did by the tens of thousands, providing many years of love and loyal dedication to their employers and their offspring whom most amahs loved as if they were the products of their own wombs.

Chinese amahs were the stock domestic servants of Hong Kong until the early seventies when they began to vanish, slipping into retirement and old age to be replaced by today's Filipina maids. Every European household had at least one and there is not a resident *gweilo* over the age of thirty-something who was not brought up by an amah. Traditionally dressed in white *sam* and black *fu*, they ran entire households – cooking, sewing, minding (and often educating) the pre-school children, cleaning the house, buying and ordering provisions, laundering and serving at table. Many took no days off save for the most important of Chinese religious festivals. They all wore their hair either in a tight bun or, in a few instances, in a short plait. Whichever was the case, the hair was scraped severely back across the crown of the head and held in place by a bone or wooden comb: *sor hei* literally translates as *combed up*.

Whilst some saved their money for retirement or were protected by charities, many were not so astute or fortunate and, after becoming too old for domestic service, left employment to run little market stalls, take on light work in factories or, in extreme cases, beg. I often wonder what some expatriate colonials, retired to the shires of England, might think or do if they knew that the loyal Ah

Mee or Ah Sun was living a hand-to-mouth existence in penury on the streets of Hong Kong with a used polystyrene cup.

The amah who begs by the Mandarin did not, I feel, work for an expatriate family for she speaks not a smattering of English but whenever I give her money – always a green $10 bill, as I do the cripple – she replies by giving me a thumbs-up sign, says 'T'ank yoo' very loudly and smiles. Her face lights up in such a way I feel humbled and filled with wonder at the human capacity for endurance and tenacity.

Where these two beggars live, I do not know: when the cripple leaves his pitch, he heads off into Western District for I once saw him making his way along the pavement and I have never seen the old amah anywhere than on the steps but she is absent at night so she does not live there.

However, there are a few dozen down-and-outs who have set up a semi-temporary camp in a wide open corridor on the exterior of the harbour-facing side of the General Post Office. Here they have erected for themselves a small community which, in the way of enigmatic Hong Kong, overlooks the section of water where the 'boats' rock awaiting a place at Blake Pier.

Each man (there seem to be no women in this little community) has taken what amounts to a bed space for himself against the post office wall. This is a near traditional if unrecognised unit of measurement for, in the old, pre-war days of coolie tenement dormitories, this was the allowance for a man sleeping on a rota basis: each bed-space was shared by two or three in eight-hour rotation.

The spaces are protected by corrals of packing case cardboard and contain an individual's worldly possessions – a mat for sleeping on, a quilt or blanket, bundles of newspapers or rags, perhaps a bicycle wheel or some other useless pieces of junk. Most of these street-sleepers, to use their official designation, are men of simple mind. Of no harm either to themselves or to society at large, they are left to go their own way rather than be incarcerated in an institution for the insane. Some are given donations from time to time by charities, some spurn any approach. None of them are mugged as they would be in London, arrested as they would be in Paris, abused or murdered as might happen in New York. They are generally just ignored.

One of the post office residents loiters around the Star Ferry. He is a man in his late middle age with unkempt, filthy locks of hair hanging in a mat to his shoulders. His skin is so indescribably soiled he looks to be as permanently sun-tanned as a Dravidian and he sports the long, straggling moustache of a wise man. His clothing is in tatters and black with dirt and he goes either barefoot or in broken sandals. Not seeking to beg, he bothers no one as he mutters incoherently to himself and dips into the litter bins to see what treasures he might discover. The milling rush-hour crowds of smartly dressed office workers steer around him, pretty Chinese secretaries or shop assistants give him not a glance while tourists ogle him and move on in dismay. His only source of alms is, thrice a day, to work the queue of those waiting for taxis at the rank. This is a shrewd move for those queuing are obliged to line up in a corridor of railings and therefore cannot escape his attentions. I would guess that at least a third of all those he touches lightly on the arm give him a coin to get him to move on.

One beggar is famous. To be more truthful, he is not so much a beggar as a scholar who gives a truth to the maxim that the line between sanity and madness is a thin one. He is known as the King of Kowloon. Living in a wooded ravine above Shek Kip Mei and So Uk, in the Kowloon foothills, the King may be a beggar but he is certainly no fool and is assuredly an eccentric of the first order. His 'castle' has what might be the most spectacular view of any hobo's property. Immediately in front of it is a highway of flyovers and bustle but beyond, stretching to the harbour, are the tenements and factories of the Kowloon peninsula and, in the far distance, the skyscrapers of Hong Kong island. Airliners glide by before him at a height of less than 300 metres and only a kilometre off. In the evenings, the warm air rising from the city shimmies so that the entire view becomes almost liquid.

If it were not for one activity of the self-styled King, he would be unknown, just another unfortunate wandering the streets to sleep in an alley or packing case. Yet he is famous – for his declarations and his poetry. These are published by being painted on either boulders overlooking the highway or, if in town, on the pillars of bridges, flyovers and underpasses. I am told by Chinese friends (for I am no judge of the matter) that his calligraphy is excellent especially considering the fact he is using a domestic paintbrush and commercial paint rather than a thick calligraphist's brush pen. His declarations of sovereignty draw smiles but his verse draws admiration and it is not unknown for it to be reprinted in the Chinese tabloid press.

On occasion, the King is to be found in the streets of Kowloon where he collects material for his home. He acquires plastic. Not just large off-cuts from factories or pieces with a second-hand or recycling value: he is not a totting rag-and-bone man, a collector of people's rubbish for pecuniary gain. His search is for anything brightly coloured – plastic sacks, broken umbrellas, discarded stretch packaging, shopping bags, bumpers and trim from traffic accidents, replaced shop hoardings. In short, anything at all. Nothing is stolen. Driving past his domain, one might be mistaken for thinking it was the entrance to a tip but, on closer inspection, it will be seen all the plastic detritus has been carefully positioned and tied in place. There is a design, albeit invisible to others, to the strewn trees, bushes and boulders. But then all artistic appreciation is solely dependent upon individual conception.

Forty years ago, the King might have had a usurper on his hands.

When I was a young child, in the years immediately after the war, Hong Kong was still the home for those whom the war had not so much displaced geographically as mentally. The local Chinese who had seen through the Japanese occupancy were busy rebuilding the colony, as were the released expatriate internees along with a flood of returning residents, refugees from Communism and fortune-hunters from Europe and the USA but there were those foreigners for whom the horrors of war had been the scissors to cut the last threads holding them to reality. They often lived only one step up from the street-sleepers of which, in the early fifties, there were tens of thousands in Kowloon, Western District and Wanchai. Sometimes living off the land, by discreet begging or on the charity of their own kind, a small percentage of these vagrants were White Russians. A few had the most menial of jobs but most were at their beam ends and beyond reliable employment.

One such was a bizarre woman. She was customarily draped in the kind of clothes I associated with my paternal grandmother who had a penchant for Edwardian dresses with frilly bits here and there: the difference, of course, was that my grandmother's were clean, in good condition and fitted her somewhat ample frame. The woman's hair was grey and piled into a loose bun that was never under control and wobbled from side to side as she walked. Her gait, somewhat like that of a seaman used to swaying decks and tilting skies, was a side-to-side wallow. I never saw her face without such a thick coating of clumsily applied make-up that she might have been a surrealist's impression of a Cantonese opera star after a night out on the town in a typhoon.

On the few occasions I came across her in the streets of Mong Kok, where I used to wander in search of adventure, she smelt of whisky and, I was subsequently to realise, opium. She spoke English with a strong Russian accent as well as French, German and something I presume was Russian. Furthermore, she also had a native command of Cantonese and Shanghainese which she spoke with all the fluent intonation and vehemence of an angry coolie. It was not unknown for her to steal food. I watched her doing this on a number of occasions, her main target being fruit stalls. The stallholders, canny to her wiles, either chased her off as one might a pigeon in a field of peas or simply ignored her in order to avoid a noisy and awkward confrontation.

For some reason, the old hag took an occasional shine to me. If I was with my Chinese friends, children of the streets and tenements, this was excruciatingly embarrassing: if I was on my own, she scared the hell out of me yet I never ran away, out of manners rather than anything else. My most memorable encounter with her took place in a little square in Liberty Avenue.

I was walking back from Mong Kok, just across the railway lines which ran past the square on an embankment. The buildings around the square were residential tenements, hung with laundry on poles and rich with the song of birds in cages. It was early afternoon, the sun high and very hot. There was no one about save an old man sitting on the curb scaling and gutting fish in a wooden tub.

Suddenly, I saw the White Russian woman appear from a doorway. She was glancing back over her shoulder as if to check she was not being followed. I thought she might have just thieved something from one of the tenements but she frequently looked over her shoulder in this fashion. Spying me, she headed straight for me. I stood quite still. If the worst came to the worst, I could run to the old man for help.

'Boy!' the woman snapped and, reaching out, she slapped her hand down hard on my shoulder.

It was the first time she had ever touched me.

'What iss your name?'

I was silent, I think, for she repeated, '*Comment appelle-tu?* What iss your name?'

'Martin,' I replied sheepishly.

'Mar-teen. Mar-teen. What the difference, eh! Alexei. Mar-teen.'

She let go of my shoulder and briefly tousled my hair in an affectionate way. Looking at her hands I felt repulsed for her fingers were grimy and her long nails black as soot.

'You know me? You know me?' she enquired, her voice suddenly angry, imperious.

I shook my head.

'I am Anastasia. Princess!' She drew herself up in a regal fashion and flicked her head up to give me a better look of her profile. The bun slung to one side. 'I am Empress of Russia. Of R-r-russia!'

As if she were wearing a ball gown, she swept her skirts up

with her grubby fingers and walked slowly, majestically across the square, past the old man who did not so much as look up from his fish, to the corner of Peace Avenue. There she stopped and turned.

'They deed-n't kill us all,' she shouted. 'Not all! Not all!'

With that, she disappeared round the corner. After a stunned moment, I ran after her but she was nowhere to be seen.

For years afterwards, well into the sixties, there were local stories circulating that Anastasia had survived the assassination of Czar Nicholas II's family at Yekaterinburg, had fled eastwards to Siberia where the royal entourage had been living in exile and then, by way of China, had drifted to Hong Kong with the White Russian migration. She was rumoured to be hiding in a squatter shack somewhere in the foothills now the dominion of the King of Kowloon but no one ever succeeded in tracking her down. A few tried but she was either not there, ran away at their approach, or was but a figment of the imagination.

Yet the fact remains that, before Kowloon had a king, it might have had an empress.

Wong Tai Sin

Once upon a time, there was a shepherd boy called Wong Tai-sin who lived on Red Pine Hill, far away in the province of Zhejiang. His was a lonely life in the mountains, tending a herd of sheep as they grazed across the grassy slopes. Then, one day when he was fifteen years old, he was approached by an old man who, announcing himself to be one of the Immortals, taught the boy the art of refining cinnabar into a miracle cure for all human illnesses. For the next forty years, it is said, Wong Tai-sin lived in isolation perfecting the drug until, eventually, he was discovered by his brother who had been sent by their father to find him and see what had become of the sheep. It was revealed, in the interim four decades, that some of the sheep had been lost so Wong Tai-sin, with the powers now vested in him, metamorphosed some boulders into replacement animals. He left his mountain solitude then to travel through China as a healer, curing the sick with his wondrous potion. In due course, he was deified in the way gods are and became an immortal sage himself. A local Hong Kong deity, his birthday is the twenty-third day of the Eighth Moon and his specialities are healing or advising the sick, assisting people with business worries and accurately prophesying the future.

As far as Hong Kong is concerned, Wong Tai-sin has two memorials – an MTR station bearing his name and the temple dedicated to him which stands above it, the largest in Kowloon. It is not an ancient structure. The image of Wong Tai Sin (as he is now known) only arrived in Hong Kong in 1915, brought by a man and his son from Canton. It was placed first in a tiny temple in Wanchai then moved to another small temple on the present site in 1921 but this was demolished and, in 1973, the present temple complex was built.

The temple is always busy: there are no set daily services but ceremonies take place at Chinese New Year when the place is jammed to a standstill with devotees thanking Wong Tai Sin for his protection and asking him to predict the coming twelvemonth. The sage's birthday is also busier than usual as are the mornings of race days when punters seek advice beyond the form card as to which horse might buck the odds.

It is the best place in Hong Kong to see not only traditional Chinese temple architecture in all its glory but also to observe the rituals of Chinese religious life and tourist inanity. The devout come to pray and understand their cosmos, tourists come to photograph, gawp and, if their guide is efficient, have their fortunes told.

As soon as the visitor leaves the MTR station, the proximity of the temple is evidenced by the long line of elderly crones begging or selling bundles of joss sticks. They form an orderly queue, the one at the head, confronting an arrival to the temple entrance then joining the end of the queue to await her turn again. At the beginning of the temple precinct are a mass of stalls selling scarlet and gold talismans with all the paraphernalia of religious devotion from mobiles to hang in car windows to fortune telling devices made of wood.

Built on a slight hill to obey the demands of *fung shui*, the temple entrance is through an ornate gate and up several flights of stone steps to a courtyard in the centre of which stands a vast bronze urn and a line of tables. These are laden with offerings of oranges, grapes, bottles of Chinese wine, paper money and, if the supplicant is particularly grateful or in need of considerable divine intervention, a whole roast suckling pig. The paper money is burned in large tubs to the side of the urn so its value may rise to heaven, the air drifting a black snow of ashes into the sky and over devotees and tourists.

From the urn, another broad flight of steps leads under a granite carved archway to the main altar building. It is a very large, exquisite building with a gold roof under vermilion supporting pillars, bright yellow latticework and azure friezes with a multitude of coloured carvings. The altar resides across a courtyard surrounded by a cloister. The image of Wong Tai Sin is a painting inside the altar hall which may not be entered, surrounded by the customary draperies and illuminated by a series of lights hanging from the dark abyss of the roof. To one side is an altar to the Monkey God, a mischievous and impish deity also known as the Great Sage Equal to Heaven.

As long as the temple is open, the courtyard is never devoid of worshippers. They kneel on little mats, on cushions or on the flags of the yard and engage either in prayer, in tendering their offerings or seeking their fortune. Over their heads drifts the blue haze of incense whilst the air around them is filled with sound – the mutter of supplication, the whispers of entreaties, the shuffle of feet, the muted sound of bird-song (although there is not a bird to be seen) and the rattle of fortune sticks.

Fortune-telling is a semi-self-service ritual. The petitioner obtains from a desk in the left-hand cloister a cylindrical bamboo holder about twenty centimetres tall containing a few dozen long bamboo splints each of which bears a number carved into it. Lighting joss sticks which may be stuck in an urn or one of the oranges being given as alms, the petitioner kneels and, holding the cylinder in both hands starts to gently shake it to and fro at a slight angle to the vertical. Gradually, the splints rise up within the cylinder until one falls out. This is then taken to the desk, the container returned in exchange for a piece of pink paper with red characters on it. This corresponds to the number of the loosened splint. The note may either be interpreted by the petitioner or taken to the fortune-telling arcade for a more thorough interpretation.

The fortune-telling ritual never fails to draw the lens of cameras and videos which click, whir and spin in competition with

277

the temple noises. The worshippers, with a patience borne of Job (or maybe Wong Tai Sin), pay no heed to this intrusion. Yet I have seen a tourist kneel right next to an old woman at prayer to obtain a better profile or finer lighting and, getting up, call to his wife that that was the shot of the trip: my caustic suggestion that he might use a long focus lens was met with a blank stare of astonishment. Few people would dream of behaving in this fashion in a cathedral in Europe and certainly no Chinese would have the effrontery to so interrupt another human conversing with his god.

To the left of the altar building is a formal Chinese garden with curiously shaped rocks, ponds and a replica of the Beijing Nine Dragon Wall whilst to the right are assorted halls, shrines, pavilions and a clinic offering Western medicine on the ground floor and Chinese herbal cures above: one of the buildings is a memorial hall for the members of a local Taoist organisation, the walls lined with spirit tablets while another is dedicated to Confucius. Old folk wander through these precincts, sit on the stone benches or walls and chat in the sunlight or read newspapers. Tourists saunter about unknowing of the fact that all the buildings, fountains, trees and urns are arranged according to the geomantic principles of the five elements – gold, wood, water, fire and earth.

Occasional sparrows hop silently under benches and bushes looking for crumbs dropped from offerings but they do not so much as cheep at each other. And yet, here, the air is even more stridently filled with bird-song. Looking up, the trees shelter no birds. None perches on the temple roofs. Then the truth dawns. This is not piped electronic bird-song nor some imitator with a flute. It is not even the gods themselves. It is the music of hundreds of caged songbirds hanging in the windows of the twenty-storey blocks of low-cost resettlement flats which tower up on all sides just over the temple wall.

Leaving the temple one passes through the fortune-tellers' arcade. Cubicles line the passageways in which sit a wide variety of soothsayers, all of them men: this is not a profession for females who seem to be as specifically excluded as they were from the old

Hong Kong Club. Despite the neon lighting and concrete floors, the place has a distinctly medieval air about it, redolent of hope and despair, faith and anguish, trust and fear.

Each cubicle is much like the next: about the size of a very large wardrobe, it contains a little table and two or three stools. The walls are lined with palmists' and phrenologists' charts, letters of thanks from satisfied customers, florid testimonials and certificates and, frequently, the faded photograph of the sage who passed on his wisdom to the present incumbent. The fortune-tellers themselves are always middle-aged or older – this is an old man's vocation – and have about themselves an immense calm, like a priest or a pilot, a surgeon or a man utterly confident of his abilities. Some dress in shirt and trousers and look like bank clerks. Others aspire to traditional Chinese clothes. One or two, either from tradition or an astute business sense, cultivate thin wispy beards like the sages of old and keep one fingernail inordinately long to prove they are not manual workers but thinkers and philosophers. Very few of them speak English and most tourists pass them by either because of the language barrier or because they do not believe although, I suspect, they are more afraid than sceptical. The last time I visited Wong Tai Sin I overheard the following conversation near the stall of one of the few prognosticators who advertises a knowledge of English. The speakers were an Australian couple in their early thirties.

He, light-heartedly – 'Go on, have your fortune told.'

She, curtly then with a hint of caution – 'No. You shouldn't mess with that sort of thing.'

He, chiding and smiling – 'Go on. It's just a bit of fun. No harm in it.'

She, adamant then teasing – 'No. If you're so keen, why don't you?'

He, after a pause and dismissively – 'No. Well, it's stupid, ain't it?'

She, argumentatively – 'It might be, it might not be. They (pointing to an old Chinese woman and her daughter paying deep attention to a fortune-teller) look to believe in it all right.'

He, dismissively then thoughtfully – 'No. It's all mumbo-jumbo. Anyway, what if he says our plane crashes . . .'

I have an abiding respect for these fortune-tellers. My life was foretold by one when I was six and his predictions have come true so far without a fault, accurate to the year. In 1989, I took my then thirteen-year-old son, Alexander, to one of the English speaking sages at Wong Tai Sin. The man, after studying his hand and brow for a moment, summed up his character with such clarity and precision – a hard-working, clever boy who did not like sport, who enjoyed puzzles and making intricate objects, who read a lot, who was sometimes stubborn in his studies and who would go far in his chosen career in business if he overcame this obdurate streak – that my son was silent for some hours afterwards, as shocked as the Australian would have been if recommended to change his flight booking.

Nothing is so frightening as a hint of possible truth.

The Land of the Precious Lotus

Lan tau means *broken head* in Cantonese: it might refer to what an infamous local brigand called Yuen did to opponents or it could reflect the result of travelling on the No. 1 bus to Tai O but, in truth, it refers to the mountains which run along the length of the island.

Known colloquially as *Tai Yue Shan* or Big Island Mountain, Lantau lies to the west of the colony and is the largest of Hong Kong's islands: at 142 square kilometres, it is almost twice the size of Hong Kong Island, its highest point rising nearly twice as high as the Peak. It is a rugged land of steep, grass- and scrub-covered mountains, wooded valleys, long white sand beaches and rocky outcrops, two dozen or so small villages, two exclusive residential developments, a reservoir, three prisons, a drinking hole of some notoriety and four monasteries. All these account for a resident population of less than 55,000 which makes Lantau the least densely inhabited area of Hong Kong.

At first, Lantau was called *Tai Hai* (or *Kai*) *Shan* on a map dated 1425 but the earliest recognisable identification, on a map of the late 1500s, named it *Tai Ho Shan* (or Big Oyster(shell) Mountain). For two centuries, the name wavered between these two and the still-used Tai Yue Shan, the name *Lantao* coming to the fore in the 1760s.

However, long before cartographers recorded the island, it was a place of settlement. At the very south-western tip of the island is a stone circle that might or might not be Neolithic or

Bronze Age, whilst a few kilometres away near the base of the Shek Pik reservoir dam, at the time of its construction the largest in the world built with loose earth, there is an assuredly Bronze Age rock carving. Above the reservoir and at Tung Chung on the northern shore are other rocks incised with grid patterns similar to those used for the Chinese board games of *sam gei* and *luk tsz gei* although their age is unknown.

Large kilns dating to the Tang dynasty can be found at Yi Long Wan, right on the beach where they were operated rendering sea shells and coral into lime which was used in cement, as a fertiliser on the salty coastal soils and for the careening of the hulls of junks. These kilns – there are fourteen of them – have suffered a similar fate to that of the Sung Wong Toi monument. Four of them have been protected and lie not in the middle of a roundabout by the airport but next to beach loungers and sail-boards ten metres from the exclusive Sea Ranch residential estate. Elsewhere, a hoard of Sung dynasty coins and a bronze dagger were found in addition to two 'taxation stones', boundary markers for the family of Li Mao-ying to whom a part of the island was ceded by the Sung emperor Ta Tsung in 1265.

Boundary stones of more recent vintage exist on the western end of the island where the land meets Chinese territorial waters. The inscription on the northernmost stone tells its tale:

1902

> This stone is in longitude 113° 52' 0" E fixed by Lieut. and Comd^r F.M. Leake, R.N. and the officers of H.M.S. "Bramble". From here the boundary line extends due North until it meets the parallel of the Southern extremity on the Nam-tau Peninsula. Southward the boundary follows the western shore of Lantau Island.

A second inscription adds, *This stone is placed 380 feet above H.W. mark for the purpose of protecting it from possible inroads of the sea.* Such was the surety of officers of the British Empire, that Hong Kong would remain sovereign, her establishing treaties unaltered or surrendered for as long as it took the oceans to rise so far: they acted without a knowledge of modern political chicanery.

At Tung Chung, on the northern shore of the island, there is a fortress. Built in the 1820s as part of the Imperial Chinese coastal defence network, primarily against pirates and foreign traders, it is eighty by sixty metres square with five metre high walls made of huge granite blocks with three arched gateways beneath squat watchtowers. The ramparts bear six early nineteenth-century cannons but the fort was constructed not as a strategic defence but as an administrative centre.

I first visited it in the winter of 1963. It was semi-derelict, overgrown with creepers and haunted by two chow dogs which barked noncommittally then slunk away into the undergrowth. The buildings within the walls were mossed, the cannons blotched with rust and a jungle of snaring weeds sprouted through the steps and flagstones. Today, the place is somewhat altered. The walls ring with infantile joy, the cannons stand burnished and the inscription over the main gate is scrubbed clean of lichen: the interior of the fort, at various times an imperial military *yamen* and a colonial police station, is now Tung Chung Primary School. How much longer this situation will remain one dare not guess. The former sleepy fishing village of Ma Wan Chung nearby, with its beached sampans and rickety pier which rocked as the ferry docked against it, is doomed. The ruined cannon battery above the village, contemporary with the fort, overlooks what was the island of Chek Lap Kok: the whole area is being levelled, reclaimed, transformed and generally adulterated to make Hong Kong's new state-of-the-art international airport.

There is another redoubt at Fan Lau, known in ancient records as the Kai Yik Kok fort: it is barely fifty metres from the curious stone circle which may be connected to it. A low ruin overgrown with bushes, it is a long hike from the nearest village but worth the effort. From its crumbled battlements which once guarded the Tiger's Mouth, one sees the South China Sea much as the pirates, Portuguese and opium-peddling sea captains did.

It stretches far off to distant hazy islands, the surface blue to one side and vaguely brown to the other where the Pearl River currents dump the last of their silt in the ocean. Only the high-speed jet-foils cutting by bound for Macau and merchant ships at anchor to the north west give away the date. Fishing junks, some under sail below their bat-wing sheets, still trawl the waters. And it is only three kilometres from here that the *Miss Macau* came down.

The main landing on Lantau is at Mui Wo, otherwise known as Silver Mine Bay. It is an easy journey from Central in an air-conditioned HYF outlying island ferry, the seats reasonably comfortable with a valuable external after-deck. This is frequently a godsend, a welcome escape from happy-go-lucky youths on the upper deck, armed with stereos capable of the volume of a discotheque against which old ladies, crocheting or knitting, furiously compete. *En route*, the ferry calls in to the island of Peng Chau as if using this as an introduction to sights to come, preparing one for a very different world from skyscrapers and traffic snarl-ups. The little harbour is crowded with sampans and a few fishing junks, some of the buildings lining the quay quaintly old, a section of them to the north reasonably new: the originals were destroyed thirty years ago when a factory making matches – Peng Chau was famous for its matches which were exported world-wide – blew up. Or was it fireworks? They made those on the island, too. What I do recall, however, is the explosion being heard in Central, thirteen kilometres away.

Arriving at Mui Wo is rather like stepping into the New Territories as they were forty years ago. There are some buses but they are rattling, rural, wretched beasts transferred here after having outlived their serviceability on the streets of Kowloon. They run on just two routes – Mui Wo to Tai O (No. 1) and Mui Wo to Ngong Ping (No. 2). Tung Chung is served by a *pak pai* line in addition to which there are forty taxis, most of which are in a similar state of decrepitude to the buses. To my mind, these vehicles add to the charm of Lantau. After the efficient air-conditioned double-decker buses of Hong Kong – not to mention air-conditioned taxis, underground railway carriages, mini-buses, hovercraft, jet-foils and ferries – it is a pleasure to drive with the window open and be assaulted by butterflies as big as sparrows rather than diesel fumes and lorries loaded with steel rods squeezing by at forty miles an hour, less than an arm's length away.

Mui Wo itself is not without attraction. The Li taxation stone sits (perhaps inevitably) in a little garden beside the bus station surrounded by trim flower-beds and, not far away along a narrow road beside the shore, a grey stone tower may be seen beside a wide creek. It is all that remains of the stronghold of one Yuen who was, arguably, Hong Kong's last real pirate, as opposed to the stockbroking variety. His gang numbered more than a hundred and he was involved in a wide variety of crimes ranging – according to rumour – from kidnapping and straight piracy to theft, opium dealing and running the deck-chair franchise on the beach. He remained powerful on Lantau until the mid-sixties, living like a little war-lord without a war until, getting on in years, he surrendered to the authorities and another aspect of the island came under the sway of the modern world.

The silver mine, high above the bay, is blocked up now. Never much more than a deep cave of galleries, it was mined for about thirty years but closed down in 1896. The quality of the ore was low – Chinese silver is notoriously brittle because of a high tin content – and the influx of foreign silver coinage, especially the release onto the market of Mexican silver dollars from which Hong Kong gained its unit of currency, flooded the market.

When I was eight, I entered the cave, hung over with tendrils of moss, damp and dripping even in the dry winter months. With a torch, I walked about five metres into the cloying air and collected a piece of ore. It was twenty years before I discovered I had the silver equivalent of fool's gold.

The main (the only!) road on Lantau runs along the southern shore, passing through quiet hamlets and beside neat paddyfields, now growing vegetables rather than rice, across a rim of wide beaches at Cheung Sha Wan (Long Sand Bay) largely unpolluted (and un populated during the week), winding over ridges and along the crest of the Shek Pik dam. Fifty metres beneath the reservoir surface lie the ruins of Shek Pik village, its fields, ancient houses and little temple through which I wandered just after the people had been evacuated but before the waters began to rise. From Shek Pik, the road rises into the mountains, twisting back on itself like a dragon's tail, crossing a pass to drop down, twenty kilometres from Mui Wo, to the fishing village of Tai O (Big Haven), the most westerly settlement, save for a few isolated houses, in Hong Kong.

For over a thousand years, the Hong Kong region was famous for its salt industry which only finally disappeared in the mid-fifties and it was salt which made Tai O famous. Salt and one god. Even before the Sung dynasty, Tai O was producing salt which was most probably shipped by junk to Tuen Mun and thence through the New Territories and up into China: here and there, fragments of the old salt road still exist . During the Sung period, it was an important centre not only for its salt but also for its strategic position at the mouth of the Pearl River estuary. When the Mongols swept across China, eradicating the Sung empire, it was between Tai O and Lingding Island where the final sea battle reputedly took place, in which the Sung fleet was sunk.

The remnants of the salt pans remain in Tai O to this day, although they are likely soon to disappear under reclamation: a few are already transformed into a car park and a building site. In the meantime they are being re-utilised as fishponds. What has not, however, vanished yet is the air of old China which pervades the village.

The bus halts at a terminus on the outskirts of the old village – a new rash of concrete boxes called the Lung Tin Estate has sprung up inland from this, a blight upon what was once paddyfields and more salt pans. None of the streets are suitable for vehicles so Tai O appears truly rural although modernity has stepped in. Coke and Pepsi signs abound and the shops sell not only dried seafood and coolie hats (for wearing, not hanging on the wall), glazed earthenware storage jars and clay braziers, noodles and rattan furniture but also televisions, hi-fi sets and green, red and white Fuji film. One shop, when I last walked down the street, had a life-size cut-out of Larry Hagman by the door, advertising a herbal cure for dandruff. Close by was a poster of Freddie Mercury overwritten in red characters with a warning against HIV infection.

At the end of the street is an unusual sight, at least for Hong Kong. Across a narrow canal bisecting the village, half of which is on an island, plies a flat punt-like sampan propelled by two old women tugging on a rope passing through runners on the side of their craft. These two have a most lucrative monopoly for they control the sole means of travelling to the island from the road. A ride costs thirty cents one way and takes less than two minutes for the canal is not much more than thirty metres wide.

The old ladies, in common with most of the people of Tai O, are of Tanka origin, fishing people descended from the first substantial tribe to settle in southern China. They wear black *sam* jackets and rattan hats with a broad, down-turned brim, their hands as hornily callused as their bare feet. Their toes, unrestricted by shoes, grip the planking with a simian surety. Everything goes by way of their punt – livestock and passengers, bicycles and motorbikes, sacks of cloth, bundles of daily papers, dried fish and even domestic appliances. I once saw three Zanussi chest freezers weigh the craft down to the gunwales.

Many of the houses in Tai O are built on stilts over the water. That they survive the merest breeze, never mind a typhoon, appears to be a miracle for they all look to be balancing on their wooden poles more by whim than design. Every house seems to be made of lengths of timber left over from the building of junks or sampans. Some are painted blue, others white and the rest varnished like the boats their constituent parts might once have made – or been. Little balconies lead down to sampans or fibreglass rowing boats with outboard motors bolted to them. Chickens cluck in narrow coops, strings of fish hang out to dry next to laundry, TV aerials project upwards from galvanised poles, potted plants flower gaudily next to plastic drums of water, buckets of flicking prawns and cage-birds twitter in the shade. It is as if the Tanka people, traditionally fisherfolk, have been obliged to settle on land but have struck an uneasy compromise with one part of their homes still at sea.

Once on the island, past a branch office of the HongkongBank – the money comes across on the punt, in the company of security guards – and through a little market, a thoroughfare called Kut Hing Back Street turns right and passes before a magnificent temple dedicated to the god, Kwan Tai. Where salt made Tai O famous in ancient times, this temple has given it a seminal part to play in the history of modern China, although few people know it, including those local residents with whom I have spoken.

Kwan Tai is the god of war, righteousness, literature and brotherhoods and, as such, is the most important deity in the pantheon worshipped by the Triads. The temple was constructed in 1784 and although it has been repaired and restored a number of times since, it retains the air of originality. One of the building's most spectacular features is an intricate tableau along the entire roof ridge depicting a village street in the Ming dynasty with ogres, gods and demons conversing with ordinary mortals, Kwan Tai in the very centre before his own pagoda.

Just inside the main door, the side pillars pasted with red banners, are the statues of two horses. That on the right is of Kwan Tai's horse, Red Hare, which he rode into battle, the one on the left that of Liu Pei, the Shu or Minor Han Dynasty emperor whom Kwan Tai served. Unlike many gods Kwan Tai, who was deified in the sixteenth century by the Ming emperor, Wan Li, is based upon a historical figure called Kuan Yu, a hero of the third century AD. Two other heavenly beings share his altar here. One is Choi San, the god of wealth and prosperity, the other Wah T'o, the physician god. The former is a purely mythical invention but the latter, like Kwan Tai, is based upon a real person, a famous doctor of the Three Kingdoms period of Chinese history who is considered to be the father of acupuncture. Needless to say, he is the patron god of herbalists and traditional medicine practitioners.

Today, the Triads are considered primarily to be racketeers, drug-smugglers and organised crime gangsters but a century ago they were just as much patriots fighting against the Manchu Ch'ing dynasty in the hope of restoring the Ming descendants to the imperial throne. Amongst their number was a doctor. He was born in Kwangtung province near Macau in 1866 and, after an early education in Hawaii, came to Hong Kong where he enrolled in Queen's College. At the age of twenty, he entered the Po-chi Hospital School in Canton and, in 1887, took up a position at the Alice Memorial Hospital in Hong Kong, graduating with a degree in medicine from the University of Hong Kong in 1894. He was a member of several Triad societies, amongst them the Chung Wo Tong society in Hong Kong and the Kwok On Wui in Hawaii. His name was Sun Yat-sen.

Engaging increasingly in republican politics, Sun Yat-sen's presence in Hong Kong became an embarrassment to the British administration which did not want to be seen to take sides: throughout history, great efforts have been made not to rock the boat of trade. In 1895, he was forced to flee China after a failed *coup d'état* and, the following year, he was deported from Hong Kong. That his political struggle continued is well-known for it culminated in 1911 with the revolution which led, on 1 January 1912, to the declaration of the Republic of China with Sun Yat-sen as the provisional president and Pu Yi, the last emperor, dethroned.

What is not known is that Sun Yat-sen, like any true Triad member, was very keen to pay homage to Kwan Tai, to ask for his support in the 1911 struggle. To this end, and probably to show support to Hong Kong patriots who had considerably financed his cause, Sun Yat-sen sneaked back into Hong Kong whilst proscribed on at least two occasions in order to worship at this very temple.

It was the most appropriate one for him to attend. Chinese territorial waters begin on the western shore of Lantau and, in those days, Tai O was no easy ferry and rattling bus ride but a full two days' journey from Central by boat and overland. Only the Royal Navy anti-piracy patrols visited this coast and then infrequently. Slipping in and out of Tai O from Macau was simplicity itself. And so Tai O has played, albeit unwittingly, an important role in the establishment of modern China: it was where the gods' assistance was requested and, seemingly, granted.

A little way beyond the temple, Sun Kit Street bears off to the right and leads to a drawbridge. It is not that ancient a structure but it looks it, constructed of planks and ropes. It leads back to Lantau but on the other side of a creek from the road so it poses no threat to the old ladies. From the bridge can be seen a panoramic view of Tai O creek, the moored sampans and junks, their masts hung with drift and trawl nets and racks of drying fish or squid, the stilt houses and, in the background, the mountains of Lantau or the wooded slopes of Tai O island. Remove the TV aerials, outboard motors and a few other modern trappings and the scene is essentially unaltered for five hundred years.

Another ten minutes' walk around Tai O island is the temple to Hau Wong, the most famous of the seven temples within a kilometre or so of the boat crossing. Hau Wong is based less tenuously than Kwan Tai upon a real person. When the Sung boy emperor fled to Kowloon, he was accompanied by a trusted bodyguard called Yeung. Whilst in Kowloon, Yeung fell seriously ill and, when the emperor left, remained behind to establish a rearguard defence against the Mongols. Sadly, however, he died and the boy emperor was drowned a short time later. In the meantime, Yeung had impressed the local people with his devotion and, on his death, he was given the title of Hau Wong, the approximate equivalent rank of a marquis.

The temple was built in 1699 which makes it possibly the oldest of its kind in Hong Kong: there are two others, one in Kowloon City near where the boy emperor stayed which was built in 1731, the other at Tung Chung, about a kilometre from the fort. The fact there are two on Lantau suggests to some the boy emperor may well have met his death on the island and not, as some of the chronicles suggest, further west.

No matter how quaint, picturesque and genuinely Chinese Tai O appears, there is another place on Lantau that is far more spectacular and is, in every respect, the crowning glory of the island. It is the Buddhist monastery of Po Lin.

I first went to the monastery at the age of eight. There were no roads at all on Lantau in those days and the journey necessitated a long walk over the mountains following centuries-old paths. A weekend in the monastery was an excursion favoured by hardy expatriates and my parents, with a number of others, decided to make the trek. Such journeys were only undertaken in the winter for the summer heat and sun posed a dangerous risk in the mountains for fair-skinned *gweilos*.

The full name of the community is *Po Lin Ching Tze* which translates as the Meditation of the Precious Lotus Monastery. It was founded in 1905 at Ngong Ping on a small, rolling plateau at an altitude of about 500 metres, just to the west of Fung Wong Shan, or Lantau Peak, the highest summit of the island. Three monks looking for a retreat settled there, building a small stone house. In the way of religious communities, others joined them and the monastery received its name in 1924, being inaugurated three years later. The war years passed it by almost unheeded. The Japanese spasmodically patrolled the mountains but left Lantau mainly well alone for few partisans were thought to operate there and, besides, the occupying forces were hard stretched for numbers from late 1943 onwards when the tide of war began to turn in the Allies' favour.

The monks built a small temple and a range of outbuildings containing dormitories, a dining hall and a cookhouse. Being Buddhists, they were all vegetarians so the plateau was cultivated, affording a self-contained if frugal existence. And so, until the early fifties, the monks remained, cut off from the thriving metropolis thirty kilometres away. From time to time, however, they received visitors. Some were devout Buddhists on retreat and some were curious foreigners: all were equally welcomed for Buddhist monasteries are bound by a strict code of hospitality. Although no charge was made for staying in the monastery, visitors left a generally accepted sum of money in exchange for a bed and a few meals.

To reach Ngong Ping, one walked up the mountain from Tung Chung. It was a hard climb of about six kilometres. The path started by the pier and wound for two kilometres across paddyfields, past the fort and a little wayside shrine to the Earth God at which point it started to climb steeply through first bushes then stunted pine trees to Tei Tong Tsai. Here was a little temple attended by a small number of resident Buddhist nuns, their heads shaved and their habits grey. Beside the path was a spring bubbling over stones, providing welcome relief to sore feet and dry throats. From the little nunnery, the path rose less steeply to a ceremonial Chinese archway in a pass between a low mountain and Lantau Peak. Dropping slightly to the plateau, it then made its way through cultivated patches and past the tombs of deceased monks to the monastery.

The memory of my first visit is still vivid. We arrived late in the afternoon, the sun going down over the mountains, night drawing quickly in. A dull bell boomed deeply in the twilight, the monks carrying guttering oil lamps on their way through the buildings. I followed them to find them at their evening meal, squatting at low tables with a bowl of rice before each of them, one of their number incanting as they all ate methodically. Nearby a monk, who must have been in a trance, swung a cylinder of wood suspended from the ceiling against a massive bronze bell shaped like an upturned tulip. He intoned every thirty seconds, as accurate as a chronometer.

After a simple vegetarian meal, our party split up by sex and I was taken to a dormitory with the men. The interior was illuminated by two oil lamps hanging from rafters bare to the roof, the floor made of flags of mountain stone. Each bed was a hard, wooden, traditional *k'ang* with a timber framework over it from which a curtain or mosquito net might be draped. The boards were covered by a sheet of rush matting and a padded quilt: for a pillow there was a lacquer wooden block. We slept in our underclothes.

Some time not long before dawn, I woke to hear the bell ringing again and feet shuffling by. I slipped from my *k'ang* and went to the window, pushing aside the wooden shutters. It was a chilly night with an ice-bright half-moon. Beneath me filed a line of monks, their closely shaven heads smooth in the cold light, going towards the temple. I quickly dressed, slipped out of the dormitory, down the stairs and outside. The temple was across a passageway between the buildings and I made for it as the last of the monks disappeared.

Cautiously, I entered the temple. The monks were kneeling on the tiled floor, facing the altar on which stood a gilded idol of Sakyamuni, the founder of Buddhism. Draperies and banners in red and gold hung on either side, coils of incense drifting smoke down from the ceiling. The altar was lit by a number of candles and small open-flame oil lamps. Everywhere there seemed to be the glowing stubs of joss sticks like a million little red eyes watching from the darkness. I secreted myself by the door and sat cross-legged on the tiles, leaning against the wall. A monk began to chant, the others joining in with responses. I kept quiet. I do not know how long the service lasted but, just before the end, one monk looked over his shoulder at me and smiled. I had assumed none of them knew of my presence for they were all kneeling with their backs to me and was somewhat perturbed. I think I smiled sheepishly in return then slipped away.

Yet I had seen something I have never forgotten. It was not that the religion captivated me so much as the incredible antiquity of it all. Despite having lived in Hong Kong for some time, it was then I felt I first saw the true China and was drawn inescapably into it.

In the morning, I said nothing to my parents. We washed in a viciously cold tub of water running straight off the mountain, used the exceptionally uncomfortable squat-down lavatories and drank bowls of tea, the latter made from leaves picked by the monks from wild tea bushes which used to grow on the plateau: it was here, at the monastery breakfast table, I discovered my lifelong dislike of *congee*. The tea drunk, we set off for a day's walk to Mui Wo and the ferry back to Hong Kong.

Over the years, I have frequently returned to Po Lin. Sometimes, I have stayed for days on end, at other times I have just stopped over for an hour or two. Needless to say, the place has changed somewhat . . .

The road up to the monastery now ends in a car park and bus terminus lined by stalls selling religious knick-knacks, talismans, ice creams and Coke. On a hillside to the right is erected the world's largest structure of its kind – a thirty-four metre high, 250 ton bronze statue of the seated Buddha. Constructed in the fashion of the Statue of Liberty, it consists of a steel skeletal framework covered by 202 ten-milimetre-thick, bronze sections individually cast in Nanking and shipped to Po Lin. The technology of this massive piece of sculpture is space-age: indeed, it is said the Chinese equivalent of NASA had a substantial hand in the engineering design. Rust-proofed with modern plastic-based paint, the statue cost HK$60 million.

Indeed, the monastery has done well from visitors and bequests, trippers and tourists, hikers and picnickers. It is now a limited company with the abbot as Chief Executive Officer and a board of directorial monks. In the sixties, they spent HK$2 million on building a range of facilities including a magnificent two-storey temple complex, part of the mortar for which I helped mix in the winter of 1963. This has a gold ceramic tile roof decorated with china animals. The Three Precious Buddha idols are three metres high and covered in gold leaf, with Sakyamuni in the centre of the temple accompanied by The Healing Buddha, the Goddess of Mercy, Kwun Yam and the Lord of the Western Paradise. In the monastery grounds, tubs of flowers cater for droves of butterflies, pools ripple with fish and terrapins and there is a huge restaurant where Buddhist food is served on a ticket basis. Not only is it exceedingly cheap but it is utterly superb.

No menu is shown: a visitor gets the *carte du jour* and that's an end to it. Unfortunately, Europeans tend not to get the real McCoy unless they ask for it: there appears to be a *gweilo* menu to cater for tourists and it is important to avoid this for it is bland and unexciting.

The meal consists of five or six courses. Black Chinese mushrooms, leaf vegetables such as Chinese cabbage and bean curd featuring prominently. The rice is plain and boiled. Each course comes in a unique sauce and – and this is the miracle of Buddhist cookery – the bean curd in one dish is somehow prepared so it looks like meat, has the texture of meat and tastes of meat but isn't. It is one of the culinary marvels of world cuisine.

Between the monastery and the ceremonial gateway on the Tung Chung pass there is now a horse riding centre and a commercial tea plantation where the monks used to have their vegetable plots. The tea plantation, the only one in Hong Kong, is idiosyncratically owned by a British barrister: its output is called *wan mo cha* (appropriately cloud and mist tea).

Po Lin is well ensconced on the tourist trail. Tour buses from Mui Wo deliver batches of people throughout the year. Around the monastery have sprung up little weekend cottages, a school and a youth hostel. The huge Buddha has a distinctly Disneyesque quality about it and, if it was to move its right hand in benediction, with laser bulbs beaming from its eyes, I would not be too taken aback.

And yet, despite all the razzmatazz of dollar earning, the old Po Lin is never far away. The original temple into which I crept as a child is still used for devotions twice a day and the monks still gather to eat in their dining room near the bell. The mountains are seasonally swathed in timeless mists and covered in grass rather than concrete and, incredibly, the old dormitory building still exists. When I last strolled in the gardens, I saw a Chinese cobra gliding in the bushes: evidently, it was aware of its security in the monastery precinct for it made no effort to accelerate away from a potential fate between a pair of chopsticks.

Certainly, jets fly by on their final approach, the derelict buses belch black smog as they start up and the sound of grasshoppers competes with that of video-cameras but, as in the rest of Hong Kong, the ancient ways of the Heavenly Kingdom are only just around the corner.

And there this chapter should end but for a recent public

announcement: Lantau is to undergo a transformation. For the worse. The new Chek Lap Kok airport, all 1248 hectares of it due to open in 1997, is to cater for thirty-five million passengers and 1.5 million tons of air freight per annum, this figure set to rise to eighty-seven and nine million respectively by the year 2040. The terminal is to have a floor area of 430,000 square metres and will be 1.4 kilometres in length, as long as the distance from Kowloon Star Ferry to Hong Kong island. A six-lane expressway will course along the north shore of Lantau to Kowloon, bridging the sea by cable-stay and suspension bridges, the little island of Ma Wan being transected by a motorway viaduct. Alongside this route will travel a parallel, new high-speed rail system running directly into Central. The Tung Chung valley is to be a city of 200,000 souls with other smaller cities sprouting up west of Tung Chung, at Tai Ho (presently a fishing hamlet with no road access) and at Yam O where the whole of Yam O Bay and the island of Cheung Sok will be reclaimed. Penny's Bay, which is currently isolated and undeveloped save for a small, 300Mw power station, is to be reclaimed and developed into a container port projecting several kilometres out to sea and a number of industrial sites are planned to rise up with the residential areas.

How long Tai O will hold out is anybody's guess. The old ladies could conceivably be put out of business by an overhead cable car system or a hovertrain.

In Hong Kong, anything is possible.

Postscript

It has taken just over four months to write this book, from March to late July 1993. Even in that short passage of time, things have changed and the first officer's comment as we touched down is given the steely ring of blunt truth.

Two press releases have arrived on my desk from the Hong Kong Government. The first reads:

> The contract for the demolition of the Kowloon Walled City, the largest single demolition project of its kind in Hong Kong, has been awarded by the Civil Engineering Department to Express-Cleveland Joint Venture at a cost of HK$42 million. The works will take 18 months to complete. The principal method of demolition will be the use of heavy mechanical demolition plant including 100 tonne crawler cranes with wrecking balls; and rigs which have booms with a maximum reach of 45 metres and equipped with concrete crushers and grapples. The some 300,000 tonnes of building debris generated will be recycled for use as fill material for reclamation projects.

And so the ancient buildings and the temples, the illegal factories and warrens of corridors, the dentists' surgeries and the coolie brothel will all end up as hard-core for the new international airport or the next container terminal. All that is to be preserved is the *yamen*, the two cannons, a granite lintel and verse couplet, two stone tablets from the Tin Hau temple and three wells. They are to be the centre-pieces for a 'Ching dynasty theme garden'

297

incorporating a park divided into various scenic areas such as ponds, bonsai garden, pine mound and rockery. This is ironic in the light of the 1947 suggestion for the building of a park which the Chinese government snubbed: it proves the Chinese adage that the bird who waits for the flower to die gets to eat the first seeds. And it would seem, in Hong Kong at least, crime does not pay – it gets bulldozed and history is prettified out of existence.

The second release concerns Tiu Keng Leng:

> Eligible residents affected by the clearance will be offered rehousing either in a public rental estate or a temporary housing area or priority in buying flats of home ownership schemes. Every effort will be made to rehouse those affected. The main public housing estate where eligible clearees will be rehoused will be the Hau Tak estate at Tseung Kwan O . . . It is also proposed that a new ex-gratia allowance of $3450 per square metre of floor area will be paid to owners . . . Having taken into account the geographical location of Tiu Keng Leng and consequently the higher cost of removal, it is also proposed that an enhanced domestic removal allowance will be paid to clearees. It is estimated that the clearance will involve about 6000 people and the total cost of the special allowance package will come to $312 million.

Somehow, I cannot class the old soldier in my mind as a *clearee*. He is – and will remain – a brave old warrior with few teeth left but a lot of will, pride, strength of character and dogged determination to survive against the odds.

Yung Long has gone. According to an acquaintance who flies helicopters in Hong Kong, Mr Cheng's house is a ruin and the beach is littered not just with flotsam but also more surveyor's poles. The highway cutting across the hills behind it is on the verge of opening to public traffic and dredgers are at work a quarter of the way to Lingding. The whereabouts of Mr and Mrs Cheng, so easily found before simply by driving past the ancient banyan tree sprouting from the boulder and down the dirt track to their ancestral home, would be hard to trace now. They are, I suppose, lost in the high-rise jungle of Tuen Mun whilst the cutting of their frangipani tree refused to take in my English house and withered away.

Blake Pier has also vanished. History is repeating itself and the pier, it seems, is to move yet further still from its original site. The sea into which it jutted is being reclaimed to accommodate the Hong Kong Island terminus for the high-speed rail link to the new airport. Whether or not another Blake Pier will eventually be erected beyond the station is anybody's guess.

The political stalemate between the old men of Beijing and the grey men of London continues in impasse. Democracy may or may not come. In the meantime, one of the most powerful Triad societies in Hong Kong is rumoured to have wined and dined the children of Li Peng, prime minister of China and architect of the Tienanmen Square butchery. Over the border, dire economic unrest threatens the stability of Chinese society and more and more Chinese money pours into Hong Kong to seek a safe haven. The future certainly looks as if it might be somewhat fraught.

And yet the hearts of fish still beat on the slabs of Spring Garden Lane, the wind still blows through the paper bark trees at Beas River, the Star Ferry still plies between Central and Tsim Sha Tsui, *wartcher beechews* still arrive to smack into street lights in early September and the crippled beggar still sits amidst the forest of rush-hour legs with his plastic mug.

Close by, a man caused a ruckus of late. His name was Chan Hon-ching. He positioned himself near the Stock Exchange entrance and instructed passers-by he wanted to give money to the street-sleepers and to queue up to receive money. People were told to take one $100 note at a time. After giving away about $20,000, a fracas occurred when he accused one man of being greedy and taking $300 at one go. The police arrived and arrested Mr Chan for causing a disturbance of the peace. He attempted, it is said, to give money to the policemen, but not by way of a bribe which must be near unique in Hong Kong. An ambulance was called and Mr Chan was unceremoniously driven away for psychiatric evaluation: it was later discovered he had another $97,000 on him and a cool million dollars in the bank, paid in compensation for a head injury received whilst working in the Kwai Chung container port. This, it appears, explained it all – it would seem that anyone giving money away in Hong Kong has to be immediately considered as certifiable.

Or perhaps this is a sign of the future, that the changes to come will be seriously fundamental and not just a matter of taller buildings and new spits of land. No mortal can say. On the other hand, Wong Tai Sin probably knows the answer but he isn't talking.

Index